Soviet
Policy-Making

Soviet
Policy-Making

STUDIES OF COMMUNISM IN TRANSITION

EDITED BY

PETER H. JUVILER

AND

HENRY W. MORTON

FREDERICK A. PRAEGER, *Publishers*
New York • Washington • London

For our parents
Adolphe and Katherine Juviler
and
Frank and Rose Morton

78060

FREDERICK A. PRAEGER, PUBLISHERS
111 Fourth Avenue, New York, N.Y. 10003, U.S.A.
77–79 Charlotte Street, London W. 1, England

Published in the United States of America in 1967 by
Frederick A. Praeger, Inc., Publishers

© 1967 by Frederick A. Praeger, Inc.

Library of Congress Catalog Card Number: 66–18913

Printed in the United States of America

This book is Number 182 in the series
Praeger Publications in Russian History and World Communism

Preface

Expert observers since the late Boris Nicolaevsky, including Nikita Khrushchev himself, have afforded us behind-the-scenes glimpses of the continuing power struggle in the leadership of the Communist Party of the Soviet Union and in segments of the ruling machinery: the army, the police, and the governmental administration. Until recently, these glimpses were all we knew of the pluralistic tendencies that obtained in the Soviet Union after Stalin, in the late 1920's, lowered the curtain on information and, with terror tactics, isolated professions, institutions, and individuals.

However, a notable change in the Soviet political climate has taken place since the dictator's death. In his impetuous search for effective economic and administrative remedies, Khrushchev acted as a catalyst in stimulating the formation of opinion groups which now voice their views on vital issues and propose reforms. With the overt threat of terror removed, meaningful public debate on crucial issues has become more commonplace. Statistics, once conspicuous by their absence, are now both more plentiful and more reliable. Soviet scholars and journalists have begun to mine areas that had remained untouched for thirty years. Their research and their polemics, together with expanded possibilities for foreigners to visit and do research in the U.S.S.R., have enabled non-Soviet observers, including the contributors to this book, to turn up fascinating evidence of extensive debate over crucial issues of policy.

The purpose of this symposium has been to point up underlying influences on Soviet policy decisions. The introductory chapter compares the Soviet political process with that of other countries. It is followed by a series of case studies of family, economic, cultural, scientific, penal, and foreign policies. With one exception (Peter Viereck's chapter is adapted from an article that originally appeared in *Tri-Quarterly*), the contributors were asked to write their chapters around the following questions: (1) How did the problem you are discussing become a political issue? (2) What were the influences—such as ideology, tradition, precedent, economic capacity, the simultaneous pressure of other issues, and institutional arrangements—that conditioned the choice among possible alternatives? (3) What evidence was there of factionalism, group pressures, and foreign Communist influences? (4) Did the issue result in a policy, and how did the final version differ from the original proposal? What part did the bureaucracy play in interpreting the decisions in its execution? Did the policy give rise to new issues and problems?

Obviously, such an ambitious questionnaire would be difficult to complete for any system, let alone for the relatively closed Soviet one. In some instances, not enough time has elapsed to gauge the impact of a decision. Moreover, contributors were drawn from various disciplines and could not always be expected to use the methodological approach suggested by two political scientists. That they cooperated to the extent that they did is deeply appreciated by the editors.

What do the case studies tell us about the Soviet political system? In general, it can be said that all the studies reveal a system in flux, with centrifugal forces straining at centralized controls. The label "totalitarian" no longer fits comfortably. The Party leadership, often more divided than monolithic, is increasingly leaning on the advice of experts in its quest to modernize the society, and is seeking popular support by decreasing internal tensions; but although forced to broaden the base of the decision-making process, it is equally determined to maintain tight reins of control. Unsure of what paths to follow, what pressures to acknowledge, and what concessions to make, the leaders, working without a blueprint and frequently divided among themselves, are attempting to grope their way toward satisfactory short-term solutions without compromising their eventual goal of establishing a Communist order.

1. *Problem-solving.*—Stalin's system gave priority to ends, not

means; to political, not economic, efficiency. A crash program of selective modernization emphasized central planning, heavy industry, and education, and was often enforced through terror. Policy initiative came from a small group of officials in the Party's Politburo, the departments of the Central Committee, the police, and the ministries. Russia's regime was like a giant that possesses great strength, a long reach, but dulled senses. Our case studies indicate a significant change. The giant's senses are keener now. Feedback from professional experts and the creative intelligentsia and the sounding out of popular attitudes play an incomparably greater role than they did under Stalin in the regime's attempt to understand what the problems are and how to solve them. Most decisions, yielding to urgent demands of the moment, are prompted by domestic needs. They are basically middle- and short-range decisions and are not of the kind that will radically transform the social and economic structure of the nation.

2. *Influences on policy-making.*—It is, of course, impossible to know precisely and to what extent ideology, national interest, personal power, empirical considerations of efficacy, and desire for support condition Party choices. Yet despite the enormous problems of quantifying and of correlating cause and effect, a few tentative generalizations can be ventured.

Where internationalist, equalitarian, or antistatist elements of Marxist ideology have clashed with more immediate practical political considerations, they have had to give way. We find this in the conservatism of family law, in the innovation in economic management, and in the manipulation of cultural controls. Yet although it can be overruled, ideology nevertheless remains a vital societal factor, and it performs several functions. In the Soviet Union, it is a compendium of experience, a justification of policy, and a legitimization of one-party rule. It acts as a socially integrating code of values and is an element of continuity and even of conservatism. In this respect, official ideology induces caution and encourages those groups that want to preserve the status quo. The Party gave Libermanism no serious hearing and allowed no public debate on it until compelled to do so by failing growth rates. In the same manner, the institutionalized principles of socialist realism hold up cultural liberalization.

Ideology, however, can also be a more positive force. It can spur policy initiative from below, as in the survival of the socialist principle of female emancipation, invoked by the family-law reformists, and from above—the anti-parasite decrees originated not only in certain traditional Russian methods of social control but also in Khrushchev's conviction that the human personality is malleable and responsive to social pressures and that popular justice is better than professional justice.

3. *Personalities, factionalism, pressures—foreign and domestic.*—Policy decisions reflect a complex tangle of influences and motivations. This is shown by all our case studies. The chapter on foreign policy, which serves as a capstone of the studies, indicates what any Soviet leader is up against if he tries to take policy into his own hands, as Khrushchev did. In his conduct of relations with the United States, he will be swayed by his perception of American intentions, capabilities, and resolution. He will also face a melange of domestic pressures from his rivals (who gain strength from his failures), and from the industrial-military complex, the intelligentsia, the imperatives of economic priorities, and other sources. Conversely, as several chapters show, foreign-policy needs influence the leaders' choices of domestic policy on a range of issues from birth control to industrial management, cultural relations, and book publishing.

The balance of power within the Soviet leadership is of great significance and deserves further comment. The selection of a particular policy depends upon which group prevails. It would appear that if Suslov, Kozlov, and Shelepin—Khrushchev's opposition after 1959—had taken power, they would have imposed a harder line in domestic and foreign policy. Yet they might have surprised us. After all, Beria, Stalin's police chief and a member of the post-Stalin triumverate until his liquidation in 1953, became associated with the advocacy of socialist legality and, apparently, with a much more liberal policy for Eastern Europe. We can say that Kosygin stands for a more rational and technocratically inclined policy than does Brezhnev, who is probably by inclination more of an umpire and manipulator. But we must also realize that the vast administrative apparatus over which Kosygin presides is itself divided and crisscrossed with a multitude of interests which will persevere no matter what form the succession struggle takes.

Our case studies support the conclusion that the "totalitarian" model of an all-powerful command system with self-perpetuating controls no longer serves to explain Soviet reality. In Soviet politics, totalitarian controls counterweight not only "democratic forms"* but also pluralistic pressures (rooted in the Party's need for wide consultation) which grind against these controls. If this is true, then our studies would seem to confirm the need for more research which will emphasize not only the many differences between Soviet and Western systems but also the emerging similarities.

How can we describe the Soviet system as it functions today? The system remains indubitably a one-party political monopoly. It is still far removed from the ideological relativism and pluralism that characterize the one-party system of Yugoslavia and, to an even greater extent, of Mexico. The CPSU still claims to be the guardian and oracle of one ideology, which it attempts to impose through its system of schooling and indoctrination, vigorously combating, to the extent of its power, all competing ideologies. (For example, it fights religion more vigorously than does any other Communist country with the possible exception of China.) As is pointed out in Chapter 1, since Stalin the Soviet Union has acquired certain features often associated with traditional authoritarian states. Social policy has become more conservative as the various vested-interest groups, repressed under Stalin, have successfully resisted both threats of further revolutionary social engineering from above and equalitarian pressures from below.

But the system also contains a rational element. Considerations of ideology and power are tempered by the need for rationalization of an increasingly complex society, judging at least from the case studies in this book.

4. *Policy output and implementation.*—Implementation is often the heart of the policy-making process. Laws and Party resolutions (the results of decisions) are merely plans of action. They are theoretical solutions until proven in application. Soviet policy, although decided at the highest levels, may be distorted in application (as all our chapters show), and it is often unenforceable without administrative and popular support. The imperfection of

---

* John N. Hazard, *The Soviet System of Government* (3d ed.; Chicago: University of Chicago Press, 1964), p. 10.

a decision will stimulate new attempts to resolve the issue. This has been the brief history of the parasite laws, which have raised many more problems than they have solved. Thus most decisions in the Soviet Union, as elsewhere, become a series of stop-gap measures where the proposed solution repeatedly falls short of the mark and requires rethinking and new application.

Khrushchev's fall on October 14, 1964, surprised most Sovietologists and prompted them to review their assumptions about the Soviet system. Fifty years ago, Russia stood at a crossroads between parliamentary democracy, traditional authoritarianism, and Communist one-party government. Perhaps no one man is waiting in the wings to take power as dramatically as Lenin did. Whatever the future, however, Sovietologists have recently been abandoning the concept of self-perpetuating totalitarianism they so cogently expounded in the 1950's. As the Soviet Communist regime approached its fiftieth anniversary, Western analysts ceased to emphasize the efficiency and dynamism of Party leadership and instead tended to describe it as increasingly incompetent, impersonal, unimaginative, and incompatible with the modernizing society it attempted to rule. Peter Grose, the Moscow correspondent of *The New York Times*, has written that "the Communist Party is unchallenged—this goes without question—but in the society at large, the Party seems to have lost its creative and driving force. The motivating power has passed elsewhere: to the professional organizations, to special interest groups and to individuals kindred through geographic, economic, and social positions. In the changing Soviet society the Party is following and not leading."

Our case studies support his conclusion, at least in many areas of domestic policy. The Party leaders still claim the right to determine which major issues will be debated, and they manipulate the debates. But doors have been opened in the Kremlin walls to admit warnings, suggestions, and demands from administrators, experts, intellectuals, and an awakened public opinion. This revived feedback helps to shape Party policy.

On April 5, 1966, Lunik I transmitted the "International" to an assembly of nearly 5,000 Twenty-third Party Congress delegates from all over the world. But the realities of Soviet policy in 1966 seemed more sober, empirical, pragmatic, and nationally oriented than this symbolic act would indicate. Government by fiat has become government by consultation, by reconciliation of conflicting interests. The generic term given to this complex interaction is *politics*. In the Soviet Union, political ground rules are different from those in the United States. Yet they are not so alien that the Soviet system can be described by such an unrefined term as "totalitarian." The Party leadership may be impersonal, but it is not mediocre, nor incompetent. Soviet leaders today have in fact shown surprising diplomatic, administrative, and political skill in steering the country through the difficult period of adjustment in domestic and foreign policy that followed the fall of Khrushchev. We must end, however, on a note of caution: our case studies show no justification for ruling out the possibility that a forceful leader or faction may seize power and sharply curtail debate and consultation, even at the expense of efficiency.

This symposium was made possible largely through the assistance rendered to various of its members by the Inter-University Committee on Travel Grants, the American Council of Learned Societies, the Social Science Research Council, the United States Office of Education, the Hays-Fulbright Foreign Area Travel Grants program, the Brookings Institution, and our respective universities. Their support is gratefully acknowledged. The editors would like to express their appreciation to the contributors for their balanced yet revealing case studies, to the staff of Frederick A. Praeger, and especially to Arnold Leo, who helped to prepare the final manuscript.

P. H. J.
H. W. M.

New York City
November, 1966

Contents

THE CONTRIBUTORS

MARIANNE ARMSTRONG holds a Master of Arts degree in Russian Area Studies from the City University of New York. She is currently a technical analyst for the Library of Congress.

MAURICE FRIEDBERG, Professor of Slavic Languages and Literatures at Indiana University, is the author of *Russian Classics in Soviet Jackets* and the editor of two volumes of *A Bilingual Collection of Russian Short Stories*.

MARSHALL I. GOLDMAN is Associate Professor of Economics at Wellesley College and an Associate of the Russian Research Center at Harvard University. He is the author of *Soviet Marketing: Distribution in a Controlled Economy, Comparative Economic Systems: A Reader,* and *Soviet Foreign Aid*.

LOREN R. GRAHAM is Assistant Professor of History at Columbia University and a faculty member of the university's Russian Institute. The author of *The Revolution in Russian Science: the Soviet Academy of Sciences, 1927–1932,* he is presently working on a study of the role of Marxist ideology in science.

PETER H. JUVILER is Associate Professor of Government at Barnard College and an Associate of the Russian Institute of Columbia University. He is now completing a study of Soviet family policy.

HENRY W. MORTON is Associate Professor of Political Science at Queens College of the City University of New York. The author of *Soviet Sport: Mirror of Soviet Society,* he is currently working on a study of Soviet politics.

ROBERT M. SLUSSER is Associate Professor of History at The Johns Hopkins University. He is the author of numerous articles on Soviet history, politics, and culture, and the co-author of *Soviet Secret Police* and *The Theory, Law, and Policy of Soviet Treaties*.

PETER VIERECK, poet, literary critic, and historian, is Professor of Russian History at Mount Holyoke College. He is the author of *Conservatism Revisited, Metapolitics: the Roots of Nazi Mind,* and *A New Russian Revolution*.

Soviet
Policy-Making

1

The Structure of
Decision-Making in the U.S.S.R.

A COMPARATIVE INTRODUCTION

Henry W. Morton

I

"The essence of ultimate decision," John F. Kennedy wrote of the Presidency, "remains impenetrable to the observer—often indeed to the decider himself."[1] But even if all the factors that shape a decision—the personalities, the political, economic, and social pressures, the forces of tradition and ideology, to mention only a few—can never be fully assembled for analysis, it is possible to define some of the aspects of the political process by which policy is constructed.

In the case of the Soviet Union, the apparent monolithic political structure and the informational curtain surrounding most decisions may lead some to assume that the necessary facts cannot be gathered. Yet the Soviet process differs only in degree from that of other systems, and this "degree differential" is an important measurement in comparative studies.

Similarly, the assumption that information on policy decisions in the West is qualitatively and quantitatively greater than hard news released by Soviet sources must be scrutinized. All governments seek to present their efforts in a positive light, and this often entails manipulation of the flow of information.

Then, too, politicians may withhold information because they prefer to deliberate in private. Secrecy in deliberation affords public officials the freedom to arrive at decisions without having to defend every step of the process before a fault-finding public. An equally expedient reason for secrecy is that it limits the scope of conflict. By keeping deliberations secret until a decision is reached, politicians seek to restrict political participation so that the initiative does not slip from their control, though they usually explain their restrictive measures on some other grounds.[2] This is a general rule, with universal application.[3]

The extent to which policy considerations are made public is determined by the traditions of a political system, by the issue in question, by the government's relative degree of responsibility to the public, and by the nature of the press. The personality of the executive leader also plays an important role. Within a political system, a Kennedy may be more informative than a Johnson, a Khrushchev more loquacious than a Stalin.

Although the American political scene is notable for a relatively abundant flow of information on policy deliberations, Presidents are frequently and justly accused of news management. Considered realistically, the accusations are hardly surprising. In 1965, President Johnson stated that his decisions to bomb North Vietnamese targets and commit American ground troops to South Vietnam had been prompted by the conclusion that the anti-Communist regime in Saigon was mortally threatened by Ho Chi Minh–controlled Viet Cong guerrillas. Prior to the first bombing raid, the U.S. Government issued a lengthy White Paper that supported the President's appraisal of the Vietnamese situation. The report no doubt was intended to curtail further discussion of the issue. However, several facts *not* mentioned in the White Paper indicated that the Saigon regime, having lost legitimacy in the eyes of the great majority of Vietnamese peasants, was losing a civil war and faced extinction unless the United States intervened directly.

In Britain, too, the flow of political information is limited by secrecy in the decision-making process. The custom of Cabinet responsibility requires of Cabinet ministers that they resign from office if they choose to differ publicly with their colleagues on policy. This custom is reinforced by the Official Secrets Act, which places severe penalties on government officials who divulge information to the press. The effectiveness of these restraints may be judged from the fact that most Conservative Members of

Parliament who were below Cabinet level at the time of the Suez crisis of 1956—to say nothing of the interested public—have remained uninformed as to which members of the government supported the war and which opposed it. Strong party discipline further augments the blanket of privacy that covers past as well as present deliberations.[4] Major policy decisions are more often taken in private meetings than publicly during a parliamentary debate.[5] Thus, the content of the debate that led the Labour Party to elect Harold Wilson as leader in 1963, and the outstanding differences between the contestants, were never revealed—in contrast with American Presidential primary contests, which often reveal so much that it becomes difficult to smooth over party differences. Further, each house of Parliament can imprison anyone it finds in contempt. Although this power has not been used against the press for many years, its existence has served as a forceful restraint.[6]

In France, the deliberative process is well screened by President de Gaulle's singlehanded control of French national policy. Neither the Premier, nor the Council of Ministers, nor an enfeebled National Assembly can challenge his authority. The Algerian crisis, which seriously threatened his regime and also his life, and which he hoped to resolve by granting independence to Algeria without destroying French unity at home, was handled by him with deliberative ambiguity and deception.[7] Even his ministers were often uninformed on his thoughts. During the long negotiations with the Algerian National Liberation Front, "de Gaulle gave orders directly to the French delegates without even the usual token consultation of the Council of Ministers."[8] A French witticism had it that "the British have a Shadow Government [the leaders of the opposition party in Parliament], and so have we, but ours is in office."

These brief examples illustrate that the informational curtain is a device used by many governments. Sometimes, in isolated instances, we have greater knowledge of Soviet political machinations than of the internal workings of the British Cabinet. For example, by 1961 all major figures who had plotted to overthrow Khrushchev in 1957 (the so-called anti-Party group, consisting of Molotov, Malenkov, Bulganin, Kaganovich, Shepilov, Voroshilov, Saburov, and Pervukhin) had been exposed and a version of their participation given by Khrushchev. Contrast this with our lack of knowledge of what stand the British leadership took in the Suez crisis, or of what factors induced Sir Alec Douglas-Home to resign as leader of the Conservative Party in July, 1965.

II

Policies (*outputs*) are the products of the decision-making process. They are initially stimulated by pressures and demands (*inputs*) and formulated, vetoed, temporarily blocked, or reshaped in accordance with the assumptions of the political system. The nature of the decision-making process is determined in any society primarily by two factors:

1. The *political culture*, which consists of the political beliefs held by elites and by the citizenry and the orientation of these groups to political action. The political culture may be either relatively unified and homogeneous, as in Great Britain, Australia, and the United States, or sharply divided, as in Weimar Germany or present-day Greece, Japan, and India, where the conflicting interests of numerous subcultures prevent consensus.

2. The *authority pattern*, that is, the interaction of leaders of institutions on important issues. The leaders may be executive, legislative, judicial, bureaucratic, military, or party, to name a few.

The realities of international relations, the limitations of human and natural resources, and economic conditions are also important input considerations.

After almost fifty years of Soviet rule in the U.S.S.R., the decision-making process, though influenced by the Czarist heritage, has taken on distinctly Soviet traditions and norms of operation. The authority pattern is autocratic and firmly anchored in the executive, which both formulates and executes policy. The detailed application of decisions is delegated to a centrally controlled bureaucracy which is entrusted to administer policy with a minimum of distortions—but which does not necessarily do so.*

---

* A chronic problem affecting the implementation of Soviet policies is bureaucratic mismanagement. At times, resolutions issued under the joint signature of the Central Committee (CPSU) and the Council of Ministers (U.S.S.R.) have to be repeated because they were not carried out. Such a joint resolution was issued in March, 1955. Its purpose was to grant greater production-planning initiative among managers of collective and state farms.

Soviet regimes, characterized by rules of *supreme leader* (Lenin, Stalin), of *first among equals* (Khrushchev, 1957–64), and of *collective leadership* (oligarchies, 1923–28, 1953–57, 1964–)—the three dominant patterns of Soviet power—have been nonrepresentational. Instead of meaningful electoral contests for the political offices, the political elite has been selected from above.* Soviet power is not responsible in the sense that the regime's over-all performance can be protested at the polls. Nor are restraints on political power present in constitutional or legal guarantees that might provide citizens with specific inalienable rights against the state, and there is no rooted tradition that might prevent the use of unrestrained force by the government,[9] although a tendency in this direction has developed in the wake of two decades of Stalinist excesses.

Pluralistic restraints—such as the church, the nobility, landowning, industrial, and commercial interests, and regional and cultural groups, which stand between rulers and ruled and force concessions from an otherwise unbridled executive power—are present in one form or another in traditional authoritarian, as well as in Western industrialized, societies. These intermediary groups do not exist in the Soviet Union; they were eliminated during the revolutionary restratification of Russian society that followed upon the Bolshevik seizure of power. The new ruling group, the Communist Party, having annihilated the old oligarchy, formed its own institutional pattern, which it sought to control by infiltrating every newly created organization—whether governmental, collective farm, trade union, artistic, or athletic—with cellular Party units. The aim was to make these organizations responsible to the Party leadership rather than to their own group leaders, whose aspirations might clash with Party policy, and to prevent them from acquiring an independent material or social base of support.

Yet the Soviet political system does not operate perfectly and is far less monolithic than it may appear to be on superficial

---

Because it was poorly enforced, another joint decree appeared in *Pravda*, March 24, 1964, which charged "Party, Soviet and agricultural agencies to be strictly guided by the March 9, 1955, resolution . . . 'On Revising the Practice of Planning in Agriculture.' "

* Selection is based on achievement and connections and is not restricted to specific sectors or classes of the society.

examination.[10] The freedom of Soviet policy-makers is impinged
on by several forces, which, broadly speaking, fall into two categories. The first can be classified as the *alienated and unincor-
porated sectors* of Soviet society—"latent oppositions"—which
react negatively to specific Party policies but are not necessarily
opposed to the entire value structure. Such sectors remain largely
amorphous and unorganized, though not by choice. They consist
of millions of peasants and unskilled workers, who account for a
large proportion of the population but who, living a marginal
existence, do not have the economic incentives that would encourage their positive response to policies; certain nationalities,
particularly those residing in the Baltic and Caucasian regions,
who desire greater autonomy, if not independence; members of
religious groups, who wish to practice their faith without external
threats and deprivations; and great numbers of the young generation who remain dissatisfied with the slow rate of material progress
and are highly critical of their elders for condoning Stalinism.
These sectors represent uncharted and overlapping subcultures
in the sense that although they have been discovered, their con-
tours and boundaries remain vague, the intensity of feelings within
them is still unmeasured, and their sense of identity continues to be
denied a means of expression. Although deprived by the Party of
independent leadership and organization, they are prominent obstacles to the realization of Party objectives and a continuing pre-
occupation and despair of the decision-makers. For example, the
Party leadership's efforts to solve the agricultural crisis by per-
suading the peasants to work enthusiastically within the collective-
farm system have repeatedly failed. The peasants' slowdown strike
of three decades has served as an effective veto of the persistent
Party decrees aimed at improving farm output.*

The presence of latent oppositions is testimony that the Party
leadership has been only partially successful in changing the
strongly held social values, attitudes, and traditions of prerevolu-

---

* The Party leadership, well aware of "latent oppositions," tries to win them
over by offering some incentives. When agricultural production lags, peasants
are permitted to extend their private holdings and are offered higher prices
for their crops. In its nationality policy, national pride is catered to by providing limited federalism in the form of separate republics for large ethnic
groups, by sponsoring national-language schools, newspapers, theaters, and so
on.

tionary Russia by constructing a new kind of industrialized society along the guidelines of the current ruling ideology, which, although Communist, is subject to fluctuations. Because the transformation from the old society was wrought by application of ruthless terror, with little attempt to provide the people with material incentives, the long period of this revolution-from-above resulted in serious economic and social dislocations that have bequeathed a troublesome legacy to the present leadership.*

If the continuing existence of latent oppositions indicates the failure of the Soviet experiment to gain unqualified support from significant sectors of the population, the emergence of "loyal oppositions" attests to the achievements of the system. Basically loyal to the socialist system, the loyal oppositions are critical of particular CPSU policies or organizational arrangements.[11] This challenge to the monopolistic decision-making power of Party leaders, a power that ranges from determining the price of a liter of milk to declaring war, is an important consequence of the rapid industrialization of the U.S.S.R. The many technical and social problems thrown up by an increasingly complex and structurally differentiated society have forced, at maximum, an informal sharing of power with ministerial bureaucrats, planners, scientists, economic managers, military leaders, technical experts, social scientists, and cultural authorities, and, at minimum, a reliance on their advice. Sometimes, however, active members of these vested-interest groups become "disloyal" in the eyes of the regime, i.e., they are potential leaders of latent oppositions. The contemporary writers who have espoused unpopular causes and the educated members of nationality groups who have been chafing at Russian domination are examples of this shift into uncondoned areas of opposition.

Yet the authority pattern is still predominantly of a *hierarchical* nature ("leaders substantially decide when, in what condition and with whom consultation takes place"[12]), rather than of a *bargaining* nature ("the cooperation of several groups each with different sources of strength and differing needs . . . required for the

* Industrialization per se creates serious social and economic dislocations wherever applied. Here the nature and speed of implementation, as well as the receptivity of a social order to new conditions, are critical factors. The fantastic toll in terms of human and material resources caused by the German invasion greatly added to the problems.

attainment of an object of government policy"[13]), and is *compartmentalized* (no group—outside of the Party—has the right to organize, to elect independent leadership, to communicate freely with its followers, or to appeal, if necessary, to the public at large for support), rather than *autonomous* (subsystems function with little direct governmental control).

Strong tendencies to bargain and to act autonomously, however, are far from absent in the hierarchical Soviet system. The process of industrialization stimulated them by increasing society's dependence on various kinds of experts. In the current period of relative normalcy that was ushered in by Stalin's death—the first such period in Soviet history since the New Economic Policy (1921–28)—these tendencies, once submerged, rose to the surface, and have remained there, due to one major factor: the leadership's tacit renunciation of terror as a fundamental means to enforce policy. At the Twenty-second Congress of the CPSU (October, 1961), Khrushchev revealed the following interchange that had taken place in June, 1957, with "anti-Party group" member Kaganovich, whose protégé Khrushchev had been in the 1930's:

I had a typical conversation with Kaganovich. This was two days after the end of the June plenary session of the Party Central Committee, which expelled the Anti-Party Group from the Central Committee. Kaganovich called me on the phone and said:

"Comrade Khrushchev, I have known you for many years, I ask you not to let them treat me in the vindictive way people were treated under Stalin."

And Kaganovich knew how people had been treated because he himself had been a participant in these reprisals. I answered him:

"Comrade Kaganovich! Your words once more confirm the methods you intended to use to achieve your disgusting ends. You wanted to return the country to the state of affairs that existed under the cult of the individual, you wanted to indulge in reprisals against people. And you measured other people by your own yardstick. But you are mistaken. We firmly observe and shall adhere to Leninist principles. You will be given a job," I said to Kaganovich. "You will be able to work and live in tranquillity if you labor honestly, as all Soviet people labor."

Such is the conversation I had with Kaganovich. This conversation shows that when the factionalists failed, they thought they would be dealt with in the same way they intended to deal with the Party cadres if they had succeeded in realizing their wicked designs. But we Communist-Leninists cannot embark on the path of abuse of power. . . .[14]

This guarantee not to practice terror was extended to the various subsystems by the curtailment, perhaps indefinitely, of the Party's commitment to imposing a "permanent revolution from above" on Soviet society.[15] Commenting in 1956 on the debilitating impact of fear on efficient work habits under Stalin, Khrushchev noted: "We should also not forget that, due to the numerous arrests of Party, Soviet, and economic leaders, many workers began to work uncertainly, show overcautiousness, feared all which was new, feared their shadows, and began to show less initiative in their work."[16] Although individuals may still be exiled to remote areas or jailed for opposition, or cowed by the fear of a return to terror, itself a form of terror,[17] privileged groups today can work at problem-solving with much greater rationality.

Under these conditions, centrifugal tendencies against the centralizing force of Party control have gained momentum, and economists, military leaders, lawyers, scientists, educators, artists, and other experts—most of them, incidentally, Party members—have acquired greater confidence to speak out on issues within their spheres of competence. Many significant debates have been held in the last decade on a wide variety of subjects, such as educational policy, improvement of centralized economic planning, legal reforms, and the role of the artist in society. This does not mean that each group has equal influence with the Party, i.e., that political resources are equal. Military counsel on strategy and planners' advice on economic allocations receive higher priority than lawyers' suggestions for changes in the family legislation.

Within some subsystems, certain journals have become identified with the views of specific groups. *Novy mir* (*New World*), under the editorship of the poet Tvardovsky, may be regarded as the house organ for liberal expression in literature, in contrast with Kochetov's *Oktyabr*. The division between innovators and conservatives among the economists is not so clear-cut, but those pressing for a computer-oriented solution to Soviet planning problems express their views most frequently in *Ekonomika i matematicheskie metody* (*Economics and Mathematical Methods*).

But the seedlings of autonomy are fragile. Bargaining among

Party leaders, experts, and representatives of interest groups tends to be carried on mainly behind the scenes, rather than in the open market of competing interests and ideas. The limited reduction of Party controls has been neither uniform nor smooth, and not every subject is open for discussion. Freudian psychology, for example, is still proscribed as a field of study, while Lysenko's harmful influence over genetics and plant biology—his stress on acquired, as opposed to inherited, characteristics, particularly of plants—remained unsuccessfully challenged until Khrushchev was removed from power, in October, 1964.

This brings us to an essential point. The important decisions and discussions are still initiated at the top, by the Party leadership, rather than from below, by the organized pressure of interest groups and experts. The growing tendencies toward bargaining and autonomy might even suffer a reverse in the unlikely, but not wholly implausible, event that an absolute ruler, in the Stalinist tradition, should seize power. Once again, societal efficiency would be sacrificed to political control.

The change from the authority pattern of Stalin to that of his successors, characterized chiefly by the abandonment of overt terror and the increased dependence on experts, has given the Soviet Union certain features often associated with traditional authoritarian states. Social policies became more conservative as the ebbing of Bolshevik dynamism brought to the fore various vested-interest groups inherent in the Soviet structure, each seeking to enhance its bargaining position. These groups, though repressed under Stalin, have been relatively successful in their efforts against threats of further revolutionary social engineering from above and egalitarian pressures from below. The educational reforms of 1958, aimed primarily at the children of the "new class," stipulated that most secondary-school graduates destined for higher education were to interrupt their schooling and work for two years. Preference in university admittance was to be given to youngsters of worker and peasant backgrounds. These policies, however, were virtually abandoned by 1965.[18] As long as Party leaders attempt to rationalize Soviet society, they must pay a price in looser social and ideological controls; restrictive policies alienate influential segments of the intelligentsia.

It is doubtful, however, that the system will become responsible and broadly representative in the Western sense. Democratization is not an inevitable consequence of modernization, nor would one expect it to be. In fact, the opposite may be argued. In societies with no strong tradition of citizens' rights against the state, with no well-established process for the formation of intermediary groups that might challenge government policies and goals, the demand for rudimentary guarantees against arbitrary acts of the state is made difficult by the realistic need in the twentieth century for Big Government. Rapid economic and social advancement, full employment, and wide-ranging social insurance benefits, to say nothing of measures taken in the name of national security, entail central direction of massive organizations. Centralization takes extreme expression in Communist countries and in developing nations with one-party regimes that are committed to rapid industrialization and radical transformation of the social order. Even though these major goals have been partially realized in the Soviet Union, the Party leaders' extensive powers to initiate and to veto will not be significantly curtailed in the foreseeable future, as some Western analysts claim, for at least four reasons:

1. Party rule is sustained by its own momentum. The leadership has always been extremely quick to meet challenges to its sovereignty, and continually justifies its right to rule. November 7, 1967, marks the completion of fifty years of Communist leadership. No meaningful alternatives to Party rule have ever been allowed to develop during this period.

2. Party leadership is needed to provide the *political integrative function*. The Party is the super-coordinating agent in Soviet society. Its function has changed in emphasis from transforming the nature of society to shaping and managing economic and sociopolitical conflict within the social structure. For example, in deciding what portion of available funds to allocate for armaments, for the space program, for agricultural tools, for hydroelectric plants, and so on, the Party Politburo* must balance conflicting demands presented by various government administrators and planning officials.

At the district level, the local Party organization is responsible

---

* The Politburo's title was changed to Presidium at the Nineteenth Party Congress (October, 1952), and changed back to Politburo at the Twenty-third Party Congress (April, 1966).

for ensuring that the economic plan is carried out in nearly all production units in its area. This includes providing policy direction for state enterprises, choosing administrative personnel, and most important, "coordinating the work of the different administrators and resolving disputes which arise among them."[19] If the Party organization were suddenly dismantled, chaos would swiftly ensue. The same holds true for any complex system, though in most nations, the government itself (rather than a party) assumes the important function of arbiter-coordinator. For this reason, the Marxist projection that the state will eventually wither away is not feasible.

3. Party leaders and the Party *apparatchiki*, the approximately 250,000 full-time functionaries who maintain the Party apparatus, from the all-union to the village level, are the only Soviet citizens who possess the labor time to function politically. Their lives are devoted to political duties. Other citizens are preoccupied with energy-consuming vocations and recreational pastimes that use up most of their labor hours and free time. Unless highly motivated, the citizen finds it far too costly to engage in political activity on a sustained voluntary basis.[20]

4. Institutional leaders, possibly excepting certain generals, high-level bureaucrats, and secret-police officials, are short on political integrative skills, lack the perspective necessary to national leadership, and are generally more concerned with increasing their bargaining powers and spheres of autonomy than with becoming political managers. As in Britain or even in the United States, so in the Soviet Union there is little circulation among economic, military, and political (Party) elites.

III

The policy process is governed to a significant extent by the political-belief system. "Every governing class tends to justify its actual exercise of power by resting it on some universal moral principle."[21] "Any well-knit way of life molds human behavior into its own design. The individualism of bourgeois society like the communism of a socialized state must be inculcated from the nursery to the grave."[22] Decision-makers manipulate political symbols, such as patria, democracy, national interest, etc., to justify their actions and to secure patriotic support among societal groups. But as products of the social order, the policy-makers are, at the same time, caught up in the web of their manipulations. Their frame of reference when defining problems and evaluating solutions is the ideology with which they have been raised. Ideology also determines the ground rules for making decisions. During the 1962 Cuban crisis, Attorney-General Robert Kennedy argued forcefully against a surprise air strike at the Soviet missile bases in Cuba, stating that it would be "a Pearl Harbor in reverse, and it would blacken the name of the United States in the pages of history."[23]

Every political system has built-in advantages and limitations for problem-solving. Tradition-oriented governments of the nineteenth and early twentieth centuries had an endemic inability to face up to the challenges of modernization; witness the collapse of the Russian, Ottoman, and Chinese dynasties. Czar Nicholas II, primarily concerned with preserving the social order he had inherited, would not enact the reforms that were drastically needed; such reforms, of course, would have undermined the foundations of the Russian monarchy and social structure.

In the United States, the belief that a free-enterprise system with a minimum of government regulation will bring the greatest happiness to the greatest numbers has been challenged in this century by social needs the American system has failed to meet, whether equal rights and economic opportunities for Negro citizens or the manufacture of a safe automobile. As a result, the national government has emerged as a powerful but reluctant Johnny-come-lately arbiter to resolve the persistent tension between social and market values.*

In the Soviet Union, the persistent tension is between social and Party values. Although the Party, an ideology-rooted elite, calls for a continuous molding of the "new Soviet man," it denies the presence of conflict between Party policy and societal needs. Yet, fulfillment of the need for more and better consumers'

---

* George Lichtheim, *The New Europe: Today and Tomorrow* (New York: Frederick A. Praeger, 1963), p. 194. The commuter transportation dilemma, were it not for the ideological blinkers of a free-enterprise tradition and of state rights, might have been rationally tackled long ago if the federal government had planned a comprehensive program for various states, including, if necessary, the nationalization of commuter railroads.

goods and services has long been frustrated by heavy investments in capital goods. The recurrent agricultural shortages that have greatly troubled Soviet decision-makers (over 75 per cent of Central Committee meetings since Stalin's death have dealt with this problem) could be alleviated most speedily if the Party admitted its mistake and abolished collective and state farms, turning the land over to the peasants. Peasants who owned private plots, which in 1962 accounted for only 3 per cent of the total acreage of collective and state farms, provided 70 per cent of the Soviet Union's potatoes and eggs, and 40 per cent of its milk, vegetables, and meat.[24] However, an open acknowledgment of the failure of collectivization would, among many far-reaching consequences, bring into question a whole range of political values, including belief in the superiority of collective labor over individual labor. Consequently, this drastic alternative cannot be considered by the leadership, and less efficient and more piecemeal solutions to the problem must be sought.

Every society views its problems and their solutions astigmatically, through lenses ground by the ruling ideology. In the Soviet Union, doctrine plays a far more overt and important role than in the West, and the leadership itself is much more ideology-oriented than Western leaders.[25] This view is difficult for many Americans to accept, due partly to a conviction, albeit erroneous, that ideology is used principally to justify official acts but has little influence on the shaping of them, and partly to a belief that as Soviet society undergoes bourgeoisification, the ideological commitment to Communism will erode.

On the contrary, one remarkable accomplishment of the Party leadership is that within decades a minority group has been able to impose, with varying degrees of success, a new belief system while ruthlessly transforming the socio-economic order. The commitment of various groups within Soviet society today is less to the Party's maximum goal of establishing a world Communist system, or to a continuation of the revolutionary transformation of Soviet society, than to the beliefs that "the fulfillment and maximum development of the individual and his potential are possible only in a socialistic, collective society . . . that this represents the only true humanism and that this is an inevitable development."[26] George Fischer, in writing of the Soviet intelligentsia, whose support of the existing value system is crucial for the regime, has noted: "The Soviet intelligentsia has been persuaded by the state as well as by its own interpretation of the course of history that it is participating in an advance which is unique and immensely valuable, that it prefers Soviet socialism to Western capitalism and that in any event no viable alternative exists in Russia nor is it at all likely to emerge soon."[27]

Despite Soviet admiration for Western capitalist achievements, there is widespread belief in the U.S.S.R. that a system based on the profitable exploitation of laborers cannot satisfy social needs. Khrushchev vividly expressed this view after he had sampled American television programs for children:

> What kind of food is this for tender young minds? And you wonder why you have a juvenile delinquency problem. Surely your capitalists, who put on those television programs, must have some conscience and can be persuaded not to make money out of deforming children's minds. And if they can't, why can't your society do something about it? Capitalism isn't just an unjust economic system. It's a way of life that leads to a corruption of important values. Television is only one example.[28]

In this connection, I was struck by a remark made by a Soviet friend of mine. He asked me in all sincerity, "What do you *feel* inside when you see a fat capitalist walking down the street?" A similar notion was revealed by the Soviet university student who reported that the increase in the number of strike days in the United States in 1963 over 1962 was a clear indication of the heightening of the class struggle in American society.

The post-Stalinist period has witnessed a somewhat undogmatic questioning of basic Soviet beliefs. Not many people in the U.S.S.R. today will accept statements such as the following one from the Party program of 1961: "The Party is the brain, the honor, and the conscience of our epoch, of the Soviet people, which is effecting great revolutionary transformations. It looks keenly into the future and shows the people scientifically motivated roads along which to advance, arouses titanic energy in the masses, and leads them to the accomplishment of great tasks."[29] The new skepticism, however, is no indication that the belief system will erode beyond recognition or that the leadership has lost faith in its prescriptive resolution of social ills.

General adherence to a Russified Communist creed—a mixture
of patriotically appealing aims and socialist welfare-state goals—is
obtained by a variety of powerful social processes, of which formal
schooling is probably the most important. "To reject the creed is
to reject one's society and one's chances of full acceptance in it—
in short to be an outcast."[30] People are inducted into political-
belief systems just as they are socialized into nonpolitical roles and
social systems.[31] Individuals seldom question what they accept on
faith, and inconsistencies and contradictions in one's political
outlook are not easily perceived. The Soviet citizen may curse
government policies yet revere Lenin's memory. The capacity to
work out a consistent set of political attitudes can be limited also
by a simple lack of information. In the Soviet Union, in particular,
there is but a weak flow of views that might challenge basic assumptions and offer meaningful alternatives.

Nevertheless, Soviet citizens do not automatically rally round
newly promulgated Party policies. On the contrary, Soviet society is marked by apoliticalness. The leadership must overcome
a political apathy that is far more widespread than in most Western countries. Soviet youth, for example, is highly apolitical. According to a poll conducted by *Komsomolskaya pravda*, of 1,000
high-school students in Smolensk between the ages of fifteen and
eighteen only 3 per cent answered in the affirmative when asked
whether they were interested in community work and other participation in the public welfare program.[32] This lack of interest and
involvement in the political process may be found even among
prominent members of elite groups. They, like the public at large,
are frequently denied a sense of participation, and this has reinforced the They-We dichotomy. The division between rulers and
ruled is, of course, present in most societies, but it will be most
clearly defined where citizens believe that (1) they play no important role in determining policy; and (2) they are powerless to
criticize and to change policy once it is announced.[33] Both beliefs
exist in the Soviet Union.

In the spring of 1964, I asked more than a dozen Soviet citizens, mostly from the intelligentsia, if they had any opinion on
who might replace Khrushchev. His ouster came half a year later,
but in early 1964 it was hardly expected. To a man they replied,
"Who knows? *They'll* decide." That his sudden and unexpected

removal was not, and could not be, protested but was passively accepted is a striking example of the cause of political apathy in the U.S.S.R. Compare this with the political turmoil that was created in Greece when King Constantine forced the resignation of his popular Prime Minister, George Papandreou (July 15, 1965), or with the brief flurry that erupted in Israel when Ben-Gurion, after his second retirement, attempted to regain power by openly challenging Premier Levi Eshkol, his personally designated successor (June 5, 1965).

By drastic restrictions on participation, the Soviet system maintains a façade of stability; the essence of conflict is lacking. However, since nonparticipation means that the various societal groups directly concerned may be neither consulted on decisions nor even aware that decisions are impending, Party leaders often find it impossible to marshal enthusiastic support for new policies. Often, therefore, the political awareness of the Soviet public must be aroused *after* decisions are reached, "the meaning of the decision must be explained, its implication in terms of new rights or obligations brought to the attention of interested sections of the population, an attitude of enthusiasm or at least acceptance created, and the significance of the decision in terms of over-all aims demonstrated. This is what in Soviet parlance is termed 'the mobilization of the masses for the fulfillment of Party decisions.' "[34]

IV

The decision-making process in the Soviet Union is organically linked to the succession struggle. In any society, any policy adopted may become the issue that results in a leader's ouster and the steppingstone to power for his successor, or—and this is especially true in Soviet politics—the smoke screen for an intense power struggle. Stalin, in the 1920's, stanchly supported the New Economic Policy until Trotsky and the Left Opposition were eliminated, then he promptly scrapped the NEP. Khrushchev, in his campaign against Malenkov, supported large-scale investment in heavy industry and a harsh line in foreign policy, only to switch positions several years later. The more nonrepresentative and nonresponsible a political system is, the more intense is the succession struggle within a ruling oligarchy, unless one man succeeds in establishing his supreme power, as Stalin did. Then, however, the struggle materializes at the next-lower level, among the lieutenants—for example, the conflict between Malenkov and Zhdanov in the 1940's.

In Great Britain, where opposite conditions prevail, the Prime Minister wields great influence over his party, Parliament, and nation. Yet he must carefully assess important policy decisions since they may affect his political life. He becomes expendable when any one of his policies suffers a severe setback, or when his personal image is stained; his continued presence in office jeopardizes his party's chances at the next election—and great pressure is brought upon him by his own followers to withdraw. Hence, Eden's and Macmillan's resignations, purportedly caused by ill health, occurred in fact because of the Suez failure in 1956 and the Profumo affair in 1962. Were our government organized along British lines, resignation, perhaps, would have been forced on John F. Kennedy after the Bay of Pigs debacle, in April, 1961. In this sense, the American system, as far as the President is concerned, is not as responsible to the electorate as is the British, chiefly because the President's term of office is guaranteed for four years, barring impeachment.

In Japan, despite free elections, the executive's responsibility to its electorate is even more nebulous than ours. The Socialists during the postwar period have so far proved themselves incapable of offering serious opposition at the polls to the dominant Liberal Democratic Party. The Japanese Prime Minister's tenure in office is secure as long as he receives support from the various factions that make up the Liberal Democrats. The leading factor in Prime Minister Kishi's resignation in 1960 was his loss of support from among the contesting factions within his party, not the Socialist and mass demonstrations protesting the ratification of a revised Japanese-American security treaty.[35]

In those societies with no periodic contest for political leadership, with leaders who are neither selected by nor responsible to the public—although they may have achieved popularity, as did Khrushchev—the *coup d'état* becomes the chief weapon for ousting the incumbent dictator. In Latin America, Asia, and Africa, the military often becomes the agent for gaining control. In these societies, the army is usually the only national organization with coercive powers that can claim to stand above party, region, or economic interest. In the Soviet Union, however, and so far this holds true for other Communist-controlled countries and to a lesser extent for non-Communist one-party regimes as well, the Party's political emasculation of its potential military and civilian competition has greatly reduced the ability of the military to effect a *coup d'état*.

Consequently, the power struggle in the U.S.S.R. takes place within the highest policy and administrative organs of the Party— the Politburo and Secretariat of the Central Committee of the CPSU. Potential leaders, supporters, and opponents thus emerge from a pool of less than thirty individuals (including candidate members of the Politburo). Since no acceptable constitutional pro- cedure—such as meaningful periodic elections—exists to regulate succession, the fact that an unceasing jockeying for power among the members of the ruling oligarchy takes place is not surprising. Members of the Politburo and Secretariat, having reached the pin- nacle of power, are, nevertheless, highly insecure because they can be (and have been) removed at any time. The Politburo usually num- bers from ten to twelve members. From March, 1953, to April, 1966, the turnover in membership reached thirty-one. Of the thirty- one, two died of natural causes (Kuusinen and Kozlov), and as far as we know, one was executed (Beria). A similar survival pattern holds for the Secretariat, usually composed of from five to twelve members, with Suslov the only survivor for the same period.

The nature and intensity of the conflict at the top depend on the type of rule operative at a given time: supreme leader, first among equals, or collective leadership. Each type has a different but in- evitable effect on the policy process.

Supreme leader. A Stalin could secure his enthronement by un- leashing a vicious reign of terror, by pitting Party, state, and police institutions against each other, by not holding full Politburo meet- ings (thus preventing potential opponents from communicating), and by promoting a continuous power struggle between his heir presumptive of the moment and counter-heirs. When a lieutenant fell in disfavor, as did Khrushchev, in March, 1951, or died, as did Zhdanov, in August, 1948, it often had an immediate effect on that lieutenant's followers and their institutional power base. With Zhdanov gone, Voznesensky, his closest associate and a Politburo member, was executed, and Zhdanov's seat of power, Leningrad, was purged of his followers, all to the political benefit of Malenkov.*

First among equals. The Khrushchev interlude, June, 1957, to October, 1964, was marked by a general characteristic that has colored the entire post-Stalin period: a great fear on the part of the ruling oligarchy of falling back under the domination of one-man rule. Khrushchev's first-among-equals leadership advanced until *ad hoc* opposition was mustered in sufficient strength to stop him.[36] This occurred in a number of instances even before his final ouster. Having reinstated the Party as the instrument of power, Khrushchev could not play institutions off one against the other, and his unwillingness or inability to unleash a Stalinist reign of terror prevented him from elevating himself above factional infighting. At no time, however, was it quite clear to what extent his powers were limited, nor could anyone have predicted his ouster. He was able to work a sweeping reorganization of the Party apparatus by splitting it, in 1962, into industrial and agricultural divisions, a change that was immediately reversed when he fell from power, indicating that it had widespread opposition. Yet he had great difficulty in expelling the "anti-Party group" from the Party.[37]

Collective leadership. Oligarchic committee rule—the true arena for factional infighting—precipitously accelerates tendencies that already exist under first-among-equals leadership and absolute rule. With the dictator removed from the scene, ambitious faction leaders, who under the supreme leader's rule had aimed principally at sharing patronage and protecting their protégés, emerge as contenders for the vacated throne. To enlarge their power base, they often disregard policy differences and form temporary alliances with leaders of other factions within the Party, the state bureaucracy, the army, the security police, the press, and the professional groupings. The leaders of the strategic elites whose support is essential to the warring factions thus gain a greater voice in the decision-making process. All this, of course, changes when a new ruler seizes control. An illustration in point is the rapid rise and fall of Marshal Zhukov. He was rewarded for his help in keeping Khrushchev

---

* Khrushchev proposed to narrow the differences between town and country by consolidating small collective farms into large ones and building agrotowns to replace small villages. Regarding Voznesensky, once he disappeared—his death was not announced until years later—his economic theories came under attack. Both cases indicate the close tie between the power struggle and policy.

in power in June, 1957, only to be removed from the Party Presidium in November of the same year for his attempt to assert for the army greater independence from Party control.

Some Western students contend that collective leadership produces indecisive and vacillating rule,[38] because of the absence of a supreme arbiter "who can reconcile conflicting claims and attitudes of divergent interests within the Soviet power structure."[39] According to these observers, this condition, if prolonged, threatens the hegemony of the Party machine. The facts, at least to this writer, indicate that these views are inaccurate. In both instances of collective rule—those of the post-Stalin and post-Khrushchev periods—many important policies were adopted: the Virgin-Land Campaign was launched in 1954; economic ministries were disbanded and replaced by economic regional councils in 1957; in November–December, 1964, the limited experiment in which several manufacturers of consumers' goods had followed a production program based on demand, rather than on central planning, was broadly expanded, and in March, 1965, Brezhnev announced a far-reaching program to improve agricultural production. Many more examples could be cited.

These decisions were possible either because majority support for them existed among the several faction leaders within the collective leadership or because the collective leadership came to be dominated by a leader whose followers constituted a majority. Khrushchev's plan for economic reorganization was passed because of the second reason.[40] Collective leadership may, of course, encourage the postponement of decisions if differences of interest or personality cannot be resolved—a common occurrence in societies with representational institutions. But decisions on important matters may be postponed also under a supreme leader, though he may default for no other reason than indifference toward a certain area or fear that a particular policy, however effective, will undermine his power. So far, however, the forceful momentum of Party rule, in particular the dynamics that enable one man rapidly to attain at minimum first-among-equals status, has prevented serious encroachments on Party hegemony.

Khrushchev's fall provided new insights into the succession struggle. He was the first first-among-equals leader in Soviet history to be deposed. Why was he unable to benefit from the purge of

June, 1957? Although no information on how his removal was
effected has so far been made public, the act was possible because
Khrushchev eschewed terror as a means of eliminating opposition.
Bulganin, in speaking of the 1957 attempt, made this point when
he confessed how the "anti-Party group met in my office to arrange
their anti-Party factional work."[41] Such a step was unthinkable
under Stalin, but it became possible under Khrushchev, when important opposition leaders could become members of the Presidium. And it is important to note here that new factions continued
to be formed even after the exclusion of the "anti-Party group."
This was to be expected, with the abject fear of terror removed. If
the "tradition" of nonterror continues, great progress in the ordering of the succession struggle will have been made.

Khrushchev presumably was ousted by a majority of the Party
Presidium (Politburo), many of whom were his hand-picked followers. The action was upheld by the Central Committee because
(if they had a choice) they opposed, among other things, the content of many of his decisions and the style in which he carried
them out. Unlike 1957, the military did not rally to Khrushchev's
support.

The next faction leader to achieve first-among-equals status under these conditions, will have greater limits placed on his powers.
With Khrushchev's fate written on the wall for all to see, the
new leader will be acutely aware that he can be removed by his
fellow Politburo members if he tries to exceed his powers at their
expense, or if he pushes through a series of policies that prove
unsuccessful. Because Soviet government is nonrepresentative and
nonresponsible, he will have less maneuverability to maintain himself in office (unless he receives the support of the military or gains
control of the security police and is willing to revive rule by terror)
than, for instance, the Prime Minister of Great Britain, who can
dismiss ministers, who can advise the Crown on his successor, and
who, as a last resort if his party lieutenants turn against him, can
ask the Crown to dismiss Parliament and to call for new elections.
A popular Prime Minister, moreover, by appealing directly to the
nation for support, has little fear of colleagues who oppose his policies. Such a range of alternatives is not available to the Soviet
leader, whose maneuverability is restricted to organizational support, since he will be stringently opposed by the Politburo mem-

bership if he seeks to build up a popular following. The limits placed upon his rule tend to be ignored by Western analysts. Even Khrushchev with his earthy wit, a past master at stealing the public spotlight, failed to form a strong bond with his countrymen, because he could never subject his popularity to a true electoral test. (He was severely criticized after his fall for appealing to the people over the heads of his colleagues, for publicizing policy before submitting it to the Presidium, and for attempting to enlarge the Presidium base by inviting lower-echelon Party secretaries to attend meetings.)

In fact it may take some time before a strong first-among-equals leader will emerge, and collective leadership may have a longer tenure than it had in the 1920's and 1950's. For, with the fear of imprisonment and death eliminated, there is no urgent movement today to select a first-among-equals leader who would maintain a terror-free policy.

NOTES

1. In the Foreword to Theodore C. Sorenson, *Decision-Making in the White House* (New York: Columbia University Press, 1963), p. xi.
2. E. E. Schattschneider, *The Semisovereign People* (New York: Holt, Rinehart & Winston, 1960), p. 8.
3. This law is also operative in non-political settings—in trade unions, corporations, churches, associations, and within the family circle.
4. Richard Rose, *Politics in England* (Boston and Toronto: Little, Brown & Co., 1964), p. 168.
5. *Ibid.*, p. 169.
6. "In 1956 the *London Evening News* published a cartoon that chivied members of Parliament for voting themselves a larger free gasoline allowance. The House of Commons referred the publication to its Committee of Privileges, which brought out a solemn report finding that the publication 'constitutes a reflection on all members and a contempt.' The committee demanded a 'voluntary withdrawal' by the *News*, and an apology. The *News* duly complied and thus presumably saved its editor from a stay in the tower." *The New York Times,* July 11, 1965.
7. Edward Ashcroft, "How de Gaulle Makes Decisions," *The New York Times Magazine,* March 18, 1962, p. 32.
8. Nicholas Wahl, "The French Political System," in Samuel H. Beer and Adam B. Ulam (eds.), *Patterns of Government* (2nd ed.; New York: Random House, 1962), p. 409.
9. See Zbigniew K. Brzezinski, "Patterns of Autocracy," in Cyril E. Black (ed.), *The Transformation of Russian Society* (Cambridge, Mass.: Harvard University Press, 1960), p. 102.
10. Frederick Barghoorn, "Soviet Russia: Orthodoxy and Adaptiveness," in Lucian W. Pye and Sidney Verba (eds.), *Political Culture and Political Development* (Princeton, N.J.: Princeton University Press, 1965), p. 451.
11. *Ibid.*, pp. 470–71.
12. Robert A. Dahl and Charles E. Lindblom, *Politics, Economics, and Welfare* (New York: Harper & Bros., 1953), p. 227.
13. Rose, *op. cit.*, p. 117.
14. *Pravda*, October 27, 1961.
15. Richard Lowenthal, "The Revolution Withers Away," *Problems of Communism*, XIV, No. 1 (January–February, 1965), 12.
16. N. S. Khrushchev, "Special Report to the 20th Congress of the Communist Party of the Soviet Union," reprinted in *The Crimes of the Stalin Era* (New York: The New Leader, 1956), p. 57.
17. Harold J. Berman, *Justice in the U.S.S.R.* (New York: Vintage Books, 1963), p. 72.
18. *Pravda*, March 20, 1965.
19. Jerry F. Hough, "The Soviet Concept of the Relationship Between the Lower Party Organs and State Administration," *Slavic Review*, XXIV, No. 2 (June, 1965), 230.
20. Robert A. Dahl, *Who Governs?* (New Haven and London: Yale University Press, 1961), p. 306. Although Dahl refers primarily to the American system, his explanation for the *raison d'être* of the political role has broad application.
21. Gaetano Mosca, *The Ruling Class* (New York: McGraw-Hill Co., 1939), p. 62.

22. Harold Lasswell, *Politics: Who Gets What, When, How* (New York: Meridian Books, 1958), p. 32.

23. Theodore C. Sorenson, "Kennedy vs. Khrushchev: The Showdown in Cuba," *Look*, September 7, 1965.

24. Allen B. Ballard, "Private Plots vs. Collective Farms," *The New York Times Magazine*, June 13, 1965, p. 74.

25. Robert Conquest, *Russia After Khrushchev* (New York: Frederick A. Praeger, 1965), p. 77.

26. Hadley Cantril, *Soviet Leaders and Mastery Over Man* (New Brunswick: Rutgers University Press, 1960), p. 2.

27. George Fischer, "The Intelligentsia and Russia," in Black (ed.), *op. cit.*, p. 273.

28. Norman Cousins, "Notes on a 1963 Visit with Khrushchev," *Saturday Review*, November 7, 1964, p. 60.

29. *Program of the Communist Party of the Soviet Union (Draft)* (New York: Crosscurrents Press, 1961), p. 123.

30. Dahl, *op. cit.*, p. 317. Dahl refers to the American creed, but his analysis can be extended to cover the Soviet creed as well.

31. Gabriel A. Almond and Sidney Verba, *Civic Culture: Political Attitudes and Democracy in Five Nations* (Boston and Toronto: Little, Brown & Co., 1965), p. 13.

32. *The New York Times*, June 23, 1965.

33. For greater detail on political alienation in the Soviet Union, see Raymond A. Bauer, Alex Inkeles, and Clyde Kluckhohn, *How the Soviet System Works* (Cambridge, Mass.: Harvard University Press, 1956), pp. 214–15.

34. T. H. Rigby and L. G. Churchward, *Policy-making in the U.S.S.R. 1953–1961: Two Views* (Melbourne: Lansdowne Press, 1962), p. 4.

35. Robert A. Scalapino and Junnosuke Masumi, *Parties and Politics in Contemporary Japan* (Berkeley and Los Angeles: University of California Press, 1962), pp. 140–45. A prolonged recession, plus the emergence of the Komeito (Clean Government Party), may force the Liberal Democrats to be more responsible. See *The New York Times*, August 22, 1965.

36. Conquest, *op. cit.*, p. 72.

37. See the speeches at the Twenty-second Congress, October, 1961. Suslov, in a strongly worded anti-Chinese speech given at the February, 1964, plenum of the Central Committee (CPSU), but not published until April 3, 1964, in *Pravda*, announced the group's expulsion, in passing, almost six years after their attempt to oust Khrushchev.

38. Richard Lowenthal, "Replies," *Problems of Communism*, XIV, No. 4 (July–August, 1965), 76.

39. Seweryn Bialer, "An Unstable Leadership," *ibid.*, p. 73.

40. On the nature of the division within the collective leadership, Conquest writes: "In general we can see that (*a*) there are issues on which the members of the ruling group are divided; (*b*) there are different divisions on different issues; and (*c*) there are circumstances in which a majority on a given issue becomes a minority, with both policy and personal position suffering sudden changes—indicating that faction is not fully polarized but that, on the contrary, there are intermediate or wavering positions." Conquest, *op. cit.*, p. 105.

41. *Plenum Tsentral'nogo Komiteta Kommunisticheskoi Partii Sovetskogo Soyuza, 15–19 dekabriya 1958 goda: Stenograficheskii otchet* (Moscow: Gosudarstvennoe Izdatel'stvo Politicheskoi Literatury, 1958), p. 338.

2

Family Reforms on the Road to Communism

Peter H. Juviler

EDITORS' INTRODUCTION

Two charts of achievement hang above the assembly line. One chart lists the workers' percentage fulfillment of production norms, the other, their children's grades in school. A furious wife writes eighty complaints about her unfaithful husband to various party and public organizations and to the institute at which he is studying. All are ignored except two: that to the courts, in which she refuses to agree to a divorce, and that to his place of study, which causes him to be expelled just before the completion of his diploma work, the decision reversible only if he should return to his wife. Dancing, singing, solemn registration, a speech by a deputy of the local soviet, these mark a "Komsomol wedding"—part of the effort of the state to implant secular ceremonials, which it recognizes, in place of the church ceremonials, from which it has taken all legal force. Families find that real property is restricted to a five-room house or a cooperative apartment, that ownership of the means of production is restricted to the small farm implements of peasant households and the tools of individual artisans.

Among industrial nations, such wide-ranging state impingements on family privacy are peculiar to the Soviet system, and to others patterned after it. Family privacy is only relative, however. One cannot quarrel with Wolfgang Friedmann's conclusion that "every modern state is taking an active and, often, a commanding part in the regulation of family life." In the Soviet Union, as in other modern states, laws governing marriage and divorce are central to this regulation. Stalin's family-law reform of 1944 attempted to increase the birth rate and family stability by a series of conservative provisions that greatly reduced individual discretion in marriage and divorce.

The Stalinist legacy in family policy has been the target of a determined and open attack by reformers who have tried, since 1954, to restore the "Leninist" principles of "freedom of marriage and divorce," of full female emancipation, and of legal equality for all children, extramarital or not. Lawyers, prosecutors, novelists, and poets, family people in trouble, "men in the street," joined the debate. By 1957, the prospect was bright that new laws would be made in response to the hue and cry. By 1963, the draft of a reformed family law was circulated for discussion, only to be mysteriously delayed. The reasons for this delay, the resumption of the reform process after Khrushchev's fall, and the political implications of these developments are the central questions of this chapter.

After the birth of Lydia Z.'s son in 1944, Lydia returned from military to civilian life. She had to part from K., her child's unmarried father, who remained at the front. K. subsequently refused her requests for help, and called her "charlatan" and "swindler." "Are you not aware of the edict of July 8, 1944?" he wrote to Lydia ten years later, in 1954, when she again asked him for moral and material support in their child's upbringing. "I have no obligation to you or your child since the child was born of an unregistered marriage. . . . You must get out of your scrape as best you can."[1]

K. was right. The Family Edict of July 8, 1944,* has protected

* The full title of the edict is: "On Increasing State Assistance to Pregnant Women, Mothers of Many Children, and Unmarried Mothers, Strengthening the Protection of Motherhood and Childhood; on Establishing the Honorific Title of Mother Heroine, and on Instituting the Order Motherhood Glory, and the Motherhood Medal."

K. and millions of other unmarried fathers from all legal consequences of their paternity, for it banned paternity and support suits
and prescribed that extramarital children born after publication of
the edict use their mothers', not their fathers' surnames, thus end-
ing their right to inheritance from their fathers. And since the edict
did not allow fathers even to acknowledge their paternity, the institution of illegitimacy, which the Bolsheviks abolished in 1917, was
in effect restored. In addition, the edict ended legal recognition of
unregistered (common-law) marriages, declaring that "only registered marriage creates conjugal rights and duties." This served to
reinforce another conservative provision of the edict: the requirement of a costly, complicated, not-always-successful divorce procedure in two stages in two courts.[2]

These Stalinist laws on family life have been the central issues
in a heated debate that has persisted for more than a decade
after Stalin. Lest the reader discount the drama of the bitter public
attacks on the Family Edict, believing that since the edict was enacted under Stalin it had become "fair game" for criticism, I shall
get ahead of my story and mention that Nikita Khrushchev, Soviet
leader during much of the debate, had a personal stake in the
measure: Khrushchev initiated the Family Edict.

Since the edict's initiator was in power during most of the period covered here, it is well to review his apparent purpose in the
edict, setting it against the background of the earliest Soviet family
reforms, those of the years 1917–26.[3]

In the first Soviet family reforms, during 1917 and 1918, the
Bolsheviks, in areas under their control, established equal rights
of support and inheritance for all children, whether born in or out
of wedlock. They swept away religious control over, and registration of, marriage and divorce, recognizing only civil marriage. Divorce became inexpensive and automatic. The 1926 family codes
removed divorce from the courts, making it a simple matter of registration and of mailing a notice to one's spouse—the so-called
postcard divorce. The 1926 codes gave unregistered marriage legal
force in most of the U.S.S.R.

The Bolshevik sponsors of these early reforms, such as, in 1926,
R.S.F.S.R. Commissar of Justice, Dmitri I. Kursky and his deputy,
Nikolai V. Krylenko, believed the reforms would help to eliminate
"counterrevolutionary" influences on and within the family, to

"emancipate women" (a traditional Marxist and Russian revolutionary ideal), and thereby to channel some of the vast reservoir of Soviet womanpower out of the home and into the economy.

Within a decade, the men who had been victorious in 1917–26 against both the advocates of free love and the champions of conservative family laws began to vanish along with their radical accomplishments. Stalin's form of conservatism meant continued lip service to the Marxist-Leninist ideal of "emancipating women," but he pursued social purposes wholly incompatible with the ideal. Ironically, Stalin, so wasteful of human lives, worried about manpower. Manpower resources for the fulfillment of his Five-Year Plans faced *qualitative* depletion due to juvenile delinquency. To help combat delinquency, Stalin, in 1935/36, re-enlisted the family as educator and sought to enforce parental responsibilities by promoting a new image of the "strong Soviet family." Manpower resources faced *quantitative* depletion because the same chaos of agricultural collectivization and of urbanization that caused increasing delinquency brought also a falling birth rate. Stalin's response was to glorify motherhood and, probably in reaction to the apparently shocking, never-published results of the 1936 census, to ban abortions for other than medical reasons. The ban on abortions was incorporated in the decree of June 27, 1936.

Stalin's regime issued the ban—after public discussion revealed bitter and widespread opposition to it—with the dubious justification that recent social progress, plus the decree's provisions for increased state aid to families, meant that mothers could now easily work and have children too. The decree also raised divorce fees and penalties for nonpayment of support, and prescribed punitive measures against "frivolous attitudes toward the family and family obligations." A higher birth rate, conscientious family upbringing, and family stability, interrelated goals of Stalin's family legislation, served one apparent central purpose: maximization of utilizable manpower.

The Family Edict of July 8, 1944, came without prior public discussion. Numerous Soviet sources indicate that the edict marked an extension of Stalin's social engineering for a strong family and, especially, for a higher birth rate. Thus, the U.S.S.R. Deputy Procurator-General for Juvenile Affairs, V. Tadevosyan, wrote in an authoritative article: "High fertility of the Soviet family was one of the socialist state's basic purposes in publishing the decree of June 27, 1936, on the banning of abortions. It is natural, therefore, that one of the most crucial goals of the edict of July 8, 1944, is to stimulate the birth rate."[4]

When the edict appeared, Soviet troops were crossing into Eastern Europe, on the way to victory. But the wartime decrease in birth rate, the loss of 20 million men in the war, and the predictable further drop in birth rate that would come in the postwar period from a surplus of women over men (especially in the most fertile age groups) had confronted Stalin with prospects of serious population depletion. Apparently, the edict was to increase the birth rate by maintaining family stability—deemed essential to fertility and proper upbringing[5]—and by encouraging unmarried and married mothers—with greatly augmented state assistance and with medals—to have their children and to eschew "underground" abortions. Maternity allowances and the number of child-care facilities, such as nurseries and kindergartens, were increased. Medals of Mother Heroine, Motherhood Glory, and Motherhood were minted for married or unmarried mothers of 10, 7–9, and 5–6 children, respectively. Unmarried mothers qualified for monthly state grants (halved since 1948) of 10, 15, and 20 rubles for 1, 2, and 3 or more children, respectively, or if they preferred, they could place the children in state homes.[6] Family stability was to be promoted (1) by sparing a man and his legal family the financial and emotional shocks that might arise from paternity and support suits,[7] from his official acknowledgment of paternity, or from an extramarital child's bearing his name, and (2) by discouraging hasty divorces. Thus, the Family Edict was not aimed at preventing extramarital relations. Rather, it was an attempt to increase the fertility rate of both married and unmarried women at a time when for every 4 men there were 6 women between the ages of 20 and 39 years.[8]

Reform Proposed

With the post-Stalin thaw, long-repressed criticisms of the justice and effectiveness of the Family Edict[9] came out into the open. Readers of *Literaturnaya gazeta* (*Literary Gazette*) for January 16, 1954, responded with special interest to journalist Elena Serebrovskaya's "Life Calls for an Amendment." She confined this first public attack on the Family Edict to a study of the traumatic experiences of extramarital children, whom the edict caused to be "fatherless." Serebrovskaya demanded that there be no more "blank space under 'father.'" "All Soviet citizens must have the same birth certificate," she declared.

Literaturnaya gazeta waited seven months to sum up the heavy mail response. Perhaps political consultations were held during that time on the advisability of going beyond Serebrovskaya's trial balloon. When at last the magazine replied, on August 28, it reported a huge, mostly favorable response. Correspondents wanted more than Serebrovskaya asked—in fact, they wanted a full program of reform: equal rights for all children and equal obligations for fathers and mothers, including for fathers the right to acknowledge their paternity. The magazine expressed its own qualified support for reform.

The conservative reply of the most eminent Soviet family lawyer, Dr. Grigori Markovich Sverdlov, soon found its way into print. Dr. Sverdlov, a scholar long connected with the Institute of Law of the U.S.S.R. Academy of Sciences, told the reformers, who were virtually advocating repeal of the Family Edict, that they should not lose sight of the issue: "How are we to revise our denial of any legal consequences of established paternity without hurting our struggle to strengthen the family?"

Dr. Sverdlov's main argument against the liberals, such as the editors of *Literaturnaya gazeta*, was that paternity and support suits, necessary to ensure the equality of all children, could shatter the otherwise stable registered families of transgressing fathers. He conceded that "old ideas about illegitimate children still survive in some people's minds." Children, then, should all have the same kind of birth certificate, he said. The father should be able to *acknowledge* paternity, and to be registered as the father, unless the mother contests his claim to paternity. These measures would entitle children to support, inheritance, father's name, and death benefits.[10] The issue of whether or not to make all children equal affected roughly 4 million illegitimate children under eighteen, their number then increasing by 300,000 annually,[11] and, of course, it also affected the millions of fathers of these children, and the fathers' registered families, if they were married.

Aleksandra Yosifovna Pergament was the leading advocate of

reform and the "friendly adversary" of Dr. Sverdlov. A respected and experienced expert on civil and family law, she worked in the government's All-Union Institute of Juridical Sciences, which was renamed the All-Union Institute of Soviet Legislation in April, 1963, a combined legislative reference service, graduate law school, and research institute. In reviewing Sverdlov's book and its arguments against sweeping reforms on illegitimacy, Pergament stated that Sverdlov had glossed over the injustices under the Family Edict. To stipulate merely that an unmarried father might acknowledge his paternity would *increase* the inequality between the sexes, since the father could choose to deny his obligations but the mother's obligations would begin with the birth of the child "regardless of her wishes."[12] Later, Pergament buttressed her position with a key article whose arguments reappeared subsequently in the works of her partisans. Not support payments but extramarital relations themselves break up the family, she wrote. Since the Family Edict encourages men to indulge in extramarital liaisons by freeing them from financial responsibility for the offspring of such ties, it actually weakens, not strengthens, the family. Pergament reminded her readers that the edict had re-established the inequality which had obtained under Czarist laws on illegitimacy and which Lenin had called "base without precedent, repulsive, filthy, beastly and crude." It is unjust, Pergament argued further, that support payments for children born in registered wedlock are larger than the grants for illegitimate children, and continue until the legitimate child reaches eighteen, but cease with the illegitimate child at age twelve.

"None of the defenders of the edict of July 8, 1944," Pergament wrote, "has showed how, in fact, social conditions can justify a departure from Leninist principles. . . . Here they usually limit themselves to obscure references to the need further to strengthen the family."[13] Perhaps in this passage, but certainly in her review of Sverdlov's book, Pergament indicated that she wished Sverdlov would defend the edict on concrete social grounds rather than try to minimize its unfairness:

> It may be possible to show that the retreat from the principle [of equality of men and women] is dictated by *more important state interests*—which is incorrect in our opinion—but one must not deny that indubitable fact. Such incorrect interpretation of the

provisions of the law hinders not only the necessary amendment of the law but also its correct application.[14]

To which "more important state interests" could Pergament have been referring? Undoubtedly she had in mind the regime's effort to replenish the reserves of Soviet manpower by raising the birth rate. This was, of course, the main goal of the Family Edict. But the public debate, in contrast with the disputes behind the scenes, remained discreetly silent on this sensitive topic until 1962.

Although possibly hampered, then, by limitations on what they could publicly discuss, the reformers maintained a determined assault, assisted by *Literaturnaya gazeta*'s now impassioned polemics and letters from the composer Dmitri Shostakovich, the writer Ilya Ehrenburg, the poet Samuel Marshak, and the outstanding specialist on children's diseases, Professor Georgi Speransky.[15]

Reformers attacked the Family Edict's divorce rules no less heatedly. "If husband and wife do not love each other and have started new families," the Chief Justice of the Ukranian Supreme Court asked an interviewer from *Literaturnaya gazeta*, "will either persuasion or court proceedings make them live together?" And the Deputy Chief Justice of the Kiev Provincial Court stated: "When the provincial court has refused divorce, husband and wife almost never go on living together. Usually these husbands and wives go to court again later, or start new families, this time unsanctioned by law. Divorce procedure is excessively complicated and needs simplification."[16]

Conservatives and reformers agreed in most cases that reform of the divorce law was needed. Dr. Sverdlov, who made modest proposals for change as early as 1946, began the public post-Stalin discussion of divorce in 1953, recommending a simplification of the procedure to obtain divorce, but only when by mutual consent. A. Y. Pergament and B. S. Antimonov disagreed. They wanted to go further, urging easier divorce not only in cases of mutual consent, but whenever the family had actually broken up.

Under what circumstances divorce should be simplified emerged as but one of a formidable array of questions confronting the experts and the public: Should divorce hearings in cases of mutual consent be transferred from the courts to ZAGS (the common name for the Civil Registry Bureaus, based on the first letters of the Russian words for "registration of acts of civil status"), where they were handled in 1917–26, or should *all* divorces be handled there, as in 1926–44? Should specific grounds for divorce be named, to replace the working criterion of family breakup? Should the principle of fault be applied, as in many Western and some Communist countries where the courts will not award divorce unless the respondent is guilty of legal fault—adultery, cruelty, desertion, etc.—and, in some of these countries, unless the plaintiff is legally free of such fault? If divorces remain in the courts, should the procedure not be simplified into one or two hearings in a people's court? By 1956/57, Pergament shared the view that all divorces should be given back to ZAGS when there was mutual consent and the couple seeking divorce had no children.[17]

Thrashing Out a Reform Bill

The reformers seemed nearer to victory in February, 1957, when the case for new family legislation was presented by Deputies Rumyantsev and Pusep to the U.S.S.R. Supreme Soviet, the sporadically assembling, primarily ceremonial and symbolic parliament. The prestige of E. P. Pusep came not so much from his almost powerless post of Deputy Chairman of the Presidium of the Estonian Supreme Soviet as it did from his distinguished record as combat pilot and Hero of the Soviet Union in World War II. Pusep told the Soviet of Nationalities, one of the two chambers of the Supreme Soviet, that reform of the family law was an "urgent" question. "The legal status of extramarital children, materially and psychologically worse than that of other children, can in no way be justified," he declared, and went on to denounce the difficulties in obtaining divorce, such as the long distances a plaintiff might have to travel to seek divorce in the court district in which the respondent spouse lived, or the courts' refusals on occasion to grant justified divorce. "Maintaining the legal appearance of marriage when the old family no longer exists, when a new family has formed, only violates the rights of the children. The situation approaches the ridiculous when a father who lives in unregistered marriage must adopt his own children in order to give them his name."

A. M. Rumyantsev pleaded the cause of extramarital children to the other chamber of the Supreme Soviet, the Soviet of the Union, urging that family reform be included in the ongoing campaign of legal reforms, the success of which

> . . . will depend on how much we heed the voice of the community, the proposals and comments of the toilers, who are vitally interested that codes of laws, first, serve the interests of Soviet society, of building Communism; and second, be worked out and adopted as quickly as possible. For example, the need for revising family legislation has already been voiced in the press. What is to be done about the legal status of children born out of registered marriage? By recognizing only registered marriage, the edict of the Presidium of the U.S.S.R. Supreme Soviet of July 8, 1944, puts the children born out of registered marriage in a different position from that of children born in registered marriage.[18]

Exactly what prompted Rumyantsev and Pusep to speak out for reform remains shrouded in secrecy. Their parallel pleas could hardly have been a spontaneous expression of their right of initiative as deputies to the Supreme Soviet. Their statements in the two chambers smacked of pre-planning, in which the Party leadership no doubt played a part. It is no secret in the U.S.S.R. that "legislation and all other activities" of the Supreme Soviet "proceed under the guidance of the Communist Party," that Soviet laws merely provide for the concrete fulfillment of "the goals that the Party sets for the Soviet people."[19]

Nevertheless, Rumyantsev and Pusep seemed to be more than mere mouthpieces for the Party. First, Rumyantsev, though a veteran Party publicist and *apparatchik*, had a moderately liberal preference for greater personal freedom and less Party tutelage, as evidenced by his striking defense of intellectuals and his social criticism when editor of *Pravda* in 1965 (see Introduction to Chapter 4).[20] Second, the Party at this time was not monolithic, but was divided by Khrushchev's battle with the "anti-Party group."

The true origin of the legislative initiative lies, then, somewhere between Party fiat and the deputies' own discretion. As a member of the elite Central Committee, editor of its theoretical journal, *Kommunist,* and thus a department head in the Central Committee's apparatus, Rumyantsev stood close to the winds of conflict and change at the Party summit. He must have had the approval of at least a portion of the Party leadership for an attempt to draft new rules on marriage and divorce. He himself might have introduced the case for reform before the Secretariat of the Central Committee or even before the Presidium (Politburo). In the absence of a clear Party endorsement through a Central Committee resolution, an editorial, etc., Rumyantsev's remarks to the Supreme Soviet come the closest to an unequivocal Party stand. But he did not speak in the name of the Party. Perhaps the Party leaders had done no more than agree that attempts should be made to legislate family reform, while reserving judgment on how far the reform should go.

Certainly, Rumyantsev did not speak for Khrushchev. He was not a "Khrushchev man." In fact, he succeeded a Khrushchev supporter, Satyukov, as editor of *Pravda* after Khrushchev's fall. Moreover, was it possible for Khrushchev to share Rumyantsev's aversion for the Family Edict in 1957? Khrushchev had advocated the edict in 1944 and still supported it twenty years later.

Despite the unpromising stand of the Party, virtually all experts with any claim to speak on family policy soon joined in a comprehensive effort to draft liberal laws for the family. After the 1957 Supreme Soviet meeting, Pergament launched this effort in a speech before a large audience of jurists during a conference on codification at the All-Union Institute of Juridical Sciences.[21]

True, revision of the civil law and the criminal law took priority. (That had been the center of attention also in the Supreme Soviet's sessions on legal reforms.) However, the first attempts at drafting a new family law that would resolve the complex issues of illegitimacy and divorce appeared soon after the meeting at the Institute of Juridical Sciences. Various proposals were made during exchanges at the 1959 regional conferences on codification, in which some republics produced drafts of republic family codes; in the governmental drafting commissions of the union republics; in the professional journals and newspapers; and eventually, in a working commission on family law of the Juridical Commission of the U.S.S.R. Council of Ministers. (By the end of 1961, the commission had prepared a preliminary draft of Basic Family Law, which was to replace the 1944 edict and other all-union acts.)

The reformers seemed even closer to success when the Legislative Committees of the two chambers of the Supreme Soviet met jointly (the usual procedure) in the Kremlin on December 3, 1961.

The committees heard the comments and reports of "ministers of the U.S.S.R., leaders of central agencies and institutions, representatives of the community scholars," the committees' report disclosed. Heads of the Ideological Department and other departments of the Central Committee probably attended among the "leaders of central agencies and institutions." The committees "decided to prepare a draft of a Basic Family Law of the U.S.S.R. and the union republics," the official report stated.[22] It would be based on the preliminary version drafted in the Juridical Commission.

Legislative work and controversy centered in 1962 around the special subcommittee on family reform appointed by the Legislative Committees. The subcommittee consisted of about thirty-five jurists (including Pergament and Sverdlov), a number of experts in such fields as education, public health, child-care institutions, and law enforcement, and several government and Party officials. In addition, many experts were invited in for consultation on specific problems. Olga Pavlovna Kolchina, Second Secretary of the Moscow Province Party Committee, newly elected to the Supreme Soviet on March 18, 1962,[23] presided at the meetings. Reportedly, these discussions were very open and frank, and sometimes heated. Participants used unpublished statistics on population, divorce, illegitimacy, and crime to prove their points and to formulate policies.

The Legislative Committees announced that they had "approved in the main" a first draft of the Basic Family Law and had "decided to complete work on the draft" so as to prepare it "for approval by the U.S.S.R. Supreme Soviet."[24] From informed sources, one gathers the impression that law faculties and law institutes, the republic governments, and central and republic agencies concerned with the family received a copy of the unpublished draft for further discussions. The discussions were frequently attended by members of the special subcommittee on family reform, who went out from Moscow to advise, comment, gather opinion, to work, in a word, toward uniformity of the Basic Family Law and the fifteen republic family codes that would be based on it.[25] Comments then streamed back to the offices of the Legislative Committees. Every one of the scores of legal scholars, judges, and ZAGS officials whom I interviewed in Moscow, Leningrad, Riga, Alma-

Ata, and Tashkent had participated in such discussions, and most of them had previously worked on the central drafting subcommittee or similar committees in the republics.

Unexpected Difficulties

"The draft is in preparation—that means it will soon be law. All those who cherish the welfare of women and the family await it impatiently," wrote the young lawyer-turned-littérateur Arkadi Vaksberg, in February, 1963. "Drafting the new family law is nearly completed," the September, 1963, issue of *Semya i shkola* (*Family and School*) announced enthusiastically. "Now the Khrushchev thaw is reaching women," Edmund Stevens reported from Moscow in April, 1964.[26]

Upon my arrival in Moscow two months earlier, I had received, between the tenth and the fifteenth of February, a much more pessimistic story from several jurists long active in the movement for legal reforms.[27] I was surprised to hear that no reform of family law was pending after all. Prospects brightened temporarily on February 16—*Trud* published Deputy Kolchina's forecast, tinged with doubt, that the draft of the Basic Family Law would "apparently" (*vidimo*) be issued soon for public discussion.[28] But the bill never reached the stage of public discussion, let alone passage. The disappointment of the reformers was keen. The head of Moscow ZAGS, for example, said in an interview in April: "How many children and adults have been hurt by that blank space on the birth certificate under 'father'! How many emotional articles and letters about it have been published! But all to no avail. They have all been awaiting a new law on marriage and the family for many years."[29]

According to informed opinion in early June, 1964: "The reforms were stopped at the top, for how long we don't know." And the otherwise detailed report of the Legislative Committees' meeting of July 9 and 10, 1964, contained not a word on the Basic Family law.[30] Why had the reforms been stopped? Almost all the informed sources I questioned about the delays referred to the "complexity" of the issues. Did the complexity deadlock the legislative drafters, or was the suspension imposed "at the top"? Let us turn for clues to the various levels of Soviet society that participated in making the reform.

The Mass Public

The Soviet mass public has influenced family legislation by
its behavior, rather than by its articulated opinions. The 1926
R.S.F.S.R. code recognizing unregistered marriage and the 1936
decree banning abortions were enacted despite the apparently overwhelming public opinion expressed against them. The public
had no chance to discuss the 1944 edict. During the recent attempts to amend it at least one very influential Soviet social
scientist (supported by a sizable, but not precisely ascertainable,
proportion of the involved professionals and officials) argued before his colleagues and the drafting committees that the public
would react emotionally rather than rationally to any published
proposals for a new family law. He maintained that there should
be no public discussion, therefore, until the experts had researched,
clarified, and made basic decisions on all major provisions of the
new law. When the Basic Law does come up for nationwide consideration, the discussion will probably follow standard procedures
which reflect this cautious philosophy. For nationwide discussions
are carefully controlled: "The Communist Party is the initiator,
organizer, and leader of our nationwide discussion of the most
important bills; that has become a tradition with us . . . it leads
and directs the participation of the broad masses of the toilers in
Soviet lawmaking."[31]

Feedback to policy-makers about the impact of the Family
Edict on the mass public took two forms: (1) comments by administrators (e.g., judges and ZAGS officials) and by other
interested persons in relatively small power and professional elites,
and (2) ascertained hard facts about birth rates, sexual behavior,
social discipline, and family relations.

To indicate that the delay could not have been due to the
simplest possible reason—i.e., a significant decrease in the pro-
reform feedback—let us look at the 1963/64 feedback favoring
reform. The following example is taken from Vaksberg's account
of the plight of a couple whose case he had followed for years.

Sergei left Katya and their child in 1961. Katya, like Lydia Z.,
could make no legal claims on Sergei for support based on his
paternity, because he was not her registered husband. The child

could bear only its father's surname. This might have caused him shame and embarrassment later at school. Katya herself was the victim of anachronistic prejudices and double standards. She was told at work that she had "disgraced the collective" and "besmirched the honor of her brigade." "Sergei? He's a man . . . what can you expect from him?" Katya received the regular state help to all mothers, and, as an unwed mother, a monthly allowance and special priority for her child to enter nursery and kindergarten. But her small monthly allowance of five rubles did not begin to cover the child's maintenance. Sergei married another woman, but returned undivorced to Katya in 1963.

At the time Vaksberg wrote, the couple was expecting another child. They could not get a larger place to live and had to remain in Katya's small room. Sergei was denied a permanent residential permit to be with her, because the Family Edict stipulated that "only registered marriage creates the rights and duties of spouses." Paradoxically, social-security agencies recognized the unregistered marriage—because Katya was living with the father of her child, the agencies cut off the grant she had been receiving as an unwed mother. Divorce his wife and marry Katya? Sergei could not. He was earning 70–80 rubles a month. The petition cost 10 rubles and the newspaper notice that was required prior to a reconciliation hearing in people's court cost 30–40 rubles. The divorce registration fee after the second and final hearing in a provincial or city court meant another 50 rubles, at minimum. Sergei's wife lived in the Urals, and since Sergei was suing, he would have had to take leave for each hearing and pay for fares there and back. Should his wife object, there was the chance that the divorce would have been refused after all. Sergei could not adopt his child, one way to "legitimize" him, because his angry wife would not give the needed consent.[32]

Few couples caught in the toils of the Family Edict experienced all the troubles of Katya and Sergei. Still, the Family Edict touched more people in 1963/64 than it had ten years earlier, when it first came under public debate. The number of illegitimate children under eighteen reached a peak of at least 6 million in 1962, according to necessarily imprecise calculations. That this total may err on the conservative side is indicated by Vaksberg's figure of

8 million illegitimate offspring (he does not specify their age span) in 1964. There were, in 1962, approximately 5 million unwed mothers.[33]

Adoption was no general solution. Though national figures on adoption rates have not been published, Soviet officials may have available from the ZAGS archives findings which indicate that probably only one illegitimate child in twenty has a father not only willing, as was Sergei, but also *able* to adopt it.

Soviet data and the first Soviet sociological publishings on divorce corroborate Vaksberg's case study of the difficulties that ensnared Katya and Sergei. Sociologist Anatoli Kharchev wrote that in the first years of the Family Edict, "families that had actually broken up greatly exceeded in number the court-granted divorces, for some judges 'overdid it' applying the edict and sometimes refused divorces when they were undoubtedly justified." The practice eased later (my impression from records and interviews is that this occurred right after Stalin). Kharchev cites valuable statistics: e.g., in Kiev, in 1939 (a relatively quiet period), there were 2,063 (court) divorces and 7,458 marriages; in 1949, under the Family Edict, there were only 824 divorces, and 6,592 marriages; in 1958, there were 1,337 divorces and 7,577 marriages.[34] The nation-wide legal divorce rate per thousand population rose from 0.4 in 1950 to 1.5 in 1964 (that of the more urbanized United States was 2.2). However, the average legal divorce rate in the urbanized non-Asian parts of the Soviet Union was at least as high as the U.S. rate; in Moscow it was 3.6.[35] This means that over 600,000 Soviet people every year managed to get through the divorce obstacle course, at a minimum fee of a hundred rubles, the approximate monthly pay of a skilled worker, farm-tractor owner, or schoolteacher. (Divorce in the United States, of course, is no less expensive, and thus also discriminates against poorer people, and in practice is sometimes more complex—involving a trip out of state. In the United States, expenses are mostly for lawyers, while in the Soviet Union, the fees go mostly to the state.) According to Kharchev, one spouse or both already have an illegitimate child in a new family in 20 per cent of a sample of Leningrad divorces, largely because of delays in obtaining divorces.[36]

The "Community"

Rumyantsev quite correctly stated in his above-mentioned speech to the Supreme Soviet that "the community has been insisting we restore the family-law norms of the first decrees of 1918, signed by Lenin. These norms made all children equal in the eyes of the law, regardless of the relationship of their parents."[37]

The "community" (*obshchestvennost'*), whose opinion Rumyantsev invoked, is defined by the Soviet unabridged dictionary as the "stratum of society that participates in public life and represents public opinion." In the movement for reform of the family law, the "community" consisted of the persons professionally or emotionally involved in the policy debates, including the legal scholars, pedagogues, psychologists, doctors, and officials of the health, police, judicial, and other agencies who had been called in as consultants or as members of governmental working committees in the effort to formulate the Basic Family Law.

The reformers in the "community" marshaled strong forces. In Uzbekistan, most lawyers and legislators approved the 1959–64 drafts of reformist family codes. Reformers won majorities on the Legislative Committees of the Supreme Soviet. Reformers wrote an overwhelming majority of the articles published during the debates. Most judges strongly supported a simplification of divorce. One judge put himself in the radical fringe by demanding such provisions as the recognition of unregistered marriage. The administrative apparatus of ZAGS, which is made up mainly of women, seemed to be for reform. No press organs came out against reform—though this may have been due to "party discipline." Popular publications such as *Literaturnaya gazeta* (at least through 1962), *Semya i shkola*, and *Vechernyaya Moskva* (*Evening Moscow*) indicated support. *Izvestia*, the government newspaper, printed many reformist articles and letters. M. Anyants, a department head in the government's Juridical Commission, which prepared the first version of the new family law, supported reform.[38]

Dr. Sverdlov and the other conservatives *appeared* to be but a small group among the active debaters. To the right of them were the ultraconservatives, who found no fault with the Family Edict. A girl is frivolous if she engages in an extramarital liaison, and she must pay the consequences, they said. The state grants are all that she deserves.[39]

Was the "community" simply deadlocked over complex issues? Questions of wedding ceremonials, marriage age, size of support payments, grounds for deprivation of parental rights, etc., had been long discussed, but not one appeared to be an issue that could have delayed the entire reform.

In February, 1964, Kolchina had outlined a few of the provisions of the draft that was "apparently soon to be released for public discussion." Divorce, one of the two main problems of reform, would be simpler, she stated; it would be conducted in only one court, the people's court, as reformers wanted, and without newspaper publication of notice.[40] I gathered that reformers and conservatives had reached a consensus on divorce when Pergament and others dropped their demand for ZAGS divorces in cases of mutual consent (80-90 per cent of divorces). On illegitimacy, the heart of the "complexity," Kolchina said that the draft specified the same kind of birth certificate for all children, allowed acknowledgment of paternity, and granted paternity suits "in certain cases." Which cases? Reform opinion had been divided, and many reformers had sought to prevent abuses and excessive turmoil by allowing suits only after prolonged, not "casual," relationships.[41] The question of when to allow paternity suits was clearly of crucial social and political importance, since there were millions of unwed mothers. Should the new law have retroactive force?

None of these questions presented insurmountable problems, however. Difficult problems had been solved before in Soviet policy-making. The informed persons I interviewed had expected reform in 1963. Nobody mentioned "deadlock" to me. Rather, when I had any answer at all to my question as to *how* the complexity caused the delay, the vague and evasive replies referred to the influence of the objections leading conservatives had raised so strongly, and to the intervention of "personalities" high up. This brings us to the issues as the Party leaders may have seen them.

The Party

Despite the intriguing implications of a much-meeting, increasingly de-atomized, cohesive "community," we must be sobered by the facts of the Party's untrammeled powers of intervention and veto. All legislation, Soviet writers emphasize, is under Party direction, and "the Legislative Committees of the U.S.S.R. Supreme Soviet and its other permanent committees work on the basis of decisions of the Party and under its direct supervision."[42]

Several knowledgeable people told me that the legislative formulation in the Legislative Committees (containing 62 of the 1,443 deputies to the Supreme Soviet)[43] proceeded under the surveillance of the Ideological Department of the Central Committee in 1963/64. This department carried out Party guidance of propaganda, schools, science, and culture. It had the day-to-day responsibility for checking the execution of all phases of family policy, including the campaign for "new Soviet rituals" of marriage, etc. (Before the Revolution, the surveillance of family morality, upbringing, and rituals was the province of the churches.) Basic questions of principle and final approval of the reforms for passage were reserved for the Presidium (Politburo) of the Central Committee.

Did the Party delay reform simply from old-fashioned notions of male prerogatives? The reform debates certainly resembled a battle of the sexes. Women such as Pergament, N. Ershova, and N. V. Orlova of the Institute of Law, M. G. Masevich of the Kazakh Academy of Sciences, Dr. Kh. S. Sulaimanova, outstanding Uzbek jurist and former Minister of Justice of Uzbekistan, and the late N. V. Rabinovich of Leningrad University were in the van of the assault on the Family Edict.[44] Ershova indignantly countered her senior colleague Dr. Sverdlov with such arguments as: it is not possible for us to raise "all-round men of the future" if we "do not demand the same high moral standards of men as of women"; how paradoxical to expect unfounded claims of paternity and support from Soviet women, "who have shown their great moral conscience as they helped alongside men in cultural and economic construction throughout the entire history of the Soviet state!"[45]

When I put these arguments to them, conservative officials and jurists responded with: "A woman is a maid only once and must guard her female honor." "We must protect the family, the male [pause] . . . and the female." Medal-winning workers scoffed at the easy morality in some Soviet films and at the ridiculous beehive hairdos affected by some young girls.[46] And in Hollywood, Khrushchev deplored the cancan.

Apparently, the moral standards of the Party elite (a more traditionalist group than the Bolshevik reformers of the 1920's) and the conservatives were, and probably still are, Victorian in family matters (though, of course, less so in the matter of the social role of women). By "Victorian" is meant not puritanical, but adhering to a double standard. Many of the generation of men to which these conservatives belonged had fathered illegitimate children during and after World War II. Thus morality and self-interest worked hand in hand to incline them toward opposing a repeal of the 1944 edict that relieved them of any obligation toward their extra marital offspring. Morality and self-interest caused them to welcome and support the delay in reforms prompted by the "more important state interests" to which Pergament alluded in her dispute with Sverdlov. These interests were, above all, the "Communist upbringing of the younger generation" and the raising of the birth rate.

Why the Party Needs the Family

Members of the "community" told me that in the conservatives' defense of the Family Edict at drafting sessions and at their own institutional meetings, the most telling argument brought against lifting the ban on paternity suits was that giving millions of unwed mothers the chance to launch paternity and support suits would threaten the stability of many legal families. This the Party leadership did not want. The family remained, for the Party, both the indispensable agent of "Communist upbringing" to counteract social indiscipline and the means of human reproduction most likely to offset the recent drop in the birth rate.

The Party showed no intention of following the widely opposed views of Academician S. Strumilin. In 1960, this venerable scholar advised that children should be raised apart from their parents because society could educate them much better than the family could.[47] To this advice, Khrushchev retorted: "Those who maintain [as Strumilin did] that the family will become less important in the transition to Communism and that with time it will disappear are entirely wrong. Actually the family will grow stronger under Communism; family relations will be finally cleansed of material considerations and will attain great purity and stability."[48]

Party spokesmen did not deny that there were "survivals of the past" in the family. The Soviet press regularly carried stories of parental misconduct, neglect of children, snobbishness, materialism, and religiosity. The Party's answer to these problems was to encourage the family to fulfill its parental duties. "We must instill in all parents a feeling of responsibility for their children's upbringing," said Khrushchev. He depicted child-rearing as a joint venture of family and state.[49]

Actual new departures in family policy after Stalin indicate that the Party has no plans to dispense with the family's part in the upbringing of children, and in particular, no plans to collectivize all child-rearing outside the family. Rather, there was a liberalization from 1954 to 1956, and again in 1964/65, separated by a period of comparatively collectivist measures under Khrushchev, from 1956 to 1964.

Briefly summed up, the new lines of policy included: (1) a more liberal interpretation of divorce law by the courts and an end to the 1947 ban on marriage to foreigners, in 1954; (2) repeal of the ineffectual ban on nontherapeutic abortions in 1955; (3) lengthening of normal maternity leaves from 77 to 112 days, as of April 1, 1956, followed in June by an increase in pensions; (4) exemption of unmarried women and married couples with only one or two children from the 6 per cent birth-stimulation income tax, effective January 1, 1958 (war widows and the disabled had been exempted in 1954); (5) attempts, beginning in 1956, to intensify communal controls over parental conduct and religious indoctrination of the children, through a network of Party-controlled grass-root social organizations; (6) the introduction of "new Soviet rituals for marriage, birth registration, etc., beginning in the late 1950's; (7) a revival, during this period, of sociological research; (8) as another of Khrushchev's more ideological gambits, a campaign, beginning in 1958, to eliminate gradually all peasant households by reducing garden plots, restricting private marketing, etc., the campaign being stopped and even partially reversed after Khrushchev; (9) allowing all courts, beginning in 1960, to use loopholes in the family codes to order fathers in some cases to make support payments to mothers of their illegitimate children, under long-uninvoked provisions of the family codes that a person who has undertaken permanent support of a child must continue it; and (10) an effort from 1956 to 1963 to create a system of mass boarding schools, and when this failed, a campaign to expand as rapidly as possible the system of extended day (meaning not just half-day) schools, and to speed up the expansion of crèches and kindergartens.[50]

In addition to the real problem of the "Communist upbringing of the younger generation," the problem of the birth rate apparently still had an impact on policy. There is plausible, if not conclusive, evidence that Khrushchev hesitated at family reform in part because he still believed (though probably mistakenly) that the Soviet Union faced future underpopulation due to the falling birth rate and that to sweep away the Family Edict would exacerbate the problem. Dr. Sverdlov and the conservatives pictured the Family Edict as the defender of the stability of the legal family, because it discouraged divorce and paternity suits. "An organic tie exists," Dr. Sverdlov wrote, between "population growth and problems of the family and family legislation."[51] In his fundamental text on family law, Dr. Sverdlov had written: "Encouraging fertility is closely connected to strengthening the family. A stable family is one of the most important prerequisites of a high birth rate. It is natural, therefore, that if rules of family law tend to strengthen the family, they simultaneously raise the birth rate."[52]

I was reliably informed that such arguments as these by Dr. Sverdlov and Academician V. Starovsky, head of the vital Central Statistical Administration, greatly influenced Party leaders. And a leading conservative specifically referred me to Starovsky's report before the U.S.S.R. Academy of Sciences, in which Starovsky stated that the Family Edict of 1944 had served a useful function "in raising the birth rate during a highly unfavorable sexual balance in the population" after World War II. He attributed the edict's effectiveness to the ban on support suits by unwed mothers and the program of state aid to unwed mothers, measures to which I referred at the beginning of this chapter. And Starovsky reminded his audience that these measures had been adopted in 1944 "at the initiative of N. S. Khrushchev, then working in the Ukraine,

who suggested them to the U.S.S.R. government."[53] Dr. Sverdlov
wrote to cite and support Starovsky's praise of the "measures
prescribed in the edict of July 8, 1944, and adopted on the initiative
of N. S. Khrushchev."[54] Several top jurists told me that Khrushchev had indeed suggested these measures.

In a revealing speech delivered to a group of young people
bound for the virgin lands, Khrushchev claimed that he had suggested to Stalin the unpopular birth-stimulation tax—and he
named his adversary Malenkov as corroborating witness! Moreover, he stressed the national importance of high birth rates and
large families:

> The more people we have, the stronger our country will be. . . .
> If we added another 100 million to 200 million, it would still be
> too little. . . . If anyone should be castigated for the law [of
> November 21, 1941, to tax bachelors and couples with two children
> or less], it is I. I proposed that law. Comrade Malenkov is present,
> he can confirm that I suggested to Comrade Stalin drafting and
> passing such a law, and that law was drafted and passed. I think
> it is a correct law. If every family has one or two children, the
> population of the country will not grow, it will decline. . . . That
> is why we must have at least three children in a family and
> raise them well.[55]

Starovsky told the Academy of Sciences that long-term Soviet
economic plans were being drafted on the basis of an estimated
30 per cent increase in the population of the Soviet Union by
1980. Khrushchev repeated a similar estimate, in December, 1963.
Surely the population-conscious Khrushchev knew that, at present
rates, the population would be far less than the estimated 280
million. For this would require a minimum annual rate of increase
per thousand population of 14.85, assuming unchanging rates of
mortality (or 14.7 if infant mortality dipped to the U.S. rate, as
Starovsky expected). But the rate of increase fell from 17.8 in
1960 to 14 in 1963, and 12.7 in 1964.[56]

One would think that the problem of feeding a growing population, together with the increasing signs of labor surpluses in the
European part of the U.S.S.R., especially the joblessness among
youths just out of school, would have convinced post-Khrushchev
policy-makers that the drop in the rate of population increase,
reflecting a war-caused drop in the birth rate, might not be such

a bad thing after all. Yet one specialist wrote that a "search of
relevant literature reveals no statements which declare or imply
that the Soviet birth rate should be reduced. Therefore we may
conclude that the stated ideal of Soviet population policy is at
least to preserve the present rather substantial birth rate or to
raise it even higher."[57] Persistent agricultural underproduction
and the growing problem of unemployment may now be convinc-
ing the regime to modify this ideal.

Epilogue

Second thoughts about the need to push up the birth rate and
Khrushchev's departure from the political scene may have smoothed
the way for the divorce-law edict of December 10, 1965, which
went into effect on January 1, 1966.[58] This moderate edict skirts
all the other issues of reform, including illegitimacy. In amend-
ments to Articles 25 and 26 of the 1944 edict, divorce was made
somewhat simpler and cheaper.

The new procedures eliminate the publication of divorce notice
in the local press, which used to precede the first stage of divorce
(a reconciliation hearing in people's court), and which would
sometimes delay the hearing for up to eight months. Now, also, the
second and final hearing on divorce is held in the same people's
court, not in the next-higher court (provincial, city, or autonomous
republic supreme court). This makes it easier to summon witnesses, should they be necessary, especially in rural areas, where the
provincial center may be many miles from the district center
where the people's court is located.

Not all proposals of the reformers have been heeded, however.
The 40 ruble cost of publication was abolished, but the plaintiff
still has to pay a 10 ruble filing fee and a share of the 50–200
ruble divorce registration fee, which the court apportions between
plaintiff and respondent. Lawyers are used only in a small percentage of cases, and their fees do not compare with the stiff charges
of Western attorneys. Still, the reformed divorce procedure is far
more costly than the reformers had envisioned. The reformers
had hoped also that distance would be no obstacle to divorce. But
the old rule still applies that a plaintiff must file and appear at
the respondent's place of residence unless he or she has minor

children or traveling would cause some other hardship, or the respondent agrees to appear at the court of the plaintiff's domicile.[59] The Soviet Union's vast area includes distances from point to point of up to 6,000 miles. A simpler procedure would have required no need of appearance in cases of mutual consent, or have allowed appearance to be made by a legal representative who lives near the distant court.

Nevertheless, the Soviet divorce, with its broad test of family breakup, but with no other specific grounds, with no need to establish fault, with no doctrine preventing the party at fault from suing, with a standard divorce law for the whole country, is now one of the most liberal and rational in the world.

Chances have improved recently that a comprehensive draft of a new family law will be issued in the foreseeable future, publicly discussed, and passed at last to supersede the 1944 edict and the stopgap divorce edict of 1965.[60] In view of the strong male opposition to unrestricted paternity suits, and of the divided counsels among the policy-makers and their advisers, one can expect, not a return to the spirit of 1926, but rather, an approach toward the spirit of 1918. Thus, unregistered marriage will almost certainly not be recognized. Probably, the differences between the birth certificates of legitimate and illegitimate children and the ban on the latters' using their fathers' surnames will be rescinded. As before 1944, paternity suits and suits for support will no doubt be recognized, but the circumstances under which these suits may be brought is a moot point: Merely when uncontested by the father? After only a casual liaison? If not, then after how long a period of cohabitation? There remain to be settled such thorny issues as the retroactivity of all reform provisions, the size of support payments for children by a separated or former spouse, and the desirability of introducing alimony payments (now provided in most of the U.S.S.R. only for a disabled spouse, and then only for one year).

The central issue of family reform in the Soviet Union has been: Are there injustices and inefficacies under the 1944 Family Edict that are so bad as to outweigh any risk of increasing the already high rate of family breakups, which may be the result of a more liberal family law? The conservative minority among family

lawyers prevailed over the more numerous reformers in 1964 because Khrushchev and many officials shared both their concern for
the family functions of child-rearing and reproduction and their
outdated double standards of sexual morality.

Khrushchev could be a liberal when he thought it politically
expedient, as for example in 1962, when he offered support to the
liberal writers in an effort to use their works and prestige against
his dogmatic opponents (see Chapter 4). Apparently, he saw no
political benefit in liberalizing family law. From a broader perspective, the draft of the Basic Family Law emerged from the
Legislative Committees at an inauspicious time. Bitterly divided,
the Soviet leadership was moreover deeply preoccupied with grave
problems of lagging economic growth, agricultural disaster, social
indiscipline, ideological scepticism among the youth, and seemingly
insoluble conflict with the Chinese fellow Communists. Since
little has changed in this regard after Khrushchev's fall, one must
conclude that his going had much to do with the small victory
for the reformists in 1965.

This case study of debate over reform of the family law prompts
some cautious generalization about Soviet policy-making. It reveals
the development after Stalin of a much wider communication of
opinion upward, from much more self-consciously cohesive groupings of interest and opinion, than Stalin ever permitted in his later
years. True, participation in family-policy formation has not been
pluralistic in the sense of autonomous centers of power and influence. But legislation by consultation has replaced Stalin's legislation by cabal. One has discerned, not autonomous interest groups
either for or against reform, but rather, groupings of reformist and
conservative opinion cutting across bureaucratic and professional
lines.

Along *professional* lines, there is now an evident sense of a legal
community among jurists, who have met across the land to exchange views and draft collective opinions on reforms. Nothing
came of a strong public request by jurists—judges, lawyers, prosecutors, and legal scholars—in 1958/59 to have their own national
professional Union of Soviet Jurists after the manner of writers,
architects, etc. Their relative de-atomization and greater professional cohesion since Stalin remains a fact, however. Greater
social controls at the grass roots and more leeway and cohesion

for the professions since Stalin are not contradictory. They are both facets of the Party's search for more efficiency and productivity in the social system. Witness also the new self-consciousness among sociologists of their standing as professionals. Jurists and sociologists are acutely aware of the limits of discretion in public, and in their work.

Along lines of *interest*, there have been wide opportunities to meet and exchange views with persons in other professions also working with the family, this procedure now encouraged by the Party's demand that various branches of science collaborate more in research.

Sex has entered in as a significant but not decisive grouping. Women have figured more prominently among reformers than among conservatives, and there have been occasional jocular or moralizing or very earnest references in interviews to the woman's position under the 1944 Family Edict.

Party membership has not been a significant determinant of opinion. Most active debaters, reformers and conservatives have been in the Party as a matter of course. The public has been significant, but because of its behavior, not its opinion.

The vagaries of reform show up the impressive power of Party leaders to intervene and to delay or quash a measure when politics, or such state interests as raising the birth rate and instilling more discipline, seem to militate against the changes. Only within this context can we soberly observe the partial de-atomization of the pulverized occupational and professional groupings left by Stalin.

NOTES

1. "Ot imeni syna: Po pis'mam chitatelei," *Literaturnaya gazeta* (henceforth cited as *LG*), August 28, 1954.
2. *Pravda*, July 9, 1944.
3. For a collection of documents on Soviet family policy up to 1944, see Rudolf Schlesinger, *Changing Attitudes in Soviet Russia: The Family in the U.S.S.R.* (London: Routledge & Kegan Paul, 1949). For interpretative accounts, differing from mine, see John Hazard, *Law and Social Change in the U.S.S.R.* (Toronto: Carswell Co., 1953); and William Petersen, "The Evolution of Soviet Family Policy," *Problems of Communism*, V, No. 5 (September–October, 1956), 29–35.
4. *Sotsialisticheskaya zakonnost'* (henceforth cited as *SZ*), No. 11 (1944), pp. 38–41; see also Stalin's speech to graduates of the Red Army Academy, *Pravda*, May 5, 1935; editorials in *Pravda*, May 28, 1935, March 11, 1936; and G. M. Sverdlov, *Sovetskoe semeinoe pravo* (Moscow: Gosudarstvennoe Izdatel'stvo Yuridicheskoi Literatury [Gosyurizdat], 1958), pp. 16–17, 33–34.
5. Sverdlov, *op. cit.*, pp. 11, 33.
6. The edict also extended the coverage of the birth-stimulation income tax of November 21, 1941, on childless persons and bachelors to persons with no more than two children. The tax applied to men over 20 and under 50 years old and to women over 20 and under 45 years old, amounting to 6 per cent of income for non-peasants. *Kodeks zakonov o brake, sem'e i opeke RSFSR* (Moscow: Gosyurizdat, 1956), p. 47. Allowances to unwed mothers were cut in half beginning in 1948, becoming 50 (old) rubles for 1 child, 75 for 2 children, and 100 for 3 children. Total grants to mothers, that had increased from 1.2 billion in 1940 to 5 billion rubles in 1947, dropped to about 3 billion in 1948 as a result of the cut. *Sbornik zakonov SSSR i ukazov Prezidiuma Verkhovnogo Soveta SSSR, 1938–noyabr' 1958 g.* (Moscow: Gosyurizdat, 1958), pp. 534–35.
7. G. K. Matveev, *Istoriya semeino-brachnogo zakonodatel'stva Ukrainskoi SSR* (Kiev: Izdatel'stvo Kievskogo Universiteta, 1960), p. 52.
8. There was a 63 per cent surplus of women over men of ages 35 to 54 at the time of the census of January 15, 1959. This was the most fertile part of the population in 1944. See Peter Juviler, "Marriage and Divorce," *Survey*, No. 48 (July, 1963), p. 111.
9. For example, E. Kovaleva's allusions to Stalinist repression of criticism by lawyers, in *SZ*, No. 12 (1956), p. 38.
10. G. M. Sverdlov, *Okhrana interesov detei v sovetskom semeinom i grazhdanskom prave* (Moscow: Izdatel'stvo Akademii Nauk SSSR, 1955), pp. 37–38, 46–48.
11. In 1954, unwed mothers received monthly allowances for approximately 3.3 illegitimate children under twelve years of age. Perhaps a third more illegitimate children did not receive grants for a variety of reasons, including at that time the still minor one that they were over twelve years old. See n. 33 below.
12. Review appeared in *Sovetskoe gosudarstvo i pravo* (henceforth cited as *SGP*), No. 5 (1956), pp. 134–38.
13. *SGP*, No. 9 (1956), pp. 65–72; this citation is from p. 72.

14. *SGP*, No. 5 (1956), p. 135. Emphasis added.
15. *LG*, October 9, 1956.
16. V. Kiselev, "Sushchestvuet li lyubov'?" *LG*, September 13, 1956.
17. Sverdlov's proposals appeared in *SGP*, No. 7 (1946), pp. 23–24, and *SZ*, No. 9 (1953), pp. 37–53; Pergament's in *SZ*, No. 4 (1957), pp. 77–79, and *Sovetskaya yustitsiya* (henceforth cited as *SYu*), No. 4 (1957), pp. 36–39. Pergament earlier expressed opposition to special procedures in cases of mutual consent, with B. S. Antimonov, in *SZ*, No. 9 (1954), pp. 24–31.
18. *Zasedaniya Verkhovnogo Soveta SSSR, chetvertogo sozyva, shestaya sessiya, 5–12 fevralya 1957 g.: Stenograficheskii otchet* (Moscow: Izdatel'stvo Verkhovnogo Soveta SSSR, 1957), pp. 471, 512–13.
19. *SGP*, No. 3 (1958), p. 24.
20. *Pravda*, February 21 and September 9, 1965. Rumyantsev was himself replaced in September, 1965.
21. *SZ*, No. 4 (1957), pp. 77–79; and *SYu*, No. 4 (1957), pp. 36–39.
22. *Vedomosti Verkhovnogo Soveta SSSR*, No. 49 (1961), p. 1256.
23. *Ibid.*, No. 12 (1962), p. 307.
24. *Ibid.*, No. 51 (1962), p. 1157.
25. The work of the Legislative Committees is described by their secretary, S. G. Novikov, in *Postoyannye komissii Verkhovnogo Soveta SSSR* (Moscow: Gosyurizdat, 1962); travels of members of the subcommittee to union republics was mentioned by Novikov, in *SGP*, No. 12 (1963), pp. 55–56.
26. *Semya i shkola*, No. 3 (to press February 18, 1963), pp. 28–29; *ibid.*, No. 9 (to press August 19, 1963), p. 29; Edmund Stevens, *The New York Times Magazine*, April 26, 1964, p. 16.
27. It is obvious where the results of field observations are used in this report. Detailed documentation of interviews is omitted. Field work, in 1958/59 and 1964, included: (1) interviews—twenty legal scholars and a dean of a law faculty, many of whom had participated in debating and drafting the missing reform bill; three practicing attorneys and a director of a legal-aid office; three officials of ZAGS civil registration system; eight judges; a chairman of a comrades' court; three sociologists; two directors of boarding schools; a director of a nursery-kindergarten; several officials of the Kalinin City Soviet and the Novopromyshlenyi Borough Soviet of Kalinin; two leading architects; a pedagogical psychiatrist; two directors of wedding palaces; the secretary of the Legislative Committees of the U.S.S.R. Supreme Soviet; and others; (2) published and unpublished sources, some unavailable in the West; and (3) observations of children at play, comrades' courts, divorce and other actions in family law in the regular courts, boarding schools, kindergartens, weddings, birth registrations, daily family life. Field work was conducted in the Russian, Latvian, Kazakh, Uzbek, and Ukrainian republics.
28. O. P. Kolchina, "Rozhdenie novogo zakona: Beseda s O. P. Kolchinoi, zam. predsedatelya komissii zakonodatel'nykh predpolozhenii Soveta Soyuza Verkhovnogo Soveta SSSR," *Trud*, February 16, 1964.
29. E. Mushkina, "Dela semeinye," *Moskovskii komsomolets*, April 15, 1964.
30. *Vedomosti Verkhovnogo Soveta SSSR*, No. 29 (1964), pp. 562–63.
31. D. A. Kerimov, in *SGP*, No. 10 (1961), pp. 77–85.
32. *Semya i shkola*, No. 3 (1963), pp. 28–29.

33. Full calculations would occupy a prohibitive amount of space. Note the following: (1) The number of children under eighteen adopted at some time by their natural fathers was approximately an estimated 312,000 in the U.S.S.R. by the end of 1961, from data on adoptions in Ya. P. Verbers, "Rodstvo kak osnovanie vozniknoveniya prav i obyazannostei po sovetskomu semeinomu i grazhdanskomu pravu" (dissertation for degree of Candidate of Juridical Sciences, Moscow University, 1963), pp. 43–44, and from data on the population of the U.S.S.R. relative to that of the R.S.F.S.R. in *Itogi vsesoyuznoi perepisi naseleniya 1959 goda, SSSR: Svodnyi tom* (Moscow: Gosudarstvennoe Statisticheskoe Izdatel'stvo [Gosstatizdat], 1962), p. 18. (2) The estimated number of illegitimate children who would have been receiving grants if cutoff age were 18, not 12 as now, was 4.5 million in 1961, 4.6 million in 1962, 4.46 million in 1963, from raw data on mothers of 1, 2, and 3 and more children receiving grants for illegitimate children in the series of handbooks entitled *Narodnoe khozyaistvo SSSR* (Moscow: Gosstatizdat), for years 1958 (p. 894), 1959 (p. 794), 1960 (p. 837), and 1962 (p. 495), and in *SSSR v tsifrakh v 1961 godu* (p. 377). This means that about 7 children were adopted for every 100 who had had grants. Adding the 7 per cent adopted plus an assumed 5 per cent not getting grants but in children's homes, 5 per cent receiving support by court order from men (including natural fathers) who had at one time undertaken their permanent support and then reneged, 15 per cent unreported or whose mothers live with their natural fathers and therefore cannot get grants—a total of 32 per cent—gives an estimated 6.1 million illegitimate children under 18 by the end of 1962, 5.9 million by the end of 1963, meaning that about 5 per cent of them were adopted by their natural fathers. If the trend to 1962 implies about 1.95 million unwed mothers receiving grants for illegitimate children in 1963 for 2.3 million children, then total mothers of all illegitimate children in 1963 equals approximately $1.95 \times \frac{5.9}{2.3}$, or 5.09 million mothers. (3) In Juviler, *op. cit.*, p. 115, the estimate was "up to 8 million illegitimate children" in 1957. This can now be written more precisely as about 5.5 million. (4) The above results tally well with one informed estimate of 6 million illegitimate children at peak and 5 million unwed mothers, and another informed estimate of "over 5 million" illegitimate children *under 18 years of age* in 1964 (the number under 18 years of age is declining slowly).

34. A. G. Kharchev, "Brak i sem'ya v SSSR: Opyt sotsiologicheskogo issledovaniya" (dissertation for the degree of Doctor of Philosophy, Leningradskaya kafedra filosofii Akademii Nauk SSSR, 1963), pp. 288–90.

35. *Vestnik statistiki*, No. 1 (1965), p. 93. Divorce rate for 1964, in *Narodnoe khozyaistvo SSSR v 1964 godu*, p. 41.

36. Kharchev, *op. cit.*, p. 360.

37. *Zasedaniya Verkhovnogo Soveta SSSR* . . . , p. 513.

38. On the Uzbek draft family code of 1959, see articles of: Kh. S. Sulaimanova, in *Izvestiya Akademii Nauk UzSSR: Seriya obshchestvennykh nauk*, No. 5 (1959), p. 21; U. Ibragimov, in *ibid.*, pp. 37–41; T. A. Ayubov, in *ibid.*, pp. 42–45; and for the reformer-conservative controversy in Uzbekistan, see F. Atokhodzhaev's article in *Tashkentskii gos. universitet: Nauchnye trudy; Vyp. 219: Pravovedenie* (1963) pp. 24–39; and G.

Tansikbaeva, in *Obshchestvennye nauki v Uzbekistane*, No. 12 (1962), pp. 34–38, and in *ibid.*, No. 3 (1962), pp. 57–59. Note that two out of six articles, those of Tansikvaeva, took Sverdlov's conservative position, opposing all paternity suits. This is a fair example of the scholarly and general press lineup for ten years, 1954–64. For other articles on reforms, see Juviler, *op. cit.*, pp. 104–17, and citations in this report. Interviews and articles, e.g., of R.S.F.S.R. Supreme Court Judge Ostroukhova, *SGP*, No. 12 (1957), pp. 97–103, show judges heavily favoring simplification of divorce procedure. M. Anyants, department head of the Juridical Commission (section for legal advice), in the U.S.S.R. Council of Ministers, supported Pergament, *SZ*, No. 6 (1958), pp. 49–52. Pro-reform tendency in ZAGS was deduced from interviews; and E. Mushkina, *op. cit.* On the attitudes of some journals and newspapers, see: "Vnov' i vnov' o tak nazyvaemykh 'vnebrechnykh detei,'" *Semya i shkola*, No. 9 (1963), pp. 26–27; "Molchanie ne zoloto: K voprosu o procherke v metrikakh," *LG*, January 23, 1962; and "Dukh ili bukva zakona?" *Vechernyaya Moskva*, March 13, 1964. Radical opinion, here in support of recognizing unregistered marriage, was expressed in *Izvestia* by Judge Mironkin, Omsk Provincial Court, in his "Zhizn' i zagovskii blank," January 17, 1962.

39. Conservative opinion, in addition to Sverdlov's, may be found in G. K. Matveev, *op. cit.*, pp. 59–62; Tansikbaeva's articles cited above, etc. Opinions of the ultra-conservative fringe were cited in "Ot imeni syna . . ." and other conservative articles listed above.

40. Kolchina, *op. cit.*

41. Full equality of all extramarital children, and paternity suits regardless of the type of relationship of their parents, Pergament's program, were questioned by some reformers who sought to avoid abuses by unscrupulous women through the requirement of various degrees of prolonged cohabitation before paternity suits could be brought. See Pergament's view, again, in *SYu*, No. 1 (1962), pp. 6–8; alternatives cited by E. A. Katkova in *Trudy irkutskogo un-ta.*, XXXII: *Seriya yuridicheskaya*, No. 6, chap. 1, 1963, 115–29.

42. S. G. Novikov, Secretary of the Legislative Committees, in *Postoyannye komissii Verkhovnogo Soveta SSSR*, p. 35.

43. *Vedomosti Verkhovnogo Soveta SSSR*, No. 17 (1962), pp. 449–51, 456–57.

44. N. V. Rabinovich's comments appeared in *Sorok let sovetskogo prava 1917–1957* (Leningrad: Izdatel'stvo Leningradskogo Universiteta, 1957), II, 282–84, 293–97; M. G. Masevich's, in *SGP*, No. 11 (1958), pp. 56–64; the others are cited elsewhere here.

45. N. Ershova, in *SZ*, No. 9 (1962), p. 39.

46. I. Greshnev, "O 'modakh,' lyubvi i poshlosti," *Vechernyaya Moskva*, March 13, 1964; and "Daite takuyu rol'l" *ibid.*, March 19, 1964.

47. S. Strumilin, "Rabochii byt i kommunizm," *Novy mir*, No. 7 (1960), pp. 203–20. Strumilin's rejection of family upbringing because it detracts from social collectivism can be traced to antecedents after the 1917 revolutions, to Engel's *Principles of Communism*, and much further back to Plato's *Republic*.

48. *Pravda*, October 20, 1961.

49. N. S. Khrushchev, *O kommunisticheskom vospitanii* (Moscow: Izdatel'stvo Politicheskoi Literatury [Politizdat], 1964), p. 109.

50. See Juviler, *op. cit.*; see also Peter Juviler, "La Famiglia in Russia: Dalla rivoluzione alle riforme," *Il Mulino*, No. 1 (1966), pp. 55–67; and "Soviet Families," *Survey*, No. 60 (July, 1966), pp. 51–61.

51. G. M. Sverdlov, *Pravo grazhdan v sem'e* (Moscow: Izdatel'stvo Akademii Nauk SSSR, 1963), p. 8.

52. *Sovetskoe semeinoe pravo*, p. 33.

53. V. N. Starovsky's speech, in *Vestnik Akademii Nauk*, No. 5 (1962), p. 45.

54. *Pravda grazhdan v sem'e*, p. 8.

55. *Izvestia*, January 8, 1955.

56. Starovsky, *op. cit.*, pp. 44–46, information on Soviet birth rates and population increase rates are from *Narodnoe khozyaistvo SSSR v 1962 godu*, p. 30; and *Narodnoe khozyaistvo SSSR v 1964 godu*, p. 34. Calculations on trends are omitted here. War caused this decline in two ways: (1) by bequeathing a sexual imbalance—a surplus of women over men—that reduced the birth rate (per thousand) in the 1950's to 80–86 per cent of prewar level; and (2) by slashing the wartime birth rate to less than half that of the prewar level, so that the dip in birth rate, beginning in 1940 with the Russo-Finnish War of 1939/40, is now causing a delayed dip in the birth rate as this depleted generation takes over the function of reproduction from its more numerous predecessors. The causes for declines in the birth rate are analyzed by B. Ts. Urlanis in a valuable work that greatly impressed some conservatives: *Rozhdaemost' i prodolzhitel'nost' zhizni v SSSR* (Moscow: Izdatel'stvo "Statistika," 1963), pp. 29–33.

57. David M. Heer, "Abortion, Contraception, and Population Policy in the Soviet Union," *Soviet Studies*, XVII, No. 1 (July, 1965), 77.

58. *Vedomosti Verkhovnogo Soveta SSSR*, No. 49 (1965), item 275.

59. See explanation of the President of the Civil Collegium of the U.S.S.R. Supreme Court, in SZ, No. 2 (1966), pp. 23–26.

60. See Arkadi Vaksberg's summary of the family-reform debates, in *Soviet Life*, No. 6 (June, 1966), pp. 60–61.

3

Economic Growth and Institutional Change in the Soviet Union

Marshall I. Goldman

EDITORS' INTRODUCTION

During the past decade, the Soviet economy has suffered severe reversals. The impressive increases in the growth rate from 1950 to 1958 in industry and agriculture, which had buoyed the hopes of the Soviet leaders and populace, proved to be illusionary. Disappointing harvests forced the government to make extensive grain purchases from the West in 1963, 1965, and 1966, to forestall rationing of food. Khrushchev's 1957 prediction that the Soviet Union would soon catch up with the United States in the per capita production of meat, butter, and milk was forgotten. Embarrassing too was his 1961 declaration that by 1970 the Soviet Union would exceed the United States in industrial production and by 1980 enjoy the highest standard of living in the world. The growth rate of Soviet industry, once apace with those of other rapidly expanding economies, declined from 9.5 per cent in 1962 to 8.5 per cent in 1963 and 7.1 per cent in 1964. (These are Soviet figures, which are higher than Western estimates.) Expansion rates for light industry, long the stepchild of Soviet production, were markedly lower: 4 per cent in 1962, 2 per cent in 1963, and 3 per cent in 1964.

The loss of economic momentum has severely troubled the Soviet leadership. Khrushchev, no less than his successors, repeatedly tried to eliminate shortcomings in agriculture and industry.

Solutions, however, were not easy to come by, and bold suggestions by economic experts faced stern opposition, both on ideological and practical grounds, from other economists and from planners and industrial managers. The fundamental question for the Soviet Union, and incidentally for most of her Eastern European allies, is how to wrest from a limited number of resources sufficient output to satisfy the vast requirements of its military, space, and foreign-aid programs as well as to meet rising consumer expectations.

This major problem has produced a number of vital issues. One of them, the concern of this chapter, was the question of what form of industrial organization would be best suited both to stimulate productivity and to improve the quality of products. This issue, fiercely debated in recent years by certain economists and some central planners, centered largely around a series of proposals made by Professor Yevsei Liberman of the University of Kharkov. Liberman criticized the existing system for thwarting the initiative of plant managers by tying the operation of each plant to a detailed production assignment that was determined by central planners. He argued for greater plant autonomy and for rewarding the achievements of a particular enterprise on the basis of profitability. As a means of motivating plant managers and their production units to search for ways of improving their economic performance, the profit incentive, he said, would be more effective than bureaucratically determined plans.

The proposal, simple on the surface, raised a host of issues that Liberman had not necessarily intended to probe, including the future of central planning and the need for introducing a limited market system. It also raised a key question: Should prices, now centrally determined, be allowed to reflect the pressures of supply and demand in order to gauge profitability more accurately?

The Twenty-third Party Congress (March 29 to April 8, 1966) did little to resolve the differences between the economists who advocate increased plant autonomy and the central planners, who fear diminution of their power or economic chaos or both. Nevertheless, significant progress in evaluating the performance of enterprises on a profitability rather than on a unit-output basis is taking place. Alexei Kosygin, the Chairman of the Council of Ministers, reported to the Congress on April 5 that enterprises *employing more than 300,000 workers had already shifted over to the new system, that in the second quarter of 1966, 180 additional plants—employing 700,000 persons in 33 branches of industry, including machine manufacturers, textile mills, coal mines, and oil fields—would follow, and that by early 1967, one-third of the total labor force in industry, some 9 million workers, would be working under the new system. These figures testify to the impact of Liberman's proposals. Moreover, a record harvest in 1966, the best in Soviet history, and an upturn in the rate of industrial growth may strengthen the hand of the economic reformers.*

How Libermanism became an issue and the grounds on which his proposals were criticized, accepted, and amended, are the subjects of Professor Goldman's study.

I

Since November, 1917, Soviet economic institutions have been formed, reformed, and abandoned with a rapidity that has left many observers two or three changes behind. Most often, the endless series of alterations and proposals for change have aroused little comment, but occasionally a particularly far-reaching suggestion has provoked a period of exceptionally intense debate. One such controversy occurred in the early 1960's. It was precipitated by the arguments and proposals of an engineering economist from Kharkov named Yevsei Liberman. The debate itself yields some valuable insights into the nature of the new economic problems that face Soviet decision-makers. The issues brought out during the Liberman discussions not only anticipated the downturn in the economic growth rate of the Soviet Union but suggested that the Soviet economy was undergoing basic qualitative changes.

In the early days of the Russian Revolution, if not before, the decision was made to industrialize the country as rapidly as possible. Although Russia was not exactly an industrial wasteland in 1921, it could not be counted among the leaders of the industrialized world. Furthermore, the still immature industrial framework of the country had been severely handicapped by the destruction of World War I, and of the Russian Civil War (1918–21).

Realizing that economic growth could be obtained only through the country's own efforts, the Soviets set out to mobilize their resources in what Stalin and his advisers believed was the most effective way. They identified economic growth with industrialization. The kind of industry they wished to establish was to be large in scale and heavily capitalized. This was the pattern of the most efficient and productive firms in the capitalist world and clearly it was the wave of the future. To the extent that machinery could take the place of manpower, economic progress would not be unduly hampered by the shortage of skilled laborers. At the same time, there were many other projects—such as dams and subways—that could absorb the mass of unskilled labor. Since capital was in such short supply and unskilled labor so abundant, it was perhaps only natural that both capital-intensive and labor-intensive projects should be constructed side by side.

To accomplish all this, it was necessary to mobilize and manage the entire agricultural and industrial resources of the country. Toward this end, in the late 1920's, the Soviets inaugurated the Five-Year Plans for industry and collectivized agriculture. By rounding up all the peasants into large farming units, Stalin assumed he would have greater political and economic control over the agricultural sector and, therefore, would be able to extract a marketable surplus much more efficiently. This surplus could then be used to feed the rapidly growing urban population and to earn foreign exchange in overseas markets. Similarly, the nationalization of all private business and the subordination of all production to central planning were meant to ensure compliance with major industrial aims and to hasten the industrialization of the country.

Soviet policy-makers recognized that it would take more than brute force and state directives to speed up industrialization. While the planners could dictate physical targets in terms of steel tonnage and machine-tool production, there were other, more subtle techniques that could also be utilized to mobilize the support of plant managers. For example, with central control the traditional cost-price relationship could be manipulated so that certain desirable decisions would be taken by the managers. Prices of many producers' goods were held constant or reduced below direct and indirect labor costs while prices of consumers' goods were generally doubled. To the extent that producers' goods, such as coal, appeared to be cheap, industrial consumers were induced to increase their use. Although the low prices often meant that producers had to receive state subsidies, the reductions in price increased the demand for such commodities and helped spread them throughout the industrial system. At the same time, the high prices on consumers' goods served to absorb consumer income, so that real consumption fell. To ensure that the high prices would not generate excess profits for state enterprises, the state imposed a turnover tax (a hidden sales tax) on consumers' goods that eventually averaged 50 per cent of the retail price. This proved a convenient method for diverting resources from consumption to investment.

Marx's doctrinal prohibition against charging interest on capital also served to reinforce the trend toward heavy industry. If the enterprise did not have to pay interest on its capital, then capital was virtually a free good. Plants therefore sought the techniques that were most capital intensive. This facilitated the introduction and extensive use of advanced methods in industrial production.

II

The central planners' manipulations had the desired effect. Despite civil strife, political repression, and World War II, the economy of the Soviet Union grew rapidly. By the time of Stalin's death, a solid industrial base had been forged. It was widely agreed that by the mid-1950's, the Soviet Union had become the world's second largest industrial power, with an impressive core of heavy industry.

Onto this expansive scene strode Professor Liberman in 1956. In an article in the Communist Party's official journal, *Kommunist*, he suggested that perhaps all was not well and that a change in planning procedure was needed.[1] He was not alone in his concern, but his suggestions, like those of other critics, generally had little practical effect. The Soviet economy was growing as rapidly as ever. According to official figures, Soviet national income was growing at an annual rate of 10–12 per cent, and even American estimates showed a rate of 7–8 per cent.[2] While most economists agreed that there were shortcomings in the existing program, no basic reforms were attempted. No one wanted to run the risk of ruining a good thing.

The prevailing system of physical planning had brought rapid industrialization to the Soviet Union. The main body of economists continued to argue that the best way to stimulate the factory manager and his workers was to tie premiums and bonuses to plan-fulfillment. Each factory and department was assigned a production plan and urged by word and material incentive to fulfill it. The goal of the plan was invariably set in some quantitative terms, such as number of units produced or weight. Each year, the goal was increased. The operating success of an enterprise was judged by how well the plan was fulfilled or overfulfilled. The success indicators of other societies, such as profits, were considered to be of secondary importance. This was reinforced by divorcing the bulk of employee bonuses from all yardsticks but amount produced.

If the economy lacked flexibility, it was a small price to pay. The task was to produce and then produce some more. In effect, it was decided to turn on the switch and let the production line pour out goods. Whatever was produced was in demand somewhere. If the products were inappropriate and inefficient, there was no cause for alarm. A "good" factory manager would find a way to utilize the supplies. The important thing was to produce and avoid "down time"—that is, production interruptions that are necessary if adjustments must be made for style and customer specifications. For example, most factories simply took it for granted that they would have to rework the metal they received from the steel-rolling mills. To speed up production, the steel mills set their rollers at one thickness and simply ran the ingots through until it was necessary to replace the rollers. By eliminating much of the down time that would have been required to readjust the rollers, the steel mills increased their output, although some of the manufacturing work was pushed off onto the fabricator. In the production of consumers' goods, the purchaser of a pair of ill-fitting shoes was usually forced to do the best he could, since the alternative sometimes was to go shoeless.

It was Liberman's contention, however, that major reforms were required in the planning system. The methods of economic development that had been so suitable heretofore, he argued, were too gross and unsophisticated for a developed economy. The minor shortcomings inherent in a system of physical planning were gradually assuming major proportions.

Liberman's pleas did not receive any special notice until 1962. Then, in September, *Pravda* carried an article by him that contained his previous arguments.[3] This time, however, his message received careful attention—from both the economists and the politicians. By 1962, Khrushchev and the other members of the Presidium were doubtless bothered by the fact that the rate of increase in national income had fallen off continuously after 1958. Subsequently, official Soviet figures indicated that whereas national income increased by more than 12 per cent in 1958, it increased by less than 6 per cent in 1962.[4] With this in mind, Khrushchev gave his official sanction to a debate over Liberman's proposals.[5]

As recounted in the pages of *Pravda, Voprosy ekonomiki,* and *Ekonomicheskaya gazeta* from 1962 to 1964, Liberman and most of his fellow reformers argued along five major lines:

1. As long as almost all goods were in short supply, the reformers stated, it did not matter too much if supplies did not fit specifications perfectly.[6] Since there were usually no substitutes, the goods were accepted willingly. If they could not be refashioned or refinished by the customer, there was always the possibility of barter with someone who had a complementary deficiency.

Gradually, however, as supplies and stocks increased, customers started to reject the thick paper and nails, the wrong-gauge steel, the ill-fitting sizes. If the product did not meet specifications, customers learned they could look around and find something that did. Nevertheless, the manufacturers kept on producing unwanted items. Since performance was judged on the basis of production, not sales, the manufacturer was not penalized if his unsold goods ended up in a warehouse. Technically, he was fulfilling his plan and his duty. But, as V. Dymshyts, then chairman of the U.S.S.R. Sovnarkhoz (Economic Council), stated: "The time for striving for quantity at the expense of quality has passed."[7]

2. Capital, the reformers argued, will inevitably be misdirected

in a system with no interest rate to act as a guide for allocation.[8] In Stalin's time, except for a few of his schemes, misallocation had been no more serious than some of the other problems facing the economy. Most of the country's investment projects ultimately proved to be successful, for there was so much to do that it was hard to go wrong. But the more lucrative projects were gradually completed, and continuation of economic growth required closer scrutiny over capital utilization. Too many projects had been undertaken and not completed. Also, because the projects were often so large, capital was tied up too long, and projects did not begin to pay for themselves for several years. Liberman and his colleagues were critical that a cement plant and canal could take more than ten years to complete, and pointed out that Khrushchev had decided it was better to build thermal-electric plants because they were less capital intensive than hydroelectric facilities. Khrushchev, in fact, even suggested a moratorium on all new investment projects for 1964, so that the available capital could be concentrated on completing existing projects. Liberman and his supporters pointed out that while the absence of an interest rate may have facilitated the introduction of large-scale capital projects in earlier years, the needs of the country were no longer the same. Growth was coming more slowly now, and some economic mechanism had to be found that could automatically provide discipline and guidance in the allocation of capital.

3. Except for products and processes that were assigned military priority and those promoted in nationwide crash campaigns, the reformers continued, there was a dearth of innovation. Because experimentation might result in the underfulfillment of the physical plan, there were few planners or managers who were willing to venture off the beaten track. Since the production of steel had been mastered, it was easier to increase steel capacity and production than to switch to other materials, such as plastics, even though they might be suitable. As Khrushchev put it so colorfully: "The production of steel is like a well-traveled road with deep ruts; here even blind horses will not turn off because the wheels will break. Similarly, some officials have put on steel blinkers; they do everything as they were taught in their day. A material appears which is superior to steel and is cheaper but they keep on shouting, 'Steel, steel!' "[9]

In some cases, new products were not even proposed. In other cases, there might be proposals but no implementation. Thus the expansion of the chemical industry had been proposed long before December, 1963.* In fact, sizable investment funds had been set aside as early as 1958, and there had been a considerable increase in chemical production. Yet Khrushchev could still complain that out of the funds that had been allocated to the Soviet chemical industry from 1958 to 1963, close to $777 million had been left untouched.[10] The planners simply ignored the proposed projects and shirked their responsibility. And when they did submit proposals, the plans were not necessarily the best. Khrushchev found that when planning bureaucrats took their plans out of the closets and onto the construction fields, the blueprints were often filled with worthless detail. This he ascribed to the fact that the state was paying for its blueprints by the page![11] The reformers maintained that some other method of promoting innovation and change was necessary.

4. The operation of the economy, the reformers argued, was further complicated by the fact that the economy had become so large. Not only were there more products and factories to plan for, but the various products were becoming more sophisticated and complex. The interactions between various sectors had been increasing at virtually multiple rates. Thus, unless changes were made, by 1980 the entire adult population would have to be employed in planning, with no one left for production.[12] While this might be the way to deal with those who found themselves unemployed because of automation, it suggested that existing planning methods were no longer adequate.

5. Finally, Liberman and his adherents were concerned about a wholly unanticipated phenomenon. There were faint, but nonetheless real indications that the Soviet system was not immune to

* Khrushchev's response to the lag in the chemical industry was to introduce another crash campaign. Since the normal planning procedures did not facilitate the introduction of unmastered and sophisticated techniques, the blitzkrieg campaign was necessary again. To many Soviet economists, this game of leapfrog offered little long-run promise. It always seemed that while the Soviet Union was caught up in the midst of one campaign, the rest of the world had leaped ahead to some other area of technology, and that another campaign and another diversion of resources would be required if the Soviets were to catch up.

the woes of underconsumption. Who would have predicted such a turn of events? After all, in the 1920's and 1930's, everything possible was done to discourage consumption in order to aid investment and capital formation. This explains the usefulness of the turnover tax and the resulting high prices on consumers' goods. But just as supply-and-demand conditions in industry had altered, so had the pressures on consumption. Although there still were depressing shortages of food and many nonfood products, the consumer was better off than ever before. He no longer had to buy "just any" shoes. In fact, since he already had several pairs of shoes, he could wait until he saw what he wanted. The shoes might even be of Czech, Italian, or English origin. The same applied to such items as fabrics, clothing, watches, cameras, bicycles, radios, and sewing machines. This did not mean that the average citizen had as much in his closet or suitcase as the West European, but it did mean he was no longer compelled to take whatever was shoved at him.

As a direct result of this, inventories piled up, sales plans were underfulfilled, and deposits in savings banks were soaring. Despite numerous promotional techniques—such as clearance sales, advertising, and installment credit—excess inventories of consumers' goods totaled close to $4 billion in 1964. Sales targets in the early 1960's were often underfilled by 1 per cent or more, even though projected increases were lower than in many previous years. New deposits in savings banks amounted to more than $1.5 billion a year, which represented as much as 3 per cent of total retail and restaurant sales.

Such developments had important implications for the future. Several economists, such as Ya. Orlov, complained about the accumulation of the unsold merchandise.[13] Wages had been expended and loans extended for the production of these items. While increased exports and style changes (planned product obsolescence) were partial solutions, it was necessary to cut back the rate of expansion in some of these industries. Sometimes, when inventories have piled up too much, production was actually reduced. Thus, sewing-machine sales and production fell close to 20 per cent in 1963 after a series of price markdowns and other sales campaigns failed to clear out the warehouses. What happened to the workers and raw materials? They might have been shifted to bicycle production. But bicycle sales also fell. Fortunately, since there were enough shortages of such items as refrigerators and washing machines—and, of course, automobiles—there could still be found many alternative uses for the displaced resources. Yet the number of items in short supply might conceivably diminish day by day, and then what would happen? Liberman and the reformers argued that something had to be done to make the production system more responsive to the consumer. Consumer tastes must be catered to, and production adjustments anticipated and made as painless as possible.

III

In the hope of resolving these shortcomings, Professor Liberman resubmitted his proposals. He and his supporters were not the only economists who had sensed impending trouble. There was almost no one in the U.S.S.R. by 1962 who would have insisted that no further improvements might be made in the planning system. Debates over the need for price reform had been going on for years. Other economists, including L. V. Kantorovich, the director of the Laboratory for Economical and Mathematical Methods and the originator of linear programming, argued that cybernetics and electronic computers would provide the answer to everything.[14] The Workers' Councils of Yugoslavia were even mentioned as a possible remedy for the Soviet Union's problems. And there were other proposals for either increasing or decreasing the amount of centralized control. Academician V. S. Nemchinov suggested the use of an auction method for matching bids and offers, and his colleague A. Arzumanyan criticized the stress given to heavy industry.[15] Liberman's proposals were especially interesting because he was one of the few to offer a comprehensive and far-reaching scheme that incorporated several suggestions at once.

Essentially, Liberman sought more authority for the factory manager and less interference from the central planners with their plans. If instead of trying to cope with the contradictions of a central plan, the manager could concentrate on producing what his customers wanted and using his resources more effectively, the economy would be better off. Liberman did not go so far as to advocate the abolition of all central plans (and this created its own contradictions, as will be shown), but he did suggest that seven or so existing planning indices might be eliminated and never be missed. For the guidance previously provided by the several plans, Liberman wanted to substitute greater reliance on profits.

Liberman's emphasis on profits is sometimes misunderstood. The use of profits in the Soviet Union is nothing new. Where possible, a Soviet manager has always sought to earn a profit and avoid a loss. A profit-and-loss system, called *khozraschet* ("economic accounting"), in which certain costs are subtracted from revenues, has long been in use. Liberman proposed that the *khozraschet* profit figure of a plant be compared with a base consisting of the plant's fixed and working capital. The resulting percentage would be called the "profitability rate." This figure would then be compared with a "profitability norm" that would be set up for plants in comparable positions. Since the profitability rate would be the sole determinant of the manager's and the plant's bonus fund, it would be the chief index for guiding managerial action.

There was no thought that this would mean turning over the factories to private ownership. It would not be much different from the system of awarding bonuses for profitable operations to the hired manager of a local Chevrolet assembly plant. But Liberman hoped that his scheme would provide certain important benefits: (1) More decision-making power would be delegated to the manager and much of the excess planning bureaucracy, which was discussed earlier, would be eliminated. (2) Since the profitability rate would be increased if costs were reduced, the manager would run his plant more "economically" than in the past. (3) Because of the diminution of the role of planning, the manager would be given increased responsibility for ensuring that his products were sold. Because failure to sell would reduce revenue and thus the profitability rate, presumably the manager would only produce what the consumers wanted. (4) Since the denominator of the profitability rate is capital (working and fixed), ideally the manager would earn a higher bonus if he could either reduce or maintain the capital at his disposal. As a disguised capital charge (interest rate), this would promote the conservation of capital funds and the completion of long-delayed projects. (5) Adjusting the profitability norm for various plants would make it easier for those who might attempt to innovate, and this could stimulate the introduction and production of new products. (6) Making it harder to earn premiums for plants that set their targets too low might induce the managers to raise their sights and increase their own goals. This would eliminate the tug of war that exists when the manager fights to pull down his targets and the planner tries to pull them up.

Inevitably, Liberman's proposals and those of his allies attracted considerable criticism. However, it is interesting to note that the exchanges were conducted without acrimony and in what seemed to be a scholarly spirit. Few economists, if any, rejected everything Liberman had to say. They simply disagreed with him on what corrective steps should be taken.

Most Soviet economists were elated at the chance to conduct a debate on the extent to which and the methods by which the system of central planning should be dismantled. Several were convinced that Liberman was definitely on the right track. Like good managers the world over, they accepted the idea that "what was good for the firm was good for the country" ("to chto vygodno predpriyatiyu dolzhno byt' vygodno i obshchestvu v tselom").[16] Some even felt that Liberman had not gone far enough. What he really was trying to do, they argued, was to recognize that capital was a source of value. Rather than beat around the bush, the late, well-known V. S. Nemchinov, an academician at the U.S.S.R. Academy of Sciences, V. Kotkin, then assistant director of the Technical Administration of the Belorussian Sovnarkhoz, and E. Slastenko, a member of the group at the U.S.S.R. Academy of Sciences that was studying the effects of material stimulation on production, all urged the introduction of a straight 10 per cent capital charge (interest rate).[17]

Such proposals were bound to evoke a frightened response from more conservative economists. In tempered tones, some conservatives said they felt the implementation of Liberman's plan would be tantamount to switching to capitalism.[18] Others, such as L. Alter of the Economic Research Institute of the U.S.S.R. Gosekonomsovet (State Economic Council), protested that the spirit of Communism had been lost. "No one speaks of obligations any more. Today nobody asks what he can do for the state, only what the state can do for him."[19]

There were other, more serious complaints about the proposals. Radical changes like these could result in the rejection of economic planning and all that the Soviet Union stood for. Conceivably, the state would be unable to implement special projects or care for special needs that might arise. As argued by G. Kosyachenko: If a project could not be justified according to the principles of profit maximization, then presumably it would not be attempted. Long-range projects and heavy-investment opportunities, which had made the Soviet Union what it was, would be abandoned. Instead, it was likely that resources and investment would be shifted to the production of consumers' goods. Four decades of neglect virtually assured that there would be enormous profits in the production of automobiles and the construction of homes and apartments. Heavy industry, the keystone of the Soviet economy, would be sacrificed for the production of trifles and the promise of high profits.[20]

Even if they agreed that there was nothing holy about heavy industry, several critics, like Kosyachenko, argued that the transition to a Liberman-type system would be chaotic. Since profits depend on prices and costs, a fundamental price reform would be needed before anything could be done. Naturally, each manager would seek to push his prices up as much as he could in the hope that his profitability rate would be high, at least in the short run. The unrealistically low prices on heavy-industrial products would have to be raised the most, and this would further hamper the growth of heavy industry.

There were others, such as D. Onika and V. Chernyavsky, who recognized that some sort of change in the direction suggested by Liberman was necessary but who felt that Liberman's plan contained too many inconsistencies.[21] Because of technical flaws, for example, it appeared that Liberman's method of determining profitability might make it possible for a firm to expand its capital stock and receive a bonus even though its profits had not increased. This was clearly the opposite of what was intended. But the objection refers more to a mechanical problem than to anything basic in the proposals.

More important, therefore, was the criticism that there would still be too much dependence on bureaucratic planning. As A. G. Zverev, formerly the Minister of Finance, pointed out, if Liberman planned to leave decisions to agencies outside the plant, the manager would inevitably find himself frustrated and once again in the midst of those so-called bureaucratic battles that Liberman presumably wanted to avoid.[22] Indeed, Liberman had suggested that the profitability norm be adjusted to fit the circumstances of each factory. The norm should reflect differences among industries and such variants as location and efficiency among plants in a particular industry. It should also reflect the number of new projects being introduced. Since new projects normally necessitated extra operating expense, plants that experimented would be assigned norms that were easier to meet. However, his critics argued, since the norms would be set by some sort of bureaucrat, there would probably be trouble. Life would no doubt be more comfortable for the factory manager if, instead of concentrating his efforts on the efficient operation of his factory, he could convince the bureaucrats that his factory deserved an easier norm. Hence, the bureaucratic juggling would be no different from what it was before.

Similarly, Liberman planned to retain at least three of the physical planning targets for the plant—quantity, quality, and destination—since he did not want to surrender all power to the plant manager. Thus he tried to anticipate those who would argue that his plan meant the abdication of state control and the introduction of competitive anarchy in the Soviet economy. But, Liberman's opponents pointed out, the continued existence of physical planning targets was a serious contradiction that would mean the retention of the worst aspects of the old system and might even eliminate the positive benefits of the new system. There would still be outside interference and there would still be the temptation to concentrate on reducing the targets rather than on increasing production.

For those with great expectations who were willing to experiment and did not automatically reject all attempts at reform, it soon became evident that Liberman's plan was not the solution it initially promised to be. On balance, it seemed to them that his system would be an improvement over existing procedures but at the same time might give rise to unpredictable problems. For example, it would be hard to determine precisely what a price reform of the scope suggested might entail when combined with an increase in the decision-making power of the manager. Could Soviet managers be entrusted with greater power? And would their power really be increased if some form of centralized control was retained?

IV

What have been the results of the debate? In mid-1963, just when the Western press began to proclaim that the profit motive was finally taking over in the Sovet Union and that the next logical step would be the emergence of capitalism, Liberman and his proposals faded into the background. However, planning difficulties continued to hamper the growth of the Soviet economy, and in mid-1964 Liberman and an enlarged core of supporters reappeared on the scene. Liberman's re-emergence was heralded by his somewhat unfair attack on a correspondent from *Time* magazine.[23] Liberman alleged that the correspondent had distorted his original proposals and their significance. It seemed as though Liberman felt the attack was necessary to show Soviet critics both economic and political that he was not a capitalist lackey and that he was writing, not for Western publicists, but for Soviet economists.

With the ideological air purified and the "noncapitalistic" nature of the plan re-established, the debate was resumed amid some intriguing experiments. Apparently as a direct by-product of the Liberman debate, the Soviet Government announced the formation of what were called "firms." These turned out to be units composed of several factories producing the same product. Primarily, these have been formed by the horizontal combination of like enterprises under a common management. There have also been vertical mergers of both supplier enterprises and retail outlets. Patterned after the large integrated American company, the firm is an attempt to generate the administrative and operative economies of scale the Soviets see in the United States. It is, in addition, a means of focusing more of the decision-making power within the operating unit. Thus, the firm may eliminate some of the outside interference that so concerned Liberman. Then, too, the firm makes it possible for the managers to obtain feedback from their customers. The Soviets apparently believe it is easier to communicate product desires and complaints if suppliers and buyers are merged under a common management.[24] This explains why some of the factories that have not been incorporated into firms, have opened up their own retail outlets. Presumably, the fewer the bureaucrats in the way, the more flexible and responsive the manufacturer can be to changes in consumer tastes.

With the explicit approval of the U.S.S.R. Sovnarkhoz and its chairman, V. Dymshyts, two plants were singled out for an even more radical experiment. As of May 1, 1964, the textile plants Bolshevichka, in Moscow, and Mayak, in Gorki, were given complete independence from central planning. The only plan handed down to these firms from above was the investment plan. This arrangement even went beyond what Liberman had proposed. The firms themselves draw up their own plans for procurement, production, assortment, quality, and labor productivity. These plans are passed on to industrial ministries (formerly to the Sovnarkhoz), but only as information, not for confirmation. The finished products are then shipped to the retail outlets according to contracts drawn up at frequent intervals. The stores take only what they can sell. Profits of the firm and its associated stores are based on what the ultimate consumer buys and no longer on what the factory produces. A portion of the firm's profits is then directed to the factory incentive fund. From 10 to 50 per cent of an employee's salary can be matched by a supplemental payment from the incentive fund. The exact amount is to be determined by the manager in conjunction with the trade union. As before, 4 per cent of the profits will go into the manager's fund. A further innovation, however, is that the plant director and the store manager can themselves set their prices within a limited range. This applies to both increases and decreases in price.

In this experiment, however, some features of Liberman's original plan were not included. There was no profitability rate nor any explicit scheme to stimulate the manager into raising his goal. Instead, in order to earn a bonus, the firm not only must make a profit but must fulfill its "delivery plan." Apparently, it was still too soon to do away with all central control.

After six months of the Bolshevichka and Mayak experiment, it was announced that the scheme was being extended to include 31 per cent of all ready-to-wear factories and 33 per cent of all shoe factories in the U.S.S.R.[25] Moreover, the new system was being pushed back to the raw-material suppliers. About 17 per cent of the textile factories that supply the clothing-makers and 10 per cent of the leather factories that supply the shoe manufacturers were to be affected. Thus, about 400 firms in all were put on the new experiment.

Liberman, who served as a consultant on reorganization for the U.S.S.R. Sovnarkhoz until its dissolution in 1965, said that somewhat less ambitious experiments were also being conducted in heavy industry. Between late 1964 and mid-1965, two coal mines near Lvov (Lwów), a truck factory, and a television assembly plant were converted to the new system, along with several meat packing plants, some dairies, and a candy factory.[26] Even more suggestive of what was to follow was the call for the adoption of the new methods in the whole machine-tool industry.[27] As introduced in heavy industry, however, there were some adjustments in the experiment. In addition to the profit and sales plans, these enterprises were required to fulfill a production plan that spelled out the units of production just as before. This was a retreat from some of the flexibility introduced earlier, but it appeared to be a compromise that was necessary to pacify those who feared that heavy industry would be dissipated if all controls were removed.

The most significant aspect of this last set of reforms was that they began in May, 1964, under Khrushchev's patronage and continued after his ouster, in October of that year. It seems fair to assume that the issue of the reforms was not, as some originally suggested, a cause of Khrushchev's removal. The movement for economic reform even gained momentum in the months that followed. Clearly, Kosygin and Brezhnev have supported the new measures.

What seemed to be the culmination of the experiment was introduced without warning at the September, 1965, plenary session of the Central Committee of the CPSU.[28] Kosygin announced that reforms in economic administration would be implemented throughout the whole of Soviet industry. As before, there were some steps backward toward increased control, but there were also steps forward toward increased flexibility. Plants in light industry were again granted the greatest autonomy. Most enterprises would be allowed to operate as had the 400 firms put on the experiment a year earlier.

The situation in heavy industry was somewhat ambiguous. There were profit, sales, and production plans to be fulfilled, as mentioned above. Furthermore, some central control over factory supplies has been retained, which means that there will also be control over factory deliveries. This system cannot match the effect that greater reliance on profits would have. However, it is interesting to note that this is a return to the proposals originally made by Liberman. In his 1962 plan, Liberman wanted to retain three physical planning targets. Although they were not included in the Bolshevichka and Mayak experiment, they were now adopted despite the fact that it meant considerable inconsistency and a moving at cross-purposes which had been criticized before. The changes in heavy industry seemingly represent a retreat, but another reform was introduced in September, 1965, that clearly is an economic advance. Kosygin declared that henceforth enterprises would be evaluated by a profitability rate. This, of course, was a direct throwback to Liberman's original proposals. Furthermore, there was to be a capital charge (interest rate) on capital lent out by the state bank. These features had all been omitted from the experiment at Mayak and Bolshevichka and the 400 plants. In many ways, the introduction of the interest rate was the most radical move of all. Marx had not taken a stand against profits, but he had denied that capital had value. The Soviet Union has now been forced to acknowledge that it does. At the Twenty-third Party Congress, Kosygin announced that by early 1967 one-third of the Soviet industrial labor force, including much of that in heavy industry, would be working under the new system.

To ensure that the local plants are not given too much power, an organization reform intended to secure some increase in centralization was announced in conjunction with the incentive reforms. All the sovnarkhozy at both the local and republic levels were abolished, and their power was transferred to reconstituted industrial ministries. This was an attempt to replace territorial with branch administration. Theoretically, the net effect of all this should be that the reforms will provide needed flexibility for the firm, while the return to the ministerial system should provide an offsetting restraint. It will be interesting to see if Soviet theory approaches practice any more successfully than it has in the past.

Institutional reforms are clearly not the only significant result of the debates. If the past suggests any pattern, undoubtedly the reforms themselves will shortly be reformed. Of much greater significance is the official recognition by the Soviet Government that the nation has reached an important economic crossroad.

Central planning served its purpose in the Soviet Union. But as the demands of both industry and the consumer became more sophisticated, central planning as it once existed became a fetter. Although the debates and reforms were initiated under Khrushchev, they have continued under Kosygin and Brezhnev. Apparently it is too late to return to the old methods. The core of a new economic structure has been completed. As Marx postulated so long ago, economic growth necessitates institutional change. The Soviet experience has proved to be no exception.

NOTES

1. *Kommunist*, No. 10 (July, 1956), p. 75.
2. *Narodnoe khozyaistvo SSSR v 1958 godu* (Moscow: Tsentral'noe Statisticheskoe Upravlenie, 1959), p. 95; Abram Bergson and Simon Kuznets, *Economic Trends in the Soviet Union* (Cambridge, Mass.: Harvard University press, 1963), p. 336.
3. *Pravda*, September 9, 1962, p. 3.
4. *SSSR v tsifrakh v 1963 godu* (Moscow: Tsentral'noe Statisticheskoe Upravlenie, 1964), p. 29.
5. *Pravda*, November 20, 1962, p. 5.
6. *Sovetskaya Rossiya*, October 17, 1963, p. 2.
7. *Nedelia*, No. 44 (1964), p. 4.
8. *Ekonomicheskaya gazeta*, November 3, 1962, p. 36.
9. *Pravda*, January 20, 1963, p. 4.
10. *Ibid.*, December 10, 1963, p. 6.
11. *Ibid.*, December 15, 1963, p. 3.
12. *Ekonomicheskaya gazeta*, November 3, 1962, p. 39.
13. *Voprosy ekonomiki*, No. 5 (May, 1964), p. 45.
14. *Ekonomicheskaya gazeta*, November 3, 1962, p. 39.
15. *Pravda*, February 24, 1964, p. 23.
16. *Ibid.*, September 9, 1962, p. 3.
17. *Ibid.*, September 21, 1962, p. 3, and October 12, 1962, p. 3.
18. *Ekonomicheskaya gazeta*, November 3, 1962, p. 43.
19. *Voprosy ekonomiki*, No. 11 (November, 1962), p. 116.
20. *Ibid.*, p. 111.
21. *Ibid.*, p. 29; *Pravda*, October 19, 1962, p. 4.
22. *Voprosy ekonomiki*, No. 11 (November, 1962), p. 94.
23. *Ekonomicheskaya gazeta*, May 30, 1964, p. 13.
24. *Ibid.*, July 6, 1963, p. 35.
25. *Ibid.*, October 28, 1964, p. 4.
26. *Ibid.*, June 16, 1965, p. 14.
27. *Trud*, July 8, 1965, p. 1.
28. *Pravda*, September 28, 1965, p. 1.

4

The Mob Within the Heart

*A NEW RUSSIAN REVOLUTION**

Peter Viereck

EDITORS' INTRODUCTION

What restraints should the Party place on creative artists? How this issue is resolved will greatly influence future relations between the Party and the whole of Soviet society. As Peter Viereck writes here, poets and writers traditionally have been the main articulators of social criticism and political opposition in Russia. According to Viereck, a "pendularity" of cultural policy—that is, swings between permissiveness and repression—is traditional as well. It is inherent in the centuries-old confrontation between dogmatists and liberals under the Russian autocracy.

Viereck captures the emotions and purposes of the latter-day dogmatists and liberals during and after the cultural crackdown of 1962/63. The near return to Stalinist repression in 1963, he writes, is "important for the future as a reminder of how precarious are the post-Stalin liberties in the absence of either constitutional roots or constitutional guarantees."

He concludes on a note of "cautious optimism," however. Cultural freedoms, he believes, can flourish in the Soviet Union even without political freedom. He would, therefore, not agree with observers such as Gleb Struve, who thinks, rather, that no "true liberalization of cultural policy" is possible under the Soviet one-party regime.

* This is an abridged and updated version of an article that appeared in *Tri-Quarterly*, Spring, 1965, pp. 7–43; it is printed with permission.

In fact, a great variety of cultural policies has existed under the Communist Party. With no claim for the exclusive correctness of the following list, we take stock here of no less than eleven key changes in Russia that help to account for this variety.

1. The Bolshevik overthrow of the Provisional Government, in 1917, reintroduced negative censorship. Writers were not told what they should say, as later under Stalin, but what they might not say.

2. The chaos of the Civil War and foreign intervention, in 1918–21, and the paper shortages, disrupted most creative activity.

3. The breathing spell of the NEP period, 1921–28, permitted a limited creative revival. The Party, led then by intellectuals, maintained a relative neutrality among the competing literary schools, declining to satisfy the "proletarian" writers' demands that the "Fellow-Travelers," the non-Bolshevik and more distinguished literary group, be forcibly assimilated into them.

4. To help carry out the First Five-Year Plan (1928–32), Stalin, having defeated the Party intellectuals, dragooned the arts as mass educator and mass mobilizer. There was to be no more "art for art's sake."

5. To make sure of this, Stalin totalitarianized the arts in the Second Five-Year Plan. Among other measures, he set up a single, Party-controlled Union of Soviet Artists in 1932, turning his inquisition on some of its members by 1936.

6. With the Great Fatherland War, Stalin, the writers, and the Soviet people found a common goal: to save their homeland. The temporary harmony of aspirations allowed a relaxation of controls.

7. The onset of the Cold War, in 1946, brought renewed repressions, including purges of Jewish writers. But contradictions in Socialist Realism, the official artistic method, became all too apparent. Art could be "socialist" only at the expense of "realism." Party-line propaganda made for unpopular, bad writing. The public refused to fill the theaters or to empty the bookstalls. A slight relaxation in Stalin's last three years permitted the launching of critical attacks on the "rotten" theory that drama should present no conflict between good and evil. Also, in 1952, Novy mir published Valentin Ovechkin's "The District Routine," an exposé of the ills of peasant life under the rural bureaucracy.

8. *Stalin died on March 5, 1953. He left in power a core of technically trained* apparatchiki, *not the intellectual types, whom they had long since displaced. Since the* apparatchiki *claimed credit for all achievements in the U.S.S.R., they laid themselves open to blame for all shortcomings. Thus their treatment of the writers was cautious and marked by distrust. But they were pragmatic enough to realize that "irreproachable heroes" set no example for the people, who, as Ehrenburg put it, "want to learn not how to be born a hero, but how to become one." The thaw of 1953 and the slight refreeze of 1954/55 wavered between the limits of NEP neutralism and Stalin's total repression without returning to either. Ehrenburg's novel* The Thaw, *which gave the era its name, appeared during the 1954 retrenchment, but it contained most of the new themes writers could touch on: police repression, the anti-Semitic frameup of the "doctors' plot," the artistic mediocrity fostered by the state (a cynical hack painter collects fat commissions while a painter of integrity endures hardship rather than give in to the official line), the callousness of the Stalinist factory manager (Juravlyov), and the importance and wonder of love (Juravlyov's wife, Lena, divorces him and marries her heart's desire).*

9. *Khrushchev's resort to overt anti-Stalinism as a weapon in the intra-Party power struggle, particularly his "secret speech" of February 25, 1956, intensified the conflict between conservative and liberal writers. In 1957, after the Hungarian Revolution, the Party-line writers and critics took advantage of Khrushchev's fears and embarrassments to launch telling attacks against their liberal adversaries. In 1958, the literary conservatives again appeared to win a battle, when Pasternak was forced amidst a staged hue and cry to refuse the Nobel Prize he had been awarded on October 23. In 1960, Khrushchev's controversial demobilization measures, the U-2 incident, and foreign-policy failures in the Congo and Berlin seemed again to give the conservatives the upper hand. But through all this the liberals emerged intact as a cultural force. Their literature was even more bold than it had been in 1953–55, exploring such new themes as youthful alienation and revolt, and marital infidelity. Khrushchev's impetuously pragmatic use of anti-Stalinism exposed the liberals to nerve-wracking, unpredictable,*

and violent shifts in cultural policy, but presented them with periodic opportunities for greater public self-expression.

10. *Khrushchev soon went even further to involve the liberals in his own fate. He used the Twenty-second Party Congress (October, 1961) to stage a new attack against his opposition in China and at home, presiding personally over the decision to move Stalin's remains from the Mausoleum to a simpler resting place. The following year, the liberal writers became his direct instruments of political struggle when he approved the publication of Yevtushenko's poem "Stalin's Heirs" and, against opposition within the Party Presidium, forced through the publication of Alexander Solzhenitsyn's concentration-camp tale,* One Day in the Life of Ivan Denisovich. *Khrushchev utilized anti-Stalinist literature, Priscilla Johnson writes in* Khrushchev and the Arts, *"to pave the way for a purge of Stalinist leftovers from the creaking economic bureaucracy." He was, in effect, striking at such reactionary bureaucrats as the Dozdrov figures of Vladimir Dudintsev's novel* Not by Bread Alone, *for which, ironically, Dudintsev had once been in serious trouble. In the novel, Dozdrov and his allies have the engineer Lopatkin sent to a labor camp, and almost defeat his efforts to introduce technical innovations. Commenting on the novel in a debate at the Moscow Writers' Club in October, 1956, the great prose writer Konstantin Paustovsky said the Soviet Union is plagued with "thousands" of Dozdrovs: "Rapacious and propertied persons," they form a new "philistine caste. . . . If it weren't for the Dozdrovs, such people as Meyerhold, Babel, Artyom Vesyoly, and many others would still be living among us. They were destroyed by the Dozdrovs. And they were destroyed in the name of the stinking comfort of these Dozdrovs."*

Khrushchev followed up his literary tactics with a political move at the November, 1962, plenum of the Central Committee: the reorganization of the local Party hierarchies into "industrial" and "agricultural" segments. This made natural allies of the Dozdrovs, Party apparatchiki in general, and the resentful diehards in the arts who had been alarmed by the recent literary developments and by the growing liberal or moderate influences within the unions of creative artists.

The close connection between Party politics at the time of the November plenum and the initiation of the cultural clampdown that followed the plenum is described by Priscilla Johnson in Khrushchev and the Arts:

> By the time the Central Committee met to decree the economic reform [*splitting the local hierarchies*] on November 19, Stalin's heirs [*headed by Frol Kozlov in the Party Presidium*] were ready to counterattack. At their initiative, the plenary session was presented with a petition from "*a large group of artists*" complaining of the growing "*formalist trends*" in art and asking the Party to intervene. This was the first link in a long chain that was to see Party conservatives destroy the recent liberal trend in art, then literature, in an attempt to halt the process of de-Stalinization and perhaps even upset the balance of power inside the Communist Party.

It had been a good year for the liberals, and they appeared blissfully ignorant of the cabal. On November 26, a private show of contemporary Soviet art opened in the apartment of the painter Belyutin. According to Ralph Blum (The New Yorker, August 28, 1965), the young artists were delighted when they received orders to move over to the "Thirty Years of Moscow Art" exhibition then at the Manezh hall. On November 30, the poet Robert Rozhdesvensky told a cheering crowd of 14,000 at a poetry reading in Luzhniky Sports Stadium: "We will no longer say someone is thinking for us." The bombshell burst the next day. Khrushchev visited the Manezh, and his earthy dressing down of the Belyutin group in the rooms set aside for them, his threats of economic reprisal, of banishment abroad, of ten-year sentences for pederasty, and his final: "Gentlemen, we are declaring war upon you" (Encounter, April, 1963), shook not only the artists but also the entire Soviet cultural world. The anti-liberal kulturkampf that built up during the next four months was punctuated by dramatic meetings of the Party and intellectual elites, beginning with the stormy meeting of December 17, 1962, and reaching a high point with Khrushchev's tirade on March 8, 1963. Yet, by mid-April, the campaign had begun to abate. It had ceased completely by the end of the summer, but left everyone sobered and shaken, with no clear winner.

However, the Manezh continued to be the scene of sudden policy changes that bewildered Soviet artists. In the summer of 1964, the Manezh exhibited a collection of paintings by Ilya Glazounov, a neo-Expressionist in the German style of the 1920's, an abstract artist by Soviet standards. The conservative Union of Soviet Artists tried to prevent the opening of the exhibition. While an angry and determined crowd waited outside the Manezh, the Deputy Minister of Culture personally opened the show. He intervened again when the union attempted to close the show prematurely. Students, shouting "We want new painters," had threatened a sit-in unless the show were kept open (Viktor Meier, Encounter, October, 1964). After the Glazounov exhibit, Moscow's First Party Secretary, Nikolai Yegorychev, attacked young scholars of the important Institute of World Economics and International Relations for staging a show of paintings by Glazounov and other young artists—apparently before the Manezh affair—and for writing a public letter defending the artist (Kommunist, No. 3, 1965).

Undoubtedly Khrushchev's clampdown of 1962/63 reflected his anti-intellectualism, his distaste for modern art, and his concern over the cultural trend he had aided. But the fury of his onslaught, it seems, was the result of pressures from his supposedly loyal Party apparatus, who were disgruntled at the organizational aspects of de-Stalinization. As fate would have it, Khrushchev's position was weakened by the failure of his Cuban missile gamble, by the continuing industrial inadequacies, by a growing food crisis that included price increases for meat and milk products (which set off riots in Novocherkask), by disputes over investment priorities, and by his China policy. Khrushchev was in a predicament, and it seems reasonable to assume that he was forced to make sacrificial lambs of his recent allies—the liberal artists.

The liberals, however, were not completely shattered, as the conservatives had hoped. Peter Viereck suggests here a variety of reasons for this: their determined self-defense; Khrushchev's liking for Novy mir's editor, Alexander Tvardovsky; the Party's failure to find more pliable but still talented alternatives to the famous but troublesome young literary stars; and the coincidence of

Kozlov's disabling stroke in April, 1963, after which the conservatives' campaign simmered down. Helping the liberals also, as
Priscilla Johnson indicates, was the disapproval of the campaign
voiced by Western Communists, whose support the Soviet Communists needed against the Chinese. The late Palmiro Togliatti,
for example, asserted that nobody, however able, should attempt
"to tell an artist how to write a poem, how to create music, or how
to paint."

11. Khrushchev's forced resignation on October 14, 1964, may
have gotten the artists off a roller coaster, but they soon discovered
they were in a rocky boat. And it undulated to the rhythm that
had characterized the policy shifts of 1953–55. "Seasickness,"
which Yevtushenko read over television in December, 1964, can be
interpreted as symbolizing the uncertain state of liberalization
(Olga Carlisle, The New York Times Book Review, March 14,
1965). Apparently in retaliation, two television station officials
lost their jobs and Yevtushenko's 5,000-line epic, Bratskaya ges,
appeared three months later than scheduled. The Dozdrov type
appears in the epic—"one of those telephone people" who shouted
"Plan!" to the desperate villages after the war, who padded statistics and kept a "well-known portrait" (presumably Stalin in tunic
and jackboots) behind the commode, saying, no, "let it stay there
for a while," when the maid wanted to throw it out (Yunost, April,
1965).

The instability in Soviet culture policy continued throughout
1965, a year of mixed as well as consecutive concessions and repressions. First came the optimism of February–September, created by
Pravda's pro-intellectual and anti-Dozdrov stance under its editor,
A. M. Rumyantsev (for another liberal role of his, see Chapter 2,
on his initiation of family-law reforms). Then came the dark
period engendered by Rumyantsev's resignation in September;
the arrest that month of the writers Andrei Sinyavsky and Yuli
Daniel; the press campaign against them for the "slanderous,"
"anti-Soviet" works they allegedly smuggled out of the U.S.S.R.
and published abroad under the pseudonyms Abram Tertz and
Nikolai Arzhak; their trial before a selected audience, February 10–
14, 1966; their sentences of seven and five years of hard labor, respectively; some delegates' attacks against their ilk and liberal

artists in general at the Twenty-third Congress; the relative silence and low representation of liberals at the Congress (e.g., Tvardovsky, prominently defending the liberal viewpoint and elected to candidate membership of the Central Committee at the Twenty-second Congress, in 1961, was not even a delegate to the Twenty-third, though his adversary Kochetov did attend).

Yet, the swing in policy was not absolute. Signs of liberal strength, courage, and access to top Party counsels never ceased. Witness, for example, the apparently successful pre-Congress petition of twenty-five leading scientists and artists (including physicist Peter Kapitsa and prima ballerina Maya Plisetskaya) against what they considered was an impending reversal, through a re-evaluation and upgrading of Stalin, of the anti-Stalinist course of the previous Congress; the petition of about forty leading intellectuals asking clemency for Sinyavsky and Daniel; Konstantin Paustovsky's attempt to serve as a defender for them in court; the wholesale refusals in the liberal camp, at the risk of imprisonment for contempt of court, to testify against Sinyavsky and Daniel; the defendants' pleas of not guilty and their spirited testimony, in contrast to the abject submission of most of the victims of Stalin's show trials; Minister of Culture Ekaterina Furtseva's implicit rejection of the dogmatist line, at the Twenty-third Congress; the fact that at that Congress many speakers ignored the scandal altogether and Kochetov lost his post as a member of the Central Auditing Commission; the fact that the writers could ask sharp questions of the presiding judge, L. N. Smirnov, after the trial, when he appeared before the Union of Soviet Writers to lecture them on the trial; some sensational modern art shows staged by intellectuals in their institutions during this period; Voznesensky's successful trip to the United States; Tvardovsky's survival, at least into the summer of 1966, and his publication of an anti-Stalinist novel by Bykov in Novy mir (Nos. 1 and 2, 1966) during the crescendo of vituperation against Sinyavsky and Daniel, and of his own articles, in which he advocated artistic veracity and courage against one's critics (they appeared after dogmatists at the Twenty-third Congress had just finished lambasting his journal).

When Ilya Ehrenburg looked ahead during the worst part of the previous clampdown, in March, 1963, he said to a younger

*colleague: "I shall never see the flowering of the Soviet arts. But
you will see it—in twenty years." Reading Peter Viereck's account
should help the reader to decide whether he agrees with Ehrenburg's forecast.*

> The mob within the heart
> Police cannot suppress
> —EMILY DICKINSON

A pendulum between thaw and freeze characterizes not only Soviet
society today but Russian society through the ages. Thus a reformist Alexander I seems forever alternating with a dogmatist Nicholas
I, a reformist Alexander II with a dogmatist Alexander III, a reformist Kerensky with a dogmatist Lenin, the NEP thaw of the
mid-1920's with Stalin. And already before Alexander I, there was
the pro-Western "eighteenth-century enlightenment" of Catherine
the Great alternating with the anti-Western dogmatist Paul. The
pendulum is not automatic. It is not swung by a capitalized attraction called "History" or by any other intellectual or economic de-
terminism. It is swung only by concrete human beings, making
efforts of will and conviction in either direction. Yet it is reasonable
to assume that both directions will continue to be actively and
effectively represented. For both directions have deep roots in Russia's past and present and are being personally passed on to the
future.

The dogmatist direction of Russian culture has been shaped for
centuries by Byzantine and Greek Orthodox traditions. Their heritage, inherited unintentionally but almost totally by the dogmatist
wing of Communism, includes a Caesaro-papist identity of state
with ideology (Czardom with theology) and an accompanying
sense of Russia's world-saving mission, whether for Christian Orthodoxy with a capital O or for a Marxist-Leninist orthodoxy with
a small o. For example, the same Russian-messianic motif appears
in the novels of the Czarist Dostoyevsky and the novels of his

Communist disciple Leonid Leonov,* with whom in Moscow I discussed precisely this parallel. Equally deep (today even deeper because of anti-Stalinist revulsion, pro-Western nostalgia, and the spread of scientific education) is the anti-dogmatist, liberationist tradition of Russian writers, whether the old nineteenth-century "Westernizers" or the current "revisionists." An example is the following parallel between a quotation of 1847 by the anti-Czarist rebel Vissarion Belinsky and a quotation of 1963 by the anti-Stalinist rebel Yevgeny Yevtushenko. In a letter secretly circulated against the tyrant Nicholas I, the libertarian socialist Belinsky exulted:

> The public . . . looks upon Russian writers as its only leaders, defenders, and saviors against Russian autocracy. . . . The title of poet and writer has eclipsed the tinsel of epaulettes and gaudy uniforms.

In 1963 the poet Yevtushenko, speaking for what he calls the "anti-dogmatist" Communist idealists, told the Paris *Express* (in an interview secretly circulated in Russia and denounced in person by Khrushchev):

> All the tyrants in Russia have taken the poets as their worst enemies. They feared Pushkin. They trembled before Lermontov. They were afraid of Nekrasov.

The old historical pendulum continues to alternate, just as much as before. But now less murderously. And quicker, more deviously: for example, one could write whole books—and the best authorities do—tracing how Yevtushenko was ousted during the 1963 freeze from the governing board of the Moscow Writers' Union but was re-elected to it in January, 1965, or tracing how the last volume of Ehrenburg's memoirs was announced by the thaw magazine *Novy mir* for 1964 publication and then mysteriously

* When I told Leonov that I consider his *Thief* the greatest Communist novel ever written (it applies to a backsliding Soviet war hero the Dostoyevsky gamut of sin-suffering-redemption), he told me how Stalin in person had underlined in red ink those passages he deemed heretical. Leonov's face lighted up with that quick-flashing sense of condensed history (a uniquely Russian look that I met in many tormented idealistic Communists) when I replied that, of course, Nicholas I had also underlined in person, and also with red ink, the Lermontov novel A *Hero of Our Time*.

failed to appear, only to be announced all over again by *Novy mir* for 1965.

More amusing as well as more revealing are the government attempts to by-pass pendularity toward these rebel writers by starting all over again with more docile specimens: the teacher's pets of Communism. In the spring of 1963, a Moscow conference of younger writers assembled 170 eager new apple-polishers from all over the U.S.S.R., hoping to substitute them in public affection for such youth idols as Andrei Voznesensky, Yevtushenko, and the latter's ex-wife, Akhmadullina. (A Polish poet, who had attended the well-directed Gorky Writers' Institute with her, told me—after hearing I addressed a class there—that Akhmadullina was hounded out of the institute by a Party hack, jealous of her proud creative individualism; "the Tartar princess," they nicknamed—for her pride—this best of Russia's younger women poets.) But despite Party funds and pressure, the above 1963 conference for "new youth" evoked little new talent. The 170 preening pets failed to catch on in terms of either sales or moral influence. The Party can do little to prevent or avenge this kind of increasingly typical fiasco. It can arrest citizens for any positive revolt but not for the negative, unprovable revolt of simply staying home from bad poetry readings and leaving unreadable books unread.

A basic continuity characterizes this cultural policy of the 1960's. In aim it is the old Stalin-Zhdanov policy of imposing ideology on intellectuals and artists. But in method it uses persuasion and relatively peaceful threats, with arrest as a last resort and without shootings. Stalin used arrest as almost a first resort for literary deviators, and shootings as a norm.

What has been the upshot of this post-Stalin cultural policy? A small number of arrests, notably of Yosif Brodsky* and Alex-

---

* In 1964 came the arrest and philistine "trial" of Brodsky, found guilty of "social parasitism" for being a pure lyricist rather than propagandist; clearly the thaw is still extremely precarious. When I met Anna Akhmatova, in 1963, she spoke extremely highly of Brodsky's objective literary merits.

[Anna Akhmatova was a renowned lyrical poetess attacked and hounded out of the Union of Soviet Writers in 1946, but grudgingly rehabilitated after Stalin; she died March 5, 1966.

Yosif Brodsky, not only a poet but also a brilliant translator of foreign verse, was detained by the police in 1962, when acquaintances of his, Umansky and Shakhmatov, were tried and convicted for "exerting harmful

ander S. Yesenin-Volpin,* and a large number of suppressions, notably of the experimentalist painters. But no Stalin-style murders, no Zhdanov-style total suppressions. Nothing that can in all fairness be compared to the stultifying Stalinist terror to which the anti-Soviet Western press sometimes draws analogies.

I do not mean to say sanctimoniously, heartlessly, the persecuted writers and artists in Russia should be "grateful" for not being tortured or killed. They have nothing to be grateful for; on the contrary, they have inherent human liberties to demand from their oppressors. But there is one historical and literary advantage in not being killed. This is the plain physical fact that the victims today can "sit out" the pendulum until the next swing in their

---

influence on young people by preaching mysticism, Yoga philosophy, and anarcho-syndicalism." According to Ralph Blum (*The New Yorker*, September 11, 1965), Brodsky had broken with Umansky and Shakhmatov before their arrest. Victor Frank wrote in *Encounter* (November, 1964), that Alexander Prokofiev, secretary of the Leningrad branch of the Union of Soviet Writers (which Brodsky had not joined), until replaced with a more liberal writer in March, 1965, arranged a rigged session of the secretariat to recommend that Brodsky be sentenced in court as a parasite. Anna Akhmatova, the famed writer of tales for children Kornei Chukovsky, the composer Dmitri Shostakovich, and the late poet and translator Samuel Marshak intervened to prevent the trial. Two years later, after the cultural clampdown had shaken the world of arts, Brodsky's liberal protectors were less successful. According to Ralph Blum, a certain Lerner, retired captain of the MVD, serving as a volunteer People's Guard, was the moving force behind the campaign against Brodsky. It concluded with his trial on February 18 and March 13, 1964 (a transcript of which appeared in *The New Leader*, August 31, 1964). In spite of his poor health, he was exiled from Leningrad north to Arkhangelsk Region for five years, with obligation to work. On March 22, 1964, he left by train for his place of exile. Apparently, the ordeal of Brodsky was to serve as a warning to other nonconformist writers.

Moreover, since Brodsky is not yet a major literary figure, and has not yet a large public following, though known to other writers, he has made an ideal victim for a dogmatist coalition of literary, judiciary, and police bureaucrats, for whom the major liberal spokesmen have remained beyond reach. He was reported at liberty in Leningrad (*The New York Times*, April 14, 1966) after serving only two years of his five-year sentence (this was after the rumor that arose in 1965, when a short visit home was mistaken for liberty.)—Eds.]

* Yesenin-Volpin, son of the peasant poet Yesenin, who killed himself in 1925, has sent abroad bitterly critical poetry. Like other cultural rebels— Chaadayev under Nicholas I, or his contemporary Valery Tarsis (allowed to go to England in 1966, subsequently deprived of Soviet citizenship)—Yesenin-Volpin found himself confined in a mental institution. Ralph Blum reported in *The New Yorker* (September 11, 1965) that he has been set free, to continue rendering scientific services to the state.—Eds.

favor. The Mandelstams and Babels and Tabidzes of the Stalin era were not able to flower in the subsequent thaw; they were dead.

The difference is not only one of actions but of atmosphere. Despite the government's intention to stultify, the atmosphere continues lively and rebellious; the persecution has only increased the popularity and the solidarity of the rebels. I can testify to this from personal experience because the government crackdown was already in full swing during my third Russian visit, that of January and February, 1963. By then, Khrushchev had made his December attack on the abstract painters; the Shostakovich performance of Yevtushenko's "Babi Yar" had been withdrawn and then resumed in censored form; and *Izvestia* was featuring its January attack on Viktor Nekrasov's favorable travelogue about America. With what results? A knowledgeable and well-known figure in the Soviet world of the arts told me: "Everyone recalls the Nazi attack on abstract art. My friends and I, who have always disliked abstract painting, are now doing everything to defend it in response to the government demand for mass meetings against it."

Then came the stronger guns of the Ilyichev* and Khrushchev barrage of March 7–8, 1963 (against Ehrenburg, Nekrasov, Aksyonov, and other rebel poets and artists); the Writers' Union meeting of March 26–28 (in a similar vein); the Party meeting of June with its resolutions for imposing more ideology upon literature—and so on, with alternating temporary relaxations, right through today. The results of all these earsplitting threats and pep talks, though sometimes grim enough, show a downright sensational disproportion between bark and bite. Just before March, 1963, the younger Russian writers and students were turning against Yevtushenko and Voznesensky because the two poets were becoming too official, were having too many trips abroad, trips allowed for not exactly aesthetic reasons by the Party. I even heard Yevgeny Yevtushenko nicknamed "Yevgeny Gapon" by a more bitter poet (after the Father Gapon who had led the protesting workers of Bloody Sunday, 1905, but turned out to be a secret

---

* Leonid Ilyichev, an expert in agitation and propaganda, rose to be a Secretary of the Party Central Committee in October, 1961, and Chairman of the Ideological Commission of the Central Committee, set up in 1962. On his demotion (to the post of Deputy Foreign Minister) after Khrushchev, see below—EDS.

government agent). But the rebel poets regained much of their lost popularity and influence *because* the government then denounced them and canceled their trips abroad. In retrospect, recalling my firsthand impressions of their public readings and their followers and discounting their necessary concessions to official lines, I am convinced they are sincere, independent, and enormously influential voices of the thaw and not puppets of any Communist—or, for that matter, anti-Communist—government.

The confessions of the denounced writers of 1963, if one studies the texts carefully, confess very little. All Voznesensky promised the Party was "to work harder." And the bravest of the lot, the novelist Viktor Nekrasov, refused to confess at all. Nekrasov is a veteran Communist hero of "the trenches of Stalingrad" (to quote the title of one of his novels). It is his Communist faith which sustains not only his refusal to confess and recant but those other positions for which *Izvestia* attacked him on January 17, 1963, and Ilyichev and Khrushchev on March 7 and 8. These positions include his defense of experimentalism in the arts and cinema, his insistence on the good as well as bad side of the West, his demand that Russian tourists in America be allowed by their government to travel alone instead of in disciplined, shadowed groups. All the West knows Yevtushenko's poem of 1961, "Babi Yar"; it protests against anti-Semitism and the lack of Soviet memorials at the site of the biggest Nazi pogrom. Very few in the West realize that already two years earlier Nekrasov (by nationality a Ukrainian) had published an equally courageous protest against Soviet plans to build a sports stadium instead of a memorial there: "On the site of such a colossal tragedy to make merry and play football!" (*Literaturnaya gazeta,* October 10, 1959).

Dogmatists vs. Liberals

On March 16, 1963, the Stalinist Vsevolod Kochetov published a threatening article in *Literaturnaya gazeta*. The article demanded "deeds" rather than "words" against the rebel poets. It proposed a giant grab-bag union to replace the separate writers' union, painters' union, etc. This giant union would gather all the arts under single centralized Party control, organized by the Party from above, and crushing the local semi-independence of separate unions. Example of semi-independence: on the issue of expanding Russia's cultural freedom, the Kochetov dogmatists were being steadily defeated by the Tvardovsky liberalizers inside the present Writers' Union (both factions being led by Party members). Therefore, the then powerful Ilyichev likewise urged such a grab-all union to discipline the individualists. But nothing came of the notion. The press has simply stopped discussing it.

Even at the height of the freeze, the leader of Leningrad's dogmatists, the poet Alexander Prokofiev, complained that the public would rather buy the rebel poets than the loyal ones (*Pravda*, March 27, 1963). Once again, the dogmatist winners were striking a plaintive note inconsistent with the decisive victory they claimed that spring. Nor were they victors long. Resented by most fellow writers, they were too dependent on Kozlov, Ilyichev, and Suslov—but Kozlov died on January 30, 1965, and Ilyichev was demoted on March 23, 1965. Early that year, the Leningrad Writers' Union was free at last to revolt against Prokofiev. The Leningraders elected a neutral figure, not thaw but neutral, to replace "this hated Party toady and bootlicker," to quote an off-the-record Soviet rebel.

A second consequence of the removal of Kozlov and Ilyichev (coming only five days after the latter's transfer to a high Foreign Office post) was the attack on Kochetov and his magazine, *Oktyabr*, for clinging to the Stalinist past and using "an extremely strong tone" against all new talents (*Pravda*, March 28). By thus conveying the views of its moderate editor, Rumyantsev, *Pravda* was signaling not a Party commitment to liberalization, but merely another minor pendulum swing. Moreover, the same *Pravda* piece went out of its way to stress that it saw nothing unusual in *Oktyabr*'s recent campaign against Solzhenitsyn, who no longer had Khrushchev to protect his indictments of neo-Stalinist bureaucrats.

During 1963/64, critics in Red China praised Kochetov as one of the few Russian writers they found ideologically sound. This fact, more likely than a new liberalization prematurely hailed by wishful thinkers, helps explain the 1965 *Pravda* attack on Kochetov; the account in *The New York Times* (March 29) failed to mention this motivating fact. Conversely, the Red

Chinese attack of August, 1964, on Voznesensky and Yevtushenko led to greater public kindliness toward them by Russia's rulers. Not what you write but who praises or attacks it abroad may determine your status back home. What has undermined Kochetov is not his intolerant authoritarianism, which he shares with Russia's rulers, but the kiss of death he received from Red China. Moreover, his freeze magazine sold less and had less influence than Tvardovsky's thaw magazine; and the Party despises failure, even among its own champions.

A word of background about Kochetov. His rather courageous stubbornness is worthy of a better cause. A lean, sinewy war veteran, Kochetov showed more guts than many thaw advocates when he defied Khrushchev by openly speaking out for the MTS (Stalin's Machine Tractor Stations, which Khrushchev denounced and abolished). Whereas Khrushchev favored Tvardovsky, inviting him to family festivities on the Black Sea, Kochetov has been publicly praised (but not really protected from severe press criticism) by Suslov, the top ideological dogmatist of post-Stalin Russia and a prime mover in overthrowing Khrushchev in October, 1964. Kochetov's novels include *The Yershov Brothers*, 1958 (a pro-bureaucrat, anti-intellectual rebuttal to Vladimir Dudintsev's pro-intellectual, anti-bureaucrat novel, *Not by Bread Alone*, 1956), and *Secretary of the Oblast Committee*, 1961, attacking among many other things the young rebel poets of the thaw. While paying the usual vigorous lip service to anti-Stalinism, the latter novel contains an insinuatingly anti-Khrushchev, pro-Stalin scene, in which the hero (a Party official) and his wife look up adoringly at a picture of the Stalin they claim to repudiate. Already the *Literaturnaya gazeta* of December 16, 1962, while still under its thaw editorship, accused Kochetov of crypto-Stalinism, putting his career in jeopardy under Khrushchev and after. In late 1963, Khrushchev attended a private preview of the movie based on the novel. At the Stalin-picture scene, Khrushchev reportedly started screaming with rage that he would never tolerate such officials in the Party and that the scene must be censored.

It was sometimes difficult to make Russian thaw zealots understand how instinctively we detest the very principle of censorship, whether by a Soviet Bircher like Kochetov, who tries to suppress Tvardovsky's magazine as "nihilistic poison kowtowing to the

West," or by liberalizers against Kochetov. We here mention Khrushchev's wrathful censorship of Kochetov (never published so far as we know) in order to stress that Khrushchev's famous rages were not solely against the thaw camp, even though the world better knows—because more public—his rages against modern paintings in December, 1962, and against Ehrenburg, Nekrasov, and Yevtushenko in March, 1962.

The Party has tried to build up anti-Western, anti-experimentalist poets such as Vladimir Firsov, who boasts of being too wholesome to look at modern art. Firsov is a thought-provoking example of the extroverted Soviet "square": his not untypical existence proves that a very young Komsomol secretary (Moscow chapter of the Writers' Union) can today still talk like a very old Stalinist. Here is a summary of his remarks of 1963 in a private conversation with a foreigner I know in Moscow: "There are tendencies that alarm us in modern Russian poetry. Influenced by jazz, the twist, and Picasso, instead of our Russian folk art, they lack Soviet national pride and grovel before Western bourgeois culture." Firsov was especially angry at Yevtushenko for his allegedly sympathizing more with Jewish than Slavic victims of Hitler in his poem "Babi Yar." (That same year Khrushchev forced Yevtushenko to add lines about the Slavic victims; Yevtushenko told friends he only yielded because of a loss of nerve on the part of Shostakovich, who set the poem to music.) Firsov fell into a fury against "Babi Yar," calling it a sinister, anti-Soviet poem. He tried to explain its popularity in the West by a secret conspiracy of "Jewish influences over the American press." These remarks reveal how easily anti-thaw and anti-cosmopolitanism can pass into anti-Semitism even today, recalling—though admittedly less bloodily—the Stalin-Zhdanov purge of leading Jewish writers after 1948. The philistine Firsov mentality about art and letters, a bourgeois kind of bourgeois-baiting, is in a small, despised minority among Communist writers. Among Communist bureaucrats—hence the dramatic tensions of the thaw—it is far from a minority.

The above mentality of Firsov and the bureaucrats may best be called National Bolshevism, a cousin to German National Socialism—and all this in the name of that international "cosmopolitan" Karl Marx. Compare Firsov's reaction to "Babi Yar," and his warning against "Jewish influences over the American press," with the earlier remarks of the literary critic Nikolai Gribachev (*Krokodil*, February 20, 1953). Gribachev is commenting on Stalin's plan to torture and shoot the "plotting" Jewish doctors as agents of the "Joint," the Jewish charity organization:

> There is weeping at the rivers of Babylon, the most important of which is the Hudson. The "Joint" has been plucked, that vulture dressed in the pigeon-feathers of charity. . . . From Jerusalem to London creeps the perplexed muttering of the Zionist leaders. . . . Let them weep; this will not move us to pity. . . . Even the grave will not reform them.

Like Kochetov, Gribachev also has savagely satirized Yevtushenko (*Pravda*, January 27, 1963).

The hounding of Yevtushenko by Kozlov, Ilyichev, Firsov, Kochetov, and Gribachev is only understood in the West when one realizes the importance of anti-Semitism (disguised as anti-cosmopolitanism) in National Bolshevik propaganda. In Kiev, I vainly tried to get permission to visit nearby Babi Yar, where a Soviet apartment house and not a memorial was to cover the graves of the biggest Nazi pogrom of the war. The issue came to a head in September, 1961, with Yevtushenko's best-known poem, which begins by lamenting the lack of a Soviet memorial. The National Bolsheviks attacked the poem ferociously the same month. One of their organs (*Literatura i zhizn*, September 27) called him un-Russian and accused him of defiling Russia with "pygmy's spittle" because he wrote about Jewish rather than Russian sufferings under Hitler. A publicized counter-poem yearned to see "the last cosmopolitan," a pogrom-inciting parody of the original poem's yearning to see "the last anti-Semite." Khrushchev, the balancer, condemned both poems by later firing both editors.

By accident, the same issue of the pro-thaw *Literaturnaya gazeta* which published "Babi Yar" (September 19, 1961) published Russian translations of poems by Richard Wilbur and me, on the occasion of our cultural-exchange visit. Thereby I was able to obtain this otherwise unobtainable issue, which speedily sold out to Yevtushenko's followers. Naturally I studied carefully this published version; neither it nor its translations in countless American books and newspapers are the full version which I heard him read in Moscow in mid-September (and which Michel Tatu of *Le Monde* assures me he witnessed on a later occasion). A significant omission states that anti-Semitic feelings in Soviet Russia today (officially denied) "still are rising on the fumes of alcohol and in conversation after drinking."

While the then twenty-eight-year-old author was reading this and other poems, I watched the reactions of the Moscow student audience. They were moved by all the lyrical poems and by a few of the social-conscience poems, but "Babi Yar"—combining both genres—was the one poem they made him read twice. During the second reading, Russian men burst into tears (and not just the "hysterical schoolgirls" Mikhail Sholokhov accuses him of bewitching). They burst into tears at the evocative metaphors about Anne Frank ("frail as a twig in April"), at the compassionate identifications ("today I am as old in years as the Jewish people"), and at the appeal to the honor of his fellow Slavs: "O my Russian people!/. . . those with unclean hands have often/loudly taken in vain your most pure name./. . . There is no Jewish blood in mine./But I am hated venomously by every anti-Semite/as if a Jew,/And for this reason—I am a true Russian."

The whole evening of poetry reading provided my most memorable personal impression of contemporary Soviet youth: its passion for the arts, its passion for liberty and racial tolerance. There, all around me, was the Russia I have learned to love, the Russia of generous aesthetic and ethical commitments. It was a young Russia that cheered, cried, and laughed out of a natural, unaffected enthusiasm of free poetic self-expression, bursting forth far beyond the intentions of the government's halfhearted halfthaw. These are the sort of people who shouted "Sonnet 66!" spontaneously at a poetry meeting during the Stalin era when they caught sight of Pasternak. The not-so-cryptic reference was to a line Pasternak had translated from one of Shakespeare's sonnets: "And art made tongue-tied by authority."

After his enforced silence of spring and summer, 1963, preceded by his publicity stunts of 1962, many Russian and American critics spoke of Yevtushenko as a flash-in-the-pan, now passé. They spoke too soon. True, his popularity has declined. Nevertheless, on December 14, 1963, he re-emerged on the public platform with one of the most effective and most enthusiastically received readings of his career. It suggests, being accompanied by a new writing streak, that his more serious literary career has only begun. His future literary stature will depend not on his politics but on his learning to tighten into disciplining beauty his sprawling rhetoric.

Westerners do Yevtushenko a disservice by exclusively praising his political contribution. The old Irish freedom fighter O'Leary once remarked to Yeats that you may be permitted almost any crime for the sake of your country except bad verse. Most of Yevtushenko's political poems are bad verse in a good cause. Meanwhile, what gets lost in the shuffle is Yevtushenko's excellent nonpolitical love poetry. At heart he is not so much the tribune of "revisionism" as the troubadour of the "conspiracy of feelings." When I asked his ally Ilya Ehrenburg why the Komsomol temporarily expelled Yevtushenko in the 1950's, Ehrenburg replied: "Puritanism is the curse of the Soviet arts. Yevtushenko's love poetry was guilty of revealing the state secret that men are physically different from women." Here, for example, is a poem from his second volume, that of 1955; in contrast with his unsensuous rhetorical abstractions in politics, note the felt concreteness of "bang the taxi door" and "slide to the floor":

> My love will come . . .
> In from the pouring dark, from the pitch night
> without stopping to bang the taxi door
> she'll run upstairs through the decaying porch
> burning with love and love's happiness,
> she'll run dripping upstairs, she won't knock,
> will take my head in her hands,
> and when she drops her overcoat on a chair,
> it will slide to the floor in a blue heap.

Even in a poem of laudable political symbolism ("Nefertiti," *Moskva*, No. 2, 1964), where the Pharaoh is the Party and Nefertiti is Art, the sole aesthetic merit—if only one could get Yevtushenko to admit it—is in the sensuous concreteness of the incidental images:

> He had armies, chariots,
> But she has eyes, eyelashes . . .
> And her throat curves astoundingly . . .
> Pharaoh was sullen in his caresses,

> Crude in his actions
> Because he felt the fragility of power
> Beside the power of this fragility.

Fundamentally, Yevtushenko is not a political animal at all, though like his hero Vladimir Mayakovsky he tries to be one. Yevtushenko is in the tradition of the magnetic, self-dramatizing Byronism of Mikhail Lermontov, with just enough narcissistic hamminess to annoy his more serious friends when he exploits his personality for the crowds, but with enough real poetic genius to make them gladly forgive him and deeply believe in him. What makes it so painful to predict his future candidly is the fact that this Russian Byronizing tradition has an undercurrent of unconscious self-destructiveness, constantly oscillating between would-be folk hero and would-be martyr, between matinee idol and Grand Pariah.

Tragedy in different ways brought early death to Pushkin, Lermontov, Gumilev, Mayakovsky, Yesenin, Mandelstam, Tsvetayeva. Their examples doubtless reinforce the innate martyr penchant I observed in Yevtushenko. Once when he playfully asked me to predict his future, I said I feared he had a compulsion someday to meet his Zhdanov—indeed to provoke his Zhdanov, as Pushkin and Lermontov partly provoked the duels that killed them and as Gumilev practically taunted the Party into shooting him. Later Yevtushenko asked me with strange excitement if I really thought my prediction would come true. Obviously, I hope it won't. But in March, 1963, it almost did. This was when Khrushchev and Ilyichev denounced him for publishing his autobiography without Soviet permission in L'Express of Paris (five installments, February 21–March 21). I don't mean to condone the detestable Soviet censorship, including the so-called Pasternak law of 1958, by which Soviet authors may not publish books abroad without prior permission. Yet Yevtushenko's 1963 martyrdom was forced upon him not by the censorship but by himself; he provoked it deliberately by his Paris publication. Nor can it be argued that he was ignorant of the "Pasternak law." He himself had mentioned this law, and his respect for it, to a friend of mine in Moscow as the reason why he did not let his manuscripts go abroad. And it is known he was aware of being shadowed by the Soviet secret police as he went to his actual Express interview.

The dogmatist faction, from Kochetov in literature to Kozlov in politics, were against Yevtushenko anyhow; because of his thaw position in general and his opposition to their anti-Semitism in particular. But his illegal Paris publication, so easily avoidable, swung the Party neutrals against him and made him the Saint Sebastian of their slings and arrows. Even Tvardovsky had to differentiate himself from Yevtushenko on this issue. Russia's *poète maudit* could no longer be protected even by Khrushchev, who in 1962 had personally authorized the October 21 appearance in *Pravda* of Yevtushenko's long-banned, but privately circulating, poem "Stalin's Heirs."

Moreover, Yevtushenko more than once hints in his poems at self-destruction. This fact, plus his temporary depression during the Ilyichev witch-hunt against him, may have caused the suicide rumors about him—false ones fortunately—which swept Russia in 1963. It is with superstitious certainty that I feel he will eventually contrive his Zhdanov, his Lermontov duel, his Mayakovsky or Yesenin darkness. It would equally suit his personality under czars or commissars, East or West; nobody can stop him. The analogy of doom is with Dylan Thomas, except that the intoxication is even more with romantic self-sacrifice than with alcohol. The Siberian Ukrainian in Moscow and the BBC Welshman in New York, two country boys too quickly jaded by early fame, are avatars of the artist as sacrificial animal.

Western books on Soviet literature classify Yevtushenko as a political poet and Voznesensky as a pure aesthete. This contrast holds true only of their more publicized poems. It ignores Yevtushenko's unpolitical love lyrics. And it ignores the essential political parts of Voznesensky's books *The Triangular Pear* and *Anti-Worlds*.

His *Pear* rapidly sold out its printing of 50,000 copies. And over 10,000 listeners attended Voznesensky's readings from it in one meeting in the autumn of 1962. Both his aesthetic and political merits would be just as great had he sold only ten copies and read to an audience of ten. We cite the figures merely in order to contrast Soviet and American attitudes toward serious poetry. Why the mass following of poets in Russia? First, because the poets, from Pushkin on, have always been regarded as the conscience of the country. Second, because now the poets offer a smuggled, underground religiosity to the religion-starved Russian people. This is why so many Soviet poets now chant their lines in precisely the manner of the Greek Orthodox liturgy. Probably they are not conscious of doing so.

Without falling into the Soviet error of putting politics above aesthetics in poetry, let us not go to the opposite extreme; let us not pretend there are no political intentions. The present writer happens to believe that narrow political aspects are irrelevant to aesthetic merit but that broad ethical aspects (for example, the racism in Pound's *Pisan Cantos*) are not irrelevant to aesthetic merit. Most American critics disagreed with the writer in regard to his ethical questioning of the Poundian aesthetic; on such issues honest minds in free debate can fruitfully disagree. But no matter how we assess them, ethical intentions and even narrowly political intentions—from Dante through Voznesensky—are emphatically there. Politically, the Soviet in-group audience substitutes "Russia" for "America" in many cases where the out-group (with which, being larger, the censor is more concerned) takes its "America" straight. The endless examples include "Song About an American Soldier" by the guitar-playing Bulat Okudzhava. This favorite Soviet student song makes no sense except as a rebellious Russian soldier song. In this light, consider the following American references in Voznesensky's *Pear*:

1. When Voznesensky says, "You are looking for India and will find America," the in-group reader substitutes America for India and substitutes Russia for America.

2. One of the poems tells of being trailed by a comically exaggerated mob of FBI men in America. Here the poet satirizes the penchant of the Soviet secret police to go gumshoeing after intellectuals. This penchant was satirized in Nekrasov's American travelogue (*Novy mir*, November, 1962, the same issue as Solzhenitsyn's *One Day*; November still remains the high point of the thaw). Nekrasov's insult to the cherished Soviet secret police was savagely attacked by the government *Izvestia* (January 20, 1963), an opening gun—after Khrushchev's anti-art outburst of December—of the 1963 freeze.

3. An ode to Lenin is set among sequoias in California. Here Voznesensky somehow manages, without disrespect for his hero Lenin, to satirize the Soviet genre of pious official propaganda.

4. Another poem is about a conversation with a racist in the American south. Here we have the familiar parallel of using foreign rightist extremists to signify domestic Stalinist-leftist extremists.* But this time Voznesensky provides the added fillip of using the American Negro to symbolize the poet oppressed by society. By Soviet society. But not only by Soviet society. There is in Voznesensky no ammunition for Cold War propaganda against his own country; the philistinism he attacks in Russia—via Aesopian Americans—is meant to be in part universal. The final choice offered by his poetry is not a national one between Russia and America, not an economic one between Russia and America, nor an economic one between Communism and capitalism, but a universal one between philistia and creativity. For Voznesensky as well as for his teacher and friend Pasternak, creativity is a revolution of the heart, not of politics or economics; it is a revolution of organic vs. mechanic attitudes. Unlike the nineteenth-century German Romantic movement, which also made this contrast, Voznesensky and the other rebel poets of the world today are adding an ethical, compassionate component to "heart." For them "heart" does not mean blind instinct, so easily diabolized into Fascist-Romantic anti-intellectualism, but means human elements, including the ethical and intellectual ones, as opposed to robot elements and the Russo-American technology cult.

To the world-wide capitalist-plus-socialist technologizing of the 1960's, the ablest philosophers of Communist Europe are daringly reapplying Marx's once neglected notes of 1844 about modern man's alienation from society. Since alienation is also the present theme of Western poets, philosophers, and rebels, here is the point of unity between anti-robot individualists on both sides of the Cold War. Assuming reader familiarity with Western examples, let us cite some Eastern ones. The fact that they are published at

---

* For two reasons, no embarrassment to Voznesensky can result from interpreting in print the above examples. First, his adherence to Soviet patriotism and an idealized Leninism has been established beyond doubt. Second, we are not giving new weapons to his Soviet dogmatist foes; they are old weapons, already being used by these foes; nothing we can say can add to their familiar case against him. For example, V. Nazarenko's July, 1962, article in *Zvezda* (*Star*) has already given the essence of the above points by saying insinuatingly that *Pear* is not really about America.

all is a measure of the very real progress toward cultural liberty under those rigid political dictatorships. The Kafka authority in Prague, Edward Goldstuecker, now free but in jail under Stalin, was allowed to publish in 1964 this almost Pasternakian appeal against materialism:

Technical civilization, alone and of itself, produces antihumanism and dehumanizing pressure on every individual. Modern civilization draws the individual from the collective, even if it creates enormous new collectives, and makes the individual lonesome. In a society where religion has ceased to be the cement and connecting link creating ethical inhibitions, it must be replaced by something else; and this something is, in the first place, art.

Such sentiments are part of an unorganized world-wide movement to return to art and heart. In a Belgrade philosophy journal, *Praxis** (November, 1964), Yugoslavia's Professor Mihajlo Markovic, while stanchly attacking the old capitalist alienation in Marxist terms, is now warning the Soviet bloc against the new kind of alienation caused by Communism. He defines it as the alienation suffered when the individual is treated as a mere object by Communist bureaucrats, dehumanized by what he calls their "cult of technology." Markovic sees these new "forms of alienation" threatening "those socialist countries where the creation of new centers of enormous power—which are no longer based on economic wealth, as in capitalism, but on unlimited political authority—has been made possible."

Parallel sentiments were voiced in the Prague Kafka conference of May, 1963. There, too, it was not anti-Communists but two Party members (one French, one Austrian) who told the Russian delegates that a Kafkaesque alienation is today inherent in all technocracies, not just those of capitalism and the West. With the 1964 publication of *In the Penal Colony* in the Moscow magazine *Foreign Literature*, Kafka is no longer the secret forbidden prophet of Soviet intellectuals. He can now be openly praised (even though cautiously, as in *Voprosy literatury*, No. 5, 1964). The results are

---

* On April 26, 1965, at the Fifth Croation Party Conference in Zagreb, such Party leaders as Mika Tripolo denounced the *Praxis* philosophers of a rehumanized Marxism as "diametrically opposed" to the Party line. The official Yugoslav Party magazine, *Komunist*, called them "un-Marxist" and "unacceptable."

electrifying: for example, the Kafka theme of the faceless bureaucracy versus individualism in one part of Voznesensky's poem "Oza." On the whole, Voznesensky opposes only the dehumanizing kind of technology. What he praises is not a return to the Middle Ages, but a "humanized technology." This attitude recalls not only the rediscovery of the humanist Marx of the early 1840's, but some of the most influential Western theology of today, such as that of Reinhold Niebuhr.

By now, the Western press has reprinted examples, like the above, of Communist attacks on Communist alienation. Still bolder statements of the theme have emerged in personal conversations with the Communist writers of Russia, Poland, Yugoslavia, Hungary, Rumania. These men are not to be dismissed as Red-baiting "lackeys of Wall Street." They are loyal anticapitalist Party members. Thus "polycentrism" is not only true internationally *between* Communist parties, in the sense intended by Togliatti's coinage of that term; it is also beginning (against his intentions) *inside* each Party. Each Party not only contains the two obvious splits noted in these pages (between cultural thaw and freeze and between political revisionism and dogmatism), but a third and subtler split: between treating people as humans and treating them as cogs, treating them as subjects or as objects. Psychologically, the third split is between the rooted and the alienated; it is between what Burkean conservatives as well as humanist socialists would call the mechanic and the organic.

For example, the Communist philosopher Leszek Kolakowski, who is trying to re-establish Marxism on a firmer, freer foundation, mentioned during a Warsaw conversation in 1962 the crucial importance—for younger Communist intellectuals and artists today—of facing the dilemma of such technological alienation. The same point has been stressed by the greatest Marxist literary critic of the century, Gyorgy Lukacs. I have heard this point made in so many ways in conversations with poets and artists in Eastern Europe. The reality of "the world republic of letters" becomes clearer every time I hear the same point made in the West—for example, by a leading New York art critic, Harold Rosenberg, in 1964: "With everything so convenient and shiny, one hardly knows what's missing. What else can it be but the person himself for whom all this was organized?"

Currently, most arty-phony middlebrows affect a chic robot-baiting, a flaunted alienation. Their glossy vulgarization does not refute—it merely parodies—the reality of the dilemma. It is a reality among the more serious articulators of both of our countries as well as among the inarticulate millions, especially the younger ones. Whether under so-called socialism or so-called capitalism, youth tends to secede from society. This is especially true of the more interesting young people, the non-squares, the students and artists. In 1965, Russian students would sometimes sing songs about Stalin's concentration camps when requested by their elders to sing songs of patriotic ideology. In current Soviet debate, the problem is called, in a curiously old-fashioned reference to the world of Turgenev and nihilism, "the fathers-and-sons problem." Even while discussing it, the Soviet official propaganda sources are constantly denying that the problem exists (for example, the speeches of Ilychev or of the Komsomol leaders).

The existence of the problem is shown in the stories with which Soviet youth most identifies: Aksyonov's *Ticket to the Stars*, 1961, his *Halfway to the Moon*, 1962 (*Novy mir*, No. 7), and the 1961 Soviet translation of Salinger's *Catcher in the Rye*. In *Ticket to the Stars*, much denounced by dogmatists and later made into a much censored and rewritten movie, a group of rebel teenagers flees westward from Moscow. Not across the Soviet border—such candor would never see print—but to the West-symbolizing Baltic states of the U.S.S.R. Their flight is not for reasons of ideology, politics, or economics, but out of psychological unrest, boredom with grayness, with bureaucracy, with their fathers. After Nikita Khrushchev denounced him in March, 1963, Aksyonov had to recant some of his heresies: "I will never forget Nikita Sergeyevich's stern but kind words to me. . . . The direction of my future work is . . . to the ideals of Communism. . . . Our enemies will not succeed in getting us into a quarrel with our fathers" (*Pravda*, April 3, 1963). But his mood of revolt-against-grayness continues as the unofficial voice of a whole generation. And artists in other genres—for example, Victor Rozov in drama—have become student favorites for writing in a similar vein.

Perhaps the most influential liberal under Khrushchev was Alexander Tvardovsky, editor of the magazine *Novy mir*. His

"surprising survival" (as the Russians called it) was another example of Soviet Russia's having more literary freedom than official
statements indicate (while having less political freedom than official statements indicate). Positions shift through gamuts rather
than through dichotomies in the fluid situation of today; battle
lines are neither clear-cut nor consistent; Soviet realities refute the
apriorist theorizers of what ought to happen.

Tvardovsky has been able to publish some of the writers attacked
so harshly in March, 1963, by Ilyichev and the entire Party press.
As Ilyichev remained propaganda boss till March, 1965, one might
have expected that Tvardovsky would be replaced as editor of *Novy
mir*. After all, in a parallel circumstance, Ilyichev on January 27,
1962, dismissed the gifted dramatist Valentin Katayev (he, too,
refused a request to recant) and replaced him as editor of *Yunost*
with the ideologist Boris Polevoi.* And indeed I did hear Moscow
rumors in 1963 that Tvardovsky was about to be replaced as editor
by V. Yermilov, the Party hatchet man who had once hounded
Mayakovsky and who now on Party orders was hurling an *Izvestia*
hatchet at the *Novy mir* publication of Ehrenburg's partly frank
memoirs. Yet Tvardovsky, appealing to Khrushchev over Ilyichev's
head, not only continued as editor; he received a Soviet passport
for an honored official visit to Italy, a special government plum
which is more than the loyal hacks like Gribachev managed to
wangle.

So once again, as when Tvardovsky openly clashed with his rival
Kochetov at the Twenty-second Congress in 1961 over the issue of

---

* Polevoi has done at least one good deed for America. He caused Howard
Fast to quit the American Communist Party. Fast had asked Polevoi if such
and such Jewish writers were still alive in Russia or had been murdered as
"cosmopolitans" by Stalin. Polevoi swore that those particular Jewish writers
were in fine fettle—he himself had seen them only the other day in Moscow—
and that the report of their death was a typical American Red-baiting slander.
It was when Fast discovered that the Jewish writers had at that time already
been murdered—and that Polevoi knew they were long dead—that Fast's
trust in Soviet dictatorship was finally shattered. Incidentally, Polevoi, as editor
of this excellent magazine, has proved more moderate and less dogmatic than
we feared on the record of his *apparatchik* past; for whatever motive, human
beings do change, and in Russia often rapidly and unexpectedly; when *Izvestia*
in 1963 attacked Voznesensky for his poems in *Yunost*, the crafty new editor
skillfully protected the vulnerable young poet by replying with a veritable fog-
curtain of just the right kind of pious, meaningless, Party jargon (*Izvestia*,
February 14, 1963, etc.).

greater literary freedom, the No. 1 thaw-leader came off better than
the No. 1 freeze-leader. Both rivals were high Party members and
both had been given high Party awards. Kochetov always had far
more backing from the bureaucratic vested interests. But Tvardovsky seemed to have worked out a better personal relationship not
only with the literary avant-garde but with the unliterary and anti-
avant-garde Khrushchev.

Even after Ehrenburg's memoirs were denounced, not only by
the declining Kochetov and Yermilov but by the rising Ilyichev,
Novy mir continued to publish the memoirs without apology up to
their final installment (Novy mir, No. 5, 1965). And they continued to make the first revelations in print in Russia about the
murders and torments inflicted on some of the best Soviet writers.
To be sure, after an Ilyichev attack, an issue with the memoirs
was delayed for two weeks by the censorship and presumably
pruned of even more shattering revelations. But the main point is
that Novy mir (which Kochetov assailed in Ogonyok as "nihilistic
poison among our intelligentsia") remains the most influential, independent, and outspoken of Russia's legal literary magazines. The
fascinating illegal ones, like Phoenix and Syntakti, get soon
squelched by the police and fail to mold so large or so influential
a body of opinion as Tvardovsky's magazine. The mere existence
of the latter refutes the blindly anti-Soviet thesis that Soviet culture today is still monolithic, servile, and sterile, as under Stalin.
Neither is the Party leadership monolithic.

Party Politics Behind Literary Policy

What is surprising, and supremely encouraging, is that Khrushchev—ever balancing between his anti-Stalinism and his fear of
too much thaw—took the calculated risk of personally authorizing
Tvardovsky to publish Solzhenitsyn's One Day in the Life of Ivan
Denisovich in Novy mir of November, 1962.* On November 23,

---

* Solzhenitsyn, until 1962 an obscure provincial schoolteacher, emerged
with One Day as a writer of superb talent. One Day was the first and best
concentration-camp saga published after Stalin. Solzhenitsyn personalizes the
grim routine of struggle for survival in Stalin's forced labor camps by tracing a
typical day of the carpenter Shukhov, whose unfounded conviction for treason
in World War II after an escape from the Germans and subsequent life in
camp he vividly describes on the basis of his own experience.—Eds.

Khrushchev told the Party Central Committee that he personally authorized the uncensored version of the novel about a concentration camp but that top officials tried to stop it. Almost certainly these two officials were not only Ilyichev but the more powerful Frol Kozlov. They obviously feared—and quite correctly so—a threat to their own standing in any literature that would openly attack the Stalinist terror, in which they had collaborated.

Yevtushenko believes that Kozlov's paralytic stroke in April, 1963 (he died on January 30, 1965), helped to save the thaw from this dogmatic witch-hunter, who in the January, 1953, issue of *Kommunist* had been Stalin's special mouthpiece against an alleged Jewish conspiracy. Kozlov probably instigated the Khrushchev freeze of December, 1962–March, 1963. As evidence, note that the worst threats of March, 1963 (for example, to expel Nekrasov from the Party and Yevtushenko from the masthead of *Yunost*) were dropped after Kozlov's stroke. Yet Kozlov remains a posthumous victor in one respect: never again (so far) has the thaw recaptured its first fine, careless rapture, namely that high point of the Yevtushenko-Solzhenitsyn anti-Stalinism of October–November, 1962.

Sovietologists should never be cocksure; too many unsolved problems remain. For example, if you accept the common view that Khrushchev favored a thaw (or our view that he favored a thaw-freeze balance), then why did he tell U.S. emissary Averell Harriman that his preferred successor was the anti-thaw Stalinoid Kozlov?

Let us suggest a tentative explanation which may also help explain the policy vacillations of 1962–64.

In politics, as opposed to cultural policy, Kozlov and Khrushchev were close allies before 1962. For example, in 1957 Kozlov swung his Leningrad bailiwick behind Khrushchev when the latter was challenged by a Presidium majority, the Malenkov-Molotov "anti-Party group." Yet even in politics Kozlov later increasingly opposed his ally. In *Leningradskaya pravda* (February 27, 1963), Kozlov openly criticized the Khrushchev plan of weakening the old local bureaucrats by splitting urban and rural Party organizations. After Khrushchev's 1964 downfall, the Party immediately abolished his rural-urban split. And although the still bouncy Khrushchev was ostensibly ousted from the Presidium for ill health, the paralyzed and incapacitated Kozlov was kept on the Presidium to the day of his death in January, 1965.

The crucial power struggle for the Leningrad organization, during the final Stalin phase of 1948–53, explains the apparent contradiction between Kozlov's pre-1962 support of Khrushchev's politics and his nonsupport of Khrushchev's cultural thaw. During Stalin's last years, Kozlov was a Zhdanov follower, both before and after Zhdanov's mysterious death. This fact means that Kozlov was strongly against Zhdanov's enemy Malenkov in politics—and thereby a close ally of the anti-Malenkov Khrushchev in politics. But Kozlov's Zhdanovism also means he was an anti-thaw thought-controller in literature—and thereby against Khrushchev's thaw-freeze balance in literature. Thus Khrushchev in 1961 chose Kozlov as his political successor, thereby excluding the remnants of the Malenkov "anti-Party group" from future politics, yet in late 1962 broke with Kozlov on cultural policy. It was their cultural clash that in 1963 almost destroyed Solzhenitsyn, Yevtushenko, Voznesensky, Nekrasov, their protector Tvardovsky, and the entire thaw.

Any Zhdanov disciple would be against all these writers anyhow, on general Agitprop principles. But Kozlov, having suffered one heart attack in 1960 and soon to suffer another, had a more specific and personal grudge against the literary rebels and their semi-protector Khrushchev. When Khrushchev allowed Yevtushenko's long-banned poem "Stalin's Heirs" to appear at last (*Pravda*, October 21, 1962), it contained the line (added later): "Not for nothing do Stalin's heirs/have their share of heart attacks."* Ever indiscreet, Khrushchev even boasted (Central Committee, November 23) of his defiance of Kozlov-style pressures against publishing this poem as well as Solzhenitsyn's novel. At this point the thaw was getting so dangerously out of hand, from a Party viewpoint, that Kozlov, Ilyichev, and the Central Committee were able to

---

* Not for nothing do Stalin's heirs
  have their share of heart attacks.
                                    Once his henchmen,
    they can't stand these times
           when the prison camps are empty
    but the auditoriums overflow with people
           listening to poets.
                              —From "Stalin's Heirs"

Khrushchev probably had Kozlov in mind, even if Yevtushenko did not. See Priscilla Johnson, *Khrushchev and the Arts* (Cambridge, Mass.: M.I.T. Press, 1965), p. 46.—EDS.

force a dramatic reversal. This reversal Khrushchev soon joined (see his remarks, published by *Encounter*, December, 1962, and March, 1963). Partly he did so under pressure; he was never so strong a dictator as the West imagined. But partly he did so voluntarily in order to continue his alternate-pendulum policy, as was soon shown by his scatological tirades against abstract art at the Manezh gallery in December.

The above is the best reconstruction we can make at present, after Khrushchev's fall, of the story of the recently ended freeze. (Its origin, the ferocious Kozlov-Malenkov split, may still lie in the unsolved mystery of whether the fifty-two-year-old Andrei Zhdanov died naturally or was murdered in 1948.) It is the story of how Kozlov, until his illness intervened, almost did succeed in replacing a Tvardovsky thaw policy and a Khrushchev pendulum policy with a return to Stalinoid Zhdanovism. These events are important for the future as a reminder of how precarious are the post-Stalin liberties in the absence of either institutional roots or constitutional guarantees.

For Solzhenitsyn's *One Day*, which provoked the almost successful return to Zhdanov, the end is not yet in sight. There is no more Khrushchev to protect *One Day*. And by himself, Tvardovsky, who again defended Solzhenitsyn in the *Novy mir* of January, 1965, is not strong enough to save him from further ordeals. So the bureaucrats in 1965 and 1966 could launch the direct attacks they had not dared when Khrushchev let Tvardovsky publish the novel in November, 1962. For example, in the journal of the Central Committee (*Kommunist*, March, 1965) the Party Secretary of Moscow attacked the novel for "disorienting" the younger generation about the Soviet past. The article admonished intellectuals to indoctrinate youth in "the heroic deeds achieved by the Soviet people" and to avoid a morbid "excessive interest" in what it admitted were "the shortcomings and mistakes" of "the period of the personality cult." This priggish diction has achieved an understatement more often found in Anglo-Saxons than Slavs; "shortcomings" is a delicate tea-party way of referring to the murder, torture, and imprisonment of millions, about which no prior novel had spoken so openly in Russia.*

* I. I. Bodyul, First Secretary of the Moldavian Party Central Committee, made a similar attack on *One Day* at the Twenty-third Party Congress. Per-

In consequence, Russia's ablest living novelist is now being dragged not only into the thaw-freeze fight (over how far to de-Stalinize) but into the fathers-sons fight (over the secession of youth from ideology). Nor is the controversy over his book a mere teapot tempest. Simultaneously it is the best book of the thaw aesthetically and the crucial book in the whole above political controversy. Both the political and the cultural controversy will be continuing long after the recent elimination of both Kozlov and Khrushchev.

The martyred hero of Solzhenitsyn's novel, "crucified" by the Stalin system, has the Everyman name of Ivan. So far as we know, no Soviet or Western critic has noted the concealed symbolism in the fact that Ivan, like the first of all Christian martyrs, is by profession a carpenter. Perhaps we may draw an analogy in part with Faulkner's victimized Joe Christmas, another symbolic name. Despite the propensity for narrow political interpretations (pro- or anti-Communism) on both sides of the Cold War, neither *One Day* nor the author's subsequent stories are the short-run realistic journalism they may seem. They are long-run works of art whose theme is not local Russian politics (any more than Faulkner's theme was local Mississippi reportage) but universal good and evil. The best of them, *Matryona's House* (*Novy mir*, 1963), has a heroine who is, in effect, a medieval Christian saint.

Such is the overlapping of literary and political debate that Western sympathizers are tempted to give freedom's defenders in Russia a higher literary rank than they deserve, and vice versa for freedom's persecutors. So doing, Western anti-Communists fall into the Communist error of subordinating literary to political judgments and blurring the distinction between them. For example, Sholokhov, who has been engaging in appalling drunken tirades against the Tvardovsky camp and against the public poetry readings, is often being denied by friends of liberty the literary greatness that his *Quiet Don* novels obviously merit. Contrariwise, though Yevtushenko is Russia's most effective rebel poet of the 1960's, he is far from being Russia's best younger poet in literary merit; not only Voznesensky, Vinokurov, and Akhmadullina but the less published Yosif Brodsky, whom I also met in Russia, are

---

haps this was meant as a slap at Tvardovsky, who had published works by Solzhenitsyn, Sinyavsky, Daniel, etc.—EDS.

purer lyricists than Yevtushenko, and Boris Slutsky is a subtler philosophical poet. (Ehrenburg told me he considers Slutsky the best younger poet of all.)

The following curious fact is of psychological but not really political interest about Tvardovsky (and about anti-Stalinism in particular, as well as anti-tyranny in general). In Poland I saw the 1954 first edition of Tvardovsky's *Hills Beyond Hills;* that edition is now withdrawn and unobtainable; almost no one seems to know of it. It contains passages, later superseded and reversed by Tvardovsky's more considered judgment, of an embarrassingly gushy adoration for Stalin as the sacred lost father-image. This is the kind of thing Kremlinologists can make too much of; though of psychological interest, it does not really discredit either the political or literary integrity of Tvardovsky. Every case is individual; Westerners must bear in mind what it meant to live under continuous totalitarian pressure; and every authority you talk to in Russia, on both the thaw and deep-freeze sides, agrees that Tvardovsky is honest and sincere and that he was also the most effective liberalizer (though often compromising with circumstances) on Russia's ruling Central Committee.*

On anything personally and emotionally connected with the daemonic figure of Stalin, not too much rationality or consistency must be expected; among his victims, one often notes a fascinated, ambivalent *amo et odi* response, and among his ex-collaborators also. A motif of both victims and ex-collaborators is their bursting into tears when their tyrant died, as their ancestors had done when Ivan the Terrible died (but as none had done when the reformist Peter the Great had died or when the reformist Khrushchev left office). In two different outbursts of 1963, Khrushchev declared that he had cried like a child when Stalin died and yet that Stalin was an insane murderer who, for the good of everybody, should have died ten years sooner. After publishing, in October, 1962, a poem warning against the vampire-like return of Stalin from his new grave, the Stalin-loathing Yevtushenko declared in an interview that he, too, had shed real tears in 1953 when the vampire

---

* Tvardovsky was not re-elected to candidate membership of the Central Committee at the Twenty-third Congress. This left on the new Central Committee (elected April 8, 1966) the conservative Aleksandr Korneichuk and the reactionaries Mikhail Sholokhov and Nikolai Gribachev as the only representatives of the writers and artists.—EDS.

died. (But thereupon Galina Semyonovna, the poet's second wife, interjected that she, for one, had not cried.)

In nineteenth-century Russian novels a familiar figure was "the nobleman with a conscience"; by helping rebels and voicing peasant grievances, he tried to atone for the social wrongs his class had perpetrated. A parallel figure, in part, is today's ex-Stalinist with a conscience. Disillusioned Stalinists predominate among the Hungarian rebels of 1956 (in their very different ways, Gyorgy Lukacs, the present dictator, Kadar, and his betrayed and martyred predecessor, Nagy), among Polish rebels (Milosz abroad, Wazyk at home), and among many though not all thaw-leaders of Russia today. Unless it is realized the apostates are exorcizing the Stalin in their own breast, the current literary split in Russia seems mere "liberals vs. conservatives" to American outsiders, a split without the tragic extra dimension of conscience and atonement.

When I visited Moscow in 1961, rebel writers were circulating the first issue of *Phoenix*, the mimeographed underground student magazine (its editor later went to jail). The magazine contained those rebel poets who, unlike Yevtushenko and Voznesensky, could not be printed officially. It also contained an open letter to Yevtushenko by a disillusioned disciple, accusing him of compromising with the Party. The accusation reflects an all-or-nothing extremism, the utopian purity of an uncompromising radicalism. In any society such radicalism is the salt of the earth as a destructive, needed corrective to any status quo. But in any society it is ever unworkable as a constructive alternative. Without some compromise with the Party, the ablest young rebels (Voznesensky, Nekrasov, Yevtushenko, Aksyonov, Slutsky, Akhmadullina) would not be published at all, and there would be no *Novy mir* thaw movement at all. The entire field would then be left by default to the literary dogmatists like Gribachev, Surkov, Kochetov, and magazines like *Oktyabr*.

Pushed too far, this argument can become a mere alibi, the alibi of all collaborationists, the opportunistic Lavals and Quislings. But when the argument is not pushed too far, it makes sense. An established society can best be liberalized and ethically corrected by working from within its framework and its slogans—and then subtly, almost unconsciously changing their meaning, rather than smashing the works from outside, with unforeseeable consequences.

Such consequences are more likely to be chaos and new tyranny than liberalization.

Whether or not one accepts this liberal-conservative, anti-radical analysis of social change, one should at least be aware that there exist not two but three camps, continually blurring into each other: (1) the freeze of the Communist dogmatists; (2) the thaw of the equally Communist revisionists and of the publishable rebels; (3) the open anti-Communism of the unpublishable rebels and their short-lived underground mimeographs (*Phoenix* and *Syntakti*). The present study concentrates largely on group 2. This is because group 2 has by far the highest literary merit and best represents Soviet youth and the future. Yet the unsung martyrs of group 3 must also be honored, even if silently; even to name most of them in the Western press can only endanger them further. Their motto is that of one of their once-confined philosophers, A. S. Yesenin-Volpin: "There is no freedom of the press in Russia, but who can say there is no freedom of thought?"

Cultural and Political Freedom

In a pro-Castro poem appearing October 22, 1962, in *Pravda*, Yevtushenko declares: a free debate between rival schools of culture—he names only Socialist Realism vs. abstract art but implies free cultural self-expression in general—can well be accompanied by the Communist one-party state in politics. According to the poem, the two schools of artists drop their rival paintbrushes to pick up their shared political rifles whenever capitalist imperialism threatens to attack. This example sustains our thesis that Western optimists err in expecting political freedom from the thaw movement but that Western pessimists err in overlooking the freedom brought by the thaw movement into other areas: cultural freedom and the self-expression of the human heart. The *boulevardier* Ehrenburg, the aesthete Voznesensky, the sober Communist war hero Tvardovsky, the lone Prometheus Nekrasov, and the tribal medicine man Yevtushenko may differ on many other issues. But these five most active voices of the thaw do share two inarticulate goals: a revolution and a restoration. Let us dare to articulate the inarticulate, by summarizing their two shared goals like this: (1) a non-Communist revolution of feelings, on behalf of the nonmonolithic private life in heart and art; (2) a Communist restoration of "Leninism," on behalf of the monolithic public life in politics and economics. Their second goal contains (as Lenin would say) contradictions. For the real Lenin probably lacked those more human, less ideological and less technocratic qualities they attribute to "Leninism."

Russia's momentum for political liberty is feeble, but here is a possibility that would strengthen it and thereby threaten Communist rule. It is the possibility that one of Khrushchev's successors may try to halt too long, in its repressive phase, the cultural pendulum between thaw and freeze, thereby forcing as a counterreaction the spilling over of cultural momentum into political momentum. This will not necessarily happen; for in Russia the two momentums are separate—they are not a single overlapping freedom as in the West—and only the frustration of Russia's very strong and unhaltable cultural momentum can arouse Russia's very weak momentum for the political kind of freedom. World Communists share with world anti-Communists a belief in greater cultural freedom for artists than Russia now permits. Thus the Italian and even the French Communist parties have refused to accept the Moscow persecution of abstract art even while accepting Moscow's far bloodier political persecutions (like the suppression of Hungary). The strength of the cultural momentum even in Russia, the feebleness of the political momentum *especially* in Russia—both kinds of freedom desirable but in Russia not equally attainable—are the two most vivid impressions remaining from my many months behind the Iron Curtain.

When I asked Ilya Ehrenburg what guarantee there was against a return to Stalinism in view of the absence of any Russian movement for political liberty (free constitution, free press, free elections) and in view of the continuance of the one-party dictatorship, he replied: "The guarantee lies not in a constitution or in political institutions nor in the whim of governing individuals but in the new knowledge and strength of the Russian people themselves. For the first time in Russian history the people has become" —we were speaking in French—"*mûr*."

Hence my cautious optimism about the future changes of Russian cultural and intellectual freedom; not because I trust the intentions of the Party bosses, who are never going to allow free elections or any freedom threatening the Communist framework, but because I trust the new maturity of the younger generation of workingmen as well as intellectuals, who will demand and often get every concession possible within the framework.

All such gains, limited but far from phony, succeed precisely because they never smash the Communist framework itself. (In contrast with Poland, no Russian writer I talked to wants to go outside that framework or restore what they rather vaguely and anachronistically call "capitalism.") The present dictatorship, harassed by Party dissensions at home and abroad and facing the two fronts of literary revisionists and Chinese dogmatists, simply lacks that monolithic strength which enabled Stalin to ignore popular pressures and to send 15 million inconvenient citizens into slave labor camps. Most observers I met, many of them Party members, agreed that the Zhdanov days cannot be repeated and that the Party itself will ultimately have to put up with a lot more cultural independence.

5

Coexistence in Culture

PUBLIC TASTE AND
THE PRESSURE OF THE RUBLE

Maurice Friedberg

EDITORS' INTRODUCTION

SIMONOV: *We must read one another's books. So long as we don't read one another, we shall not know one another.*
JOHNSON: *There we are back at the problem of transition.*
SIMONOV: *It is a difficult problem.*
GRASS: *It is not a problem of the translation.*
SIMONOV: *No, it is a publishing problem, a problem of political relationships.*
GRASS: *Now we are away from books again.*
SIMONOV: *It's inevitable. We can't take politics away from books.*
— GUENTER GRASS and UWE
JOHNSON
"Conversations with Simonov"
Encounter, January, 1965

"We can't take politics away from books" when it is a question of East–West cultural exchanges. This is especially true in the Soviet Union, where the government maintains a more vigilant political check on culture than do all but a handful of the most dogmatic Communist regimes, such as the Albanian and Chinese. Still, as Maurice Friedberg shows in this chapter, Western culture is imported by the Soviet Union on a large scale. Such importation, however, is not a neutral area in Soviet policy-making. At the Twenty-third Party Congress, the antiliberal Party leader of Moldavia, I. I. Bodyul, issued a demand for "more discrimination and

Party-mindedness in the cultural exchange with capitalist countries." The warnings against possible ideological subversion of Bodyul and some other officials speaking at the Congress probably reflect behind-the-scenes lobbying by an isolationist grouping. Nevertheless, it would appear from Professor Friedberg's study that the Party leadership has strong reasons not to accede completely to the wishes of the dogmatists. Considerations of public taste and morale, profitability, and international politics would seem to marshal against sealing off the U.S.S.R. from the West.

Since all publishing houses and theaters are state-owned, the Party has extraordinary powers of censorship over cultural activities. The publishers are supervised by the State Committee for Press and Publishing. Set up in 1963, the Committee was a super-centralized expansion of Glavlit—the Main Administration for Literature and Publishing—which has existed, in one form or other, since 1865. The theaters operate under the auspices of the Ministry of Culture. (See Professor Friedberg's article on censorship in Problems of Communism, November–December, 1964.)

For several reasons, however, Party control is neither absolute nor consistent. For example, among Party leaders and cultural authorities there are marked differences of opinion about the limits of permissibility in culture (see Chapter 4). No less important is the governmental requirement that books and plays must pay for themselves, since this means that public taste and the publishers' need to make profits play a significant role in the selection of foreign books and plays. Because the Party leaders, the cultural purveyors, and the public do not see eye to eye, ideological purity has given way to a working, if wavering, compromise.

Party ideology has also been compromised, Professor Friedberg explains, as a result of cultural contacts with the outside world. The number of East–West cultural exchanges increased greatly under Khrushchev's version of the peaceful coexistence policy, which was spurred on by considerations of economic benefit, diplomacy, prestige, and good public relations. But Party vigilance and suspicion are hard barriers to break down. The Picasso show in 1956, the Moscow Youth Festival in 1957, and other displays of "modernism," coming after a long period of cultural isolation, were met so enthusiastically by Soviet youth that the Party, already shocked by the Hungarian Revolution and the ferment elsewhere in Eastern Europe, quickly retaliated with an all-out campaign against "alien, decadent, bourgeois" ideology.

The cultural vigilance of the Party limits the influx of new forms and ideas even from the socialist countries. In an Eastern European art exhibit held in the winter of 1958/59 at the Manezh in Moscow, the Polish section consisted almost entirely of abstract and expressionistic paintings. The canvases caused a sensation and drew 600,000 visitors in three months. Heated debates broke out on the museum floor and the authorities felt impelled to hold meetings directed against "revisionism in modern art." These meetings, at Moscow institutions of higher education, were marked by even more excitement, with Polish students rising in the audience to speak out in defense of their show. Since then nothing quite as stimulating has been allowed to enter from Eastern Europe, with the possible exception of Franz Kafka's writings, which began to appear in translation in 1964.

Soviet cultural exchange, with both "bourgeois" and "socialist" countries, is affected by the ups and downs of relations with them. The plush magazine Yugoslavia disappeared from Moscow newsstands in 1958, and in 1959 the Chinese magazines Friendship and China likewise vanished, as relations with Yugoslavia and China became strained. U.S. exhibits and other cultural offerings in the Soviet Union have been harassed or even canceled as a result, it would seem, partly of the machinations of dogmatists with police connections, partly of Soviet-American diplomatic disagreements.

Selectivity in cultural imports did not originate with the Bolsheviks; it was a time-honored, self-preserving policy of Czardom. "The political system of Russia," wrote the Marquis de Custine in 1839, "could not withstand twenty years of free communications with Western Europe." By the twentieth century, however, many of the barriers had come down, and for a brief period Russia's creative artists profited from and contributed mightily to Western culture. The Bolshevik Revolution and the harsh years of Stalinism destroyed the budding cultural ties with the West. Since Stalin's death, the Party's misgivings about Western cultural influences have been eased. But, the Party insists, improved relations with the West must not signify surrender to its baneful ideological *influences. Maurice Friedberg's thesis is that the making of Soviet policies for cultural interchange is more complex than implied by such cant as "no peaceful coexistence in ideology."*

A deplorably prevalent view among social scientists is that the Western scholar who specializes in Soviet literature must be something of a cross between an ivory-tower littérateur, that is, a person unaware of socio-political reality, and a Kremlinologist—a term of opprobrium widely used as a generic label but rarely linked with specific names. It is true, of course, that some among us have, on occasion, betrayed a degree of other-worldliness sufficient to study the use of metaphor or iambic pentameter in Soviet verse. From time to time, a few of us may have yielded to the temptation of explaining current Soviet literary policies with the aid of information gathered from official (or, at the very least, unimpeachable) sources on the personal tastes of one or another Soviet leader—be he Malenkov, with his weakness for the satire of Gogol and Saltykov-Shchedrin, or Khrushchev, with his passion for the rhymes of Demian Bedny. The present essay is an attempt, with all due respect to Sir Charles Snow, to bridge the chasm between the two cultures, that of the literary scholar and that of the social scientist, in the area of Soviet studies and to present an episode in recent Soviet literary polemics with due attention to political factors which have shaped the artistic results.

The year of Stalin's passing, 1953, marked a turning point in almost all areas of Soviet life, including the cultural. One of the least explored aspects of the evolution in cultural policy after Stalin is the virtual revolution that has taken place in book publishing. Although Soviet statistics on book publishing, in terms of both numbers of titles and numbers of copies, are highly misleading, there can be no doubt that the totals of both have increased suddenly and impressively.[1] Moreover, the increases reflected the greater attention being paid to public taste. The proportion of belletristic to political books published rose from 79.5 per cent in 1946–53 to about 178 per cent in 1954–58 and 191 per cent in 1959–62.[2]

Nevertheless, if one is to judge by public demand, the quantity of political books in the stores was still too large, while that of novels, short stories, poetry, and drama remained insufficient. Thus, while political works constituted 10 per cent of all copies printed, they accounted for nearly 20 per cent of all *unsold* books. Similarly, in the public libraries, political writings accounted for almost 25 per cent of all books in the stacks, but for only 10 per cent of those on loan. In the city libraries, they were borrowed two times less frequently than the average for all books, and in the villages the demand for them was even smaller. An average political book was borrowed from a public library only once in two years.[3] However, despite greatly expanded printings, there was a continued shortage of almost all types of belles-lettres. The demand was greatest for juvenile literature,[4] for the multivolume editions of the Russian classics,[5] and, above all, for translations of Western European and American literature, of which little had been published during Stalin's declining years. Due to the acute shortages in the latter category, translated foreign books disappeared from bookstore shelves within hours after delivery from the warehouses, waiting lists in the libraries grew extremely long, and a flourishing black market in these books soon developed.

Enter Sherlock Holmes and the Three Musketeers

Decades of isolation from the Western world resulted in a generation of Soviet readers for whom hundreds of Western authors did not exist. Even entire schools of twentieth-century Western writing were unknown to them. Their knowledge of Western literature was of necessity limited to those writers whose works had been permitted under Stalin. As a result, even sophisticated Soviet readers were simply unaware of the modern classics of Kafka, Joyce, Proust, Faulkner, and other major writers. Not unexpectedly, therefore, during the post-Stalin thaw, they asked first for more books by Western writers whose works had been available during the Stalin era but had been difficult to obtain. The Soviet reading public of the mid-1950's awoke, like Rip Van Winkle, and did not

know where it was. It resumed reading the Western literature of
the late 1920's, and thus the "latest" Western writers—names that
were all but unknown in the Soviet Union in the early 1950's, particularly to the younger generation—were Erich Maria Remarque
and Ernest Hemingway. Only a handful remembered *All Quiet on
the Western Front* and *A Farewell to Arms,* and the illusion of
these writers' newness was abetted by the fact that at the time both
were still writing. Similar circumstances contributed to the clamor
for Sir Arthur Conan Doyle's tales of Sherlock Holmes—extremely
popular in Russia during the first two decades of this century—and
for the faithful childhood friends of most middle-aged Russians,
the adventurous lads of Robert Louis Stevenson, the American In-
dians of James Fenimore Cooper (whose impact on Russian boys
was once movingly described by Chekhov), and the irresistibly
dashing musketeers of Alexandre Dumas père. Another factor favored these romantic writers: Their locales and protagonists, strikingly antithetical to Russian writing both before and after the
Revolution, exerted the normal attraction of escapist literature.

In the U.S.S.R., public demand for specific types of reading matter does not necessarily have any effect on the output of the book
industry. In the mid-1950's, however, Soviet publishers were afforded an opportunity to respond, for once, to the reading public's
desires. This came about because the public's clamor for translations of Western literature coincided with renewed governmental
pressure on the publishing houses to show a financial profit and
with a series of Party pronouncements commending expansion of
cultural contacts with the West.

The effects of all this were remarkable. Between 1956 and 1957,
Doyle's tales of Sherlock Holmes were printed in 1.5 million copies,
a figure surpassed by the works of Remarque, with 3 million copies
over a somewhat longer period of time. Half a million copies of
A Thousand and One Nights were printed in the Moldavian city
of Kishinev, where the publishers also brought out huge quantities
of books by George Sand.[6]

This "veritable torrent of translated foreign 'best sellers'" trig-
gered an article in the Central Committee's official journal, *Kommunist,* which divulged that more than 1.4 million copies of the
works of Thomas Mayne Reid—the British author of westerns and
a perennial favorite with Russian readers—had been published over

a period of two years, 1955/56.[7] Moreover, the article went on, this had been supplemented by nearly 2 million copies of Jules Verne's adventure novels—more than had been printed in Russia in the preceding *eighty-six* years!—and worst of all, 3 million copies of the works of Dumas père had appeared during the same two-year period. To bring home the horror of this state of affairs, *Kommunist* declared that the printings of *The Three Musketeers, The Count of Monte Cristo,* and *Queen Margot* had "consumed almost twice as much paper as is used annually by the publishing house Sovetskii Pisatel' for the printing of all new Soviet fiction, poetry, and drama." In the first eleven months of 1956 alone, there were more than a hundred titles by sixty-one foreign authors, printed in a total of 14.5 million copies, an average of 238,000 copies per author. Most of this was "light reading." By contrast, in 1955 the corresponding figures for Soviet literature were 1.29 million copies, a mere 22,000 per author.

The Party's concern over these enormous printings was summed up in *Sovetskaya kul'tura* of May 4, 1957:

> Many publishers have adopted the erroneous policy of continually publishing large printings of such "best sellers" as *The Count of Monte Cristo, Queen Margot,* and [George Sand's] *Consuelo.* At first glance it may appear that there is nothing objectionable in this. These are not bad books and the demand for them is indeed great. The trouble, however, is that the publishers' enthusiasm for these books is not due to solicitude for the readers, but is prompted by a desire to swell the publishers' pockets the easy way. What this incorrect practice leads to may be learned from the fact that the Kirgiz State Publishing House used up last year more than half of its paper allotment on the printing of "best sellers."

Similar conditions prevailed in the nation's theaters. During the thaw, plays were selected with an eye to the box office, rather than to the Party's district committee. Given an opportunity to express its preferences, the Soviet theatergoing public voted with its rubles and leisure time in favor of escapist foreign fare and thus administered a humiliating defeat to both the native Socialist Realist product and the didactic works of modern Western left-wing authors. On July 25, 1956, *Sovetskaya kul'tura* stated:

> In the selection of plays by foreign authors, theater directors frequently pass over valuable works with important social content and

at the same time cannot cure themselves of their passion for plays that preach bourgeois morality (e.g., *Telephone Call* [the Soviet title of *Dial M for Murder*], *Dangerous Corner*) and in spite of all the justified criticism retain these plays in the repertory.

Nearly a year later, on May 16, 1957, an almost identical complaint appeared in *Sovetskaya Rossiya:*

> The theater season in Leningrad began in a rather disquieting manner. And not only because it was in Leningrad that the notorious *Telephone Call*—a cheap detective play that was sharply and justly criticized in our press—first rang. The fact is that nearly every [!] Leningrad theater got such a "telephone call." At one theater it was called *Commotion at Night,* at another, *What Every Woman Knows,* at a third, still something else. The theater managers, anxious to fill up the house, plainly lowered their repertory standards. They looked around to see what their neighbors were doing and eagerly took up the production of detective plays and farce comedies.

The Party Intervenes

The Party could not welcome this "unhealthy" infatuation with escapist foreign literature, this expression of dissatisfaction and boredom with modern Soviet writing, this sign of a possible attraction to the bourgeois values of the West. But there was no questioning the fact that British detectives, French soldiers of fortune, and American playboys were displacing Komsomol tractor drivers, bemedaled milkmaids, and district Party secretaries as the literary heroes of the average Soviet citizen. The Party felt impelled to adopt measures to combat the ideological advances of the unholy reactionary alliance led by Sherlock Holmes, Dr. Watson, Queen Margot, and the Three Musketeers.

On April 5, 1958, the Central Committee of the CPSU resolved to warn Soviet publishers against printing "worthless" books merely because they were good money-makers. The chief money-making culprits mentioned were Dumas and Doyle.[8] On September 4, 1958, the Central Committee passed a resolution limiting the circulation of multivolume editions of works of fiction, and appointed itself the arbiter for making all future decisions in the matter.[9]

On June 4, 1959, a new resolution reaffirmed those of the previous year, except that Dumas and Doyle were replaced as the
bête noire by a living English writer, Somerset Maugham. In
addition, a list of priorities in the publication of foreign books was
made public. Highest on the list were technical and political books
and works of fiction written by foreign Communists, "depicting
the struggle of the working people for their rights and for social
progress and literature revealing the decay of the capitalist system," and those written by "progressives" and "fighters for
peace."[10]

On May 31, 1960, the Central Committee accused the book
trade of betraying the Party's trust and of degenerating, in effect,
into a quasi-capitalist industry guided by the profit motive:

> Many book trade organizations order books without taking into
> account the interests of their customers, acting instead from purely
> commercial considerations, and are insufficiently active in pro-
> moting timely literature, particularly political and modern [Soviet]
> fiction. At the same time, these organizations place inflated orders
> for translations of certain foreign authors which have no artistic
> merit.[11]

Nevertheless, the book industry apparently made little or no
effort to reform its practices. On March 8, 1963, at the height of
the cultural freeze of 1962/63, Khrushchev spoke out against
ideological laxity in Soviet culture, and although the speech contained no specific reference to politically "harmful" or "worthless"
foreign literature, there could be no mistaking the implications.
Fifteen days later, *Pravda* printed a report on a meeting of the
"*aktiv* of Moscow's Creative Intelligentsia," an informal organization of the city's artistic elite:

> It was also pointed out that the repertories of Moscow's theaters
> are overloaded with plays by foreign authors, plays that are often
> philistine and shallow and that glorify life in bourgeois society.
> Yet for some reason there is no room on the capital's stages for
> some of the good plays by Soviet dramatists. There was mention
> of directors who invested much painstaking effort in the pro-
> duction of foreign plays, while devoting no comparable attention
> to Soviet plays. In this connection, there was criticism of such
> [foreign] plays as *The Third Head, Good Night, Patricia,* and
> *Two for the Seesaw.*

In the summer of 1963, a new state commission was organized to supervise the output of the country's publishing houses. On August 19, 1963, *The New York Times* reported that "Pavel G. Romanov, who had been responsible for control of foreign correspondents' dispatches before censorship was abolished two and a half years ago, was named to head the organization with the rank of a Cabinet Minister. The organization will decide what literary works will be published and what circulation they will get."[12]

Our case study is thus partly inconclusive, and this reflects, among other things, the partial decentralization of Soviet power in recent years, and the development of the various centrifugal forces that have hastened the move away from centralized management. There can be no doubt of the continued primacy of the Party, but since the death of Stalin—under Malenkov, under Khrushchev, and under his successors—the Party has appeared reluctant to use the full weight of its power to enforce decisions of less than paramount importance, and even then, for a variety of reasons, not the least of which are the absence of a charismatic leader and the factional tensions within the Party proper, it has not always been able to enforce its will effectively.

The problem in book publishing and the theater is illustrative of this development. There is reason to believe that the Party would like to have the selection and dissemination of books and plays governed by ideological considerations alone. It has exercised considerable self-restraint in this matter, however, and this must be due in part to its justifiable fear that the Soviet public, and particularly the intelligentsia, would be excessively antagonized if all ideologically "useless" or even partly "harmful" books and plays were banned. In other words, the Party has apparently displayed a degree of responsiveness to the wishes of the public that would have been unthinkable under Stalin. Another liberalizing factor is that the managers of the book industry and the theater, like their counterparts in the West, are eager to earn a profit. To do so, they are willing to cater to the wishes of their customers. Commercial instincts of this sort reinforce the Party's new responsiveness to the public's desires. Ironically, this commercialism is, in turn, strengthened by the Party's repeated demands that culture, too, prove economically profitable or, at the very least, unneedy of financial subsidies. This, of course, is not the only instance of internal contradiction in Party policy.

Naturally, the publishers and theater managers would be happiest if they could sell politically acceptable books and plays to the Soviet public. The public, however, prefers reading matter and drama that fail to meet the ideological specifications of the Party. The clash of economic and ideological interests places the managers of the Soviet cultural establishment in a predicament that is well expressed in the old Russian phrase: *"Kapital priobresti i nevinnost' sobliusti"* ("How to make one's operations pay off without losing one's innocence").

As one might expect, the official Soviet position is that no contradiction exists between the ideology and the economics of Soviet culture and that, in fact, they complement each other. Thus, a recent Soviet study declares that Soviet book publishing

> . . . produces precisely the kind of books which reflect, on the one hand, popular demand, and on the other hand, the needs of the construction of a new society. This is a special characteristic of Soviet publishing, and is one of its distinctions from bourgeois publishing, which could never possibly set before itself the task of combining in its book output readers' demands and the true interests of the people.[13]

Nevertheless, Soviet readers might question the assertion that their preferences have been neatly reconciled with the Party's interpretation of "the needs of the construction of a new society" and "the true interests of the people."

Moreover, ideology has been eroded by economics perceptibly but within limits in post-Stalin publishing policy, which has been marked by stratagems and compromises. Most important, the tastes of the Soviet reading public have continued as a factor in the making of publishing policy. As Alexander Tvardovsky warned in his editorial written for the fortieth anniversary of *Novy mir,* in January, 1965: "Most frequently it is the response of those people not involved in literary disputes and score-settling, in affirming or denying literary and artistic realities, which determines the vitality and longevity of . . . books, films, plays."

NOTES

The author gratefully acknowledges the assistance of the American Council of Learned Societies and the Social Science Research Council.

1. Registered as "books" in Soviet statistics are pamphlets of five pages or less, reprints, translations, and industrial manuals. None of these are considered books in the West, where only actually sold materials of forty-eight pages or more are designated as such. For a detailed discussion of the subject, see Maurice Friedberg, "Literary Output: 1956–1962," in Max Hayward and Edward L. Crowley (eds.), *Soviet Literature in the Sixties* (New York: Frederick A. Praeger, 1964).

2. These figures are derived from the table below, printed in A. I. Nazarov, *Kniga v sovetskom obshchestve* (Moscow: Izdatel'stvo "Nauka," 1964), facing p. 240:

SOVIET BOOK AND PAMPHLET PRODUCTION: ANNUAL AVERAGES

	1946–53	1954–58	1959–62
Political literature			
titles	6,350	7,410	10,590
copies	187,000,000	179,000,000	191,000,000
Fiction, poetry, drama			
titles	4,100	6,250	7,870
copies	149,000,000	319,000,000	365,000,000
Total book production			
titles	38,000	57,000	75,000
copies	713,000,000	1,054,000,000	1,194,000,000

3. N. I. Buzliakov, *Voprosy planirovaniya pechati v SSSR* (Moscow: Izdatel'stvo "Iskusstvo," 1957), p. 52.

4. *Ibid.*, pp. 55, 57.

5. *Ibid.*, pp. 38, 55–56.

6. Maurice Friedberg, "Soviet Books, Censors, and Readers," in *Literature and Revolution in Soviet Russia, 1917–1962: A Symposium,* ed. Max Hayward and Leopold Labedz (New York and London: Oxford University Press, 1963), p. 205.

7. Il'ya Kremlev, "V zashchitu chitatelia" ("In Defense of the Reader"), *Kommunist,* No. 8 (June, 1957), pp. 123–28.

8. *Sovetskaya pechat' v dokumentakh* (Moscow: Gospolitizdat, 1961), pp. 360–62.

9. *Ibid.*, pp. 294–95.

10. *Ibid.*, p. 368. An interesting aside was the frank directive to censor books by foreign authors. Even among books selected for translation and publication, "passages of no scholarly or practical interest are to be deleted." For a more detailed discussion of the subject, see Maurice Friedberg, "Keeping Up With the Censor," *Problems of Communism,* XIII, No. 6 (November–December, 1964), 22–31.

11. *Sovetskaya pechat' v dokumentakh,* p. 314.

12. See also Friedberg, "Literary Output: 1956–1962," *loc. cit.*

13. Nazarov, *op. cit.*, p. 86.

6

Reorganization of the U.S.S.R. Academy of Sciences

Loren R. Graham

EDITORS' INTRODUCTION

Last summer [Mr. Khrushchev] proposed the election to the Soviet Academy of one of his own men. It was a turning point in Soviet history, my friend said, when the members of the Academy voted against this official candidate. (It also made it only a matter of time, he thought, before the hated Professor Lysenko was excluded from its ranks.) Mr. Khrushchev insisted, but the scientists refused to accept this outside nominee.

Mr. Khrushchev's response was to lose his temper. He shouted that the academicians were overpaid and undisciplined, and that he would have their ivory tower disbanded (raspustit'). Eventually he was dissuaded from this impetuous move.

— *"Monitor," in The Times (London)*
April 7, 1965

The foiling of Khrushchev's attempt to foist his candidate for academician upon the scientists may not have happened as related above, but it could have; members of the creative intelligentsia had stood up to Khrushchev, and even argued directly with him, over the cultural clampdown of 1962/63. And Khrushchev might well have tried to sponsor a favorite candidate for academician; much honor and scientific significance is attached to membership in the U.S.S.R. Academy of Sciences, and there is, moreover, a well-established Bolshevik tradition of intervention in the Academy's internal affairs.

Ever since Peter the Great (1682–1725) founded the Academy in 1724, Russia's rulers have reserved for it a crucial role in their programs for modernizing Russian society. Sprawling across the fields of the natural sciences, the social sciences, law, and the humanities, the Academy occupies a more important position relative to the science of its nation than does any other academy, any foundation, agency, or university, in the world. The U.S.S.R. Academy of Sciences combines, in fact, the roles of all these institutions. It is the leading Soviet center of basic and applied research; it teaches and awards advanced degrees; it controls a huge network of 14 republic academies and 7 filials, or branches; it coordinates the pure scientific research in the academies of the union republics, the universities, and the specialized institutes; it has 181 full members and 368 corresponding members, and contains 166 institutes; in all, approximately 45,000 scientific workers are connected with the Academy system. Little wonder the reorganization of the Academy became a major issue among scientists after Stalin.

In this chapter, Loren Graham traces the debate on reorganization from its origins in the late 1950's to its conclusion in the 1960's, when reforms were effected. The principal debaters were the pure scientists, who wanted applied, technologically oriented research separated from the Academy, and the applied scientists, who rallied to resist this threat to their prestige and perquisites. But scientists in the universities and union-republic Academies of Sciences spoke up, too, for their particular interests. According to Professor Graham, Khrushchev's advocacy of the reforms, the improved status of pure science after World War II, the ideological revisions during the period of the debate all worked in favor of the pure scientists.

The reorganization of scientific research was one of a number of scattered moves after Stalin that indicated a trend toward more rationality and less ideological meddling in science and scientific policy-making. The autocratic Stalin intervened in scientific affairs more than had any of Russia's rulers after Peter the Great. Only the physical sciences enjoyed a degree of autonomy under Stalin, because of their vital importance to Soviet power. In biology, psychology, and the social sciences, dogmatism enforced by terror dried up whole fields of research, from pedology and

Freudian psychology to criminology and Oriental studies, and misdirected much of the rest.

Lysenkoism in biology is a well-known example of both aspects of this process. In 1948, Stalin saw to it that Trofim Lysenko, whose star had been on the rise since the 1930's, received the backing of the Party's Central Committee for his condemnation of the landmark work of Mendel, Morgan, and Weismann in genetics as "bourgeois reactionary," and for the imposition on an unwilling scientific community of his own scientifically unverified adaptation of the Lamarckian theory of the inheritance of acquired characteristics. Lysenko's dubious theories and experiments received Stalin's backing, it appears, because Stalin believed that they offered short cuts to needed bumper harvests and because they pandered to Stalin's grandiose vision of the "transformation of nature" under his leadership.

As the virtual commissar of biology and agricultural sciences, Lysenko caused untold billions of rubles of damage to agriculture with such unsubstantiated and ineffectual measures as the vernalization, or presprouting, of spring wheat and the massive plantings of tree shelter belts. Lysenko, moreover, shares responsibility with Stalin's regime for the liquidation of eminent scientists who disagreed with him, such as N. I. Vavilov, whom he replaced as director of the Institute of Genetics in 1940, after which Vavilov was arrested and sent to a labor camp, where he died in 1943.

Khrushchev seemed to share Stalin's faith in Lysenko. He stepped in to rescue Lysenko from the scientific disgrace into which he was slipping after Stalin. After Khrushchev had fallen, Lysenko again came under fire. In February, 1965, he was removed from his position as director of the Institute of Genetics. Subsequently, he lost his other high post of President of the Academy of Agricultural Sciences. On June 25, 1965, a Soviet biologist told a centennial meeting held in the U.S.S.R. to commemorate the work of Gregor Mendel: "We are rehabilitating an entire science that he founded." Perhaps this may eventually be said of the remaining proscribed fields of study.

In the Lysenko affair, in their participation in various recent anti-Stalinist petitions to the Party, in the above-mentioned opposition to Khrushchev's candidate for membership in the Academy, scientists have been much more united against political repression and ideological interference of all kinds than they were in the organizational issue of reforming the Academy's structure. Scientists must be counted as a significant opinion and interest grouping. Their influence, although not precisely measurable, seems to extend far beyond the walls of their laboratories and institutes, however much they may be expected, as Loren Graham points out, "to confine their professional opinions to science."

In 1932, two brilliant young men, Nikolai Nikolaevich Semenov, a physical chemist, and Ivan Pavlovich Bardin, a metallurgical engineer, were elected to full membership in the U.S.S.R. Academy of Sciences. These men represented the two distinct kinds of scientist on whom the Soviet Government relied for the next thirty years in its drive toward industrial and scientific eminence.

Semenov, a graduate of Petrograd University and an assistant to the well-known physicist A. F. Yoffe, was an adherent of pure scientific research in the tradition of German and Russian science of the late nineteenth century. As director of the Institute of Chemical Physics of the Academy of Sciences, he conducted research on the theory of chemical reactions that resulted in his being awarded a Nobel prize in 1956, the first Soviet citizen to be thus honored. Bardin, a proponent of the applied sciences, was one of the first engineers ever to be elected to the Academy, which had always been a preserve of fundamental science.[1] Bardin's name became even better known to the Soviet public than Semenov's. He was a product of the Soviet Union's Iron Age, an admirer of the steel mills at Gary, Indiana, where he had worked temporarily, and the creator in the Soviet Union of the Kuznetsk Metallurgical Combine. These two distinguished men approached science from markedly different positions: that of the theorist and that of the engineer. A quarter of a century after their election to the Academy, they emerged as two of the leading exponents of opposing schemes for the reorganization of science in the Soviet Union.

The U.S.S.R. Academy of Sciences has always occupied the most prominent position of all scientific institutions in the Soviet state. Even before the Revolution, the Academy was highly regarded as a unique institution. In the nineteenth century, the seventeenth- and eighteenth-century academies of Western Europe had yielded their positions of pre-eminence to universities and industrial research laboratories, but in Russia, the Academy remained the single most important institution in science, although the universities in the late nineteenth century challenged it in actual research, if not in prestige. After the Revolution, however, the Soviet authorities assigned the universities a primarily pedagogical function, and the Academy consequently held its position as the leading research center. Nevertheless, the Soviet Government altered the Academy's traditional pattern of activity. In the period after 1929, it was forced to accept engineers as members, and its work plan, closely controlled by the government, was directed toward subjects connected with industrialization. As a result of this compulsory elevation of the applied sciences, engineers began to play a very important role in the administration of the Academy. The Department of Technical Sciences (Engineering) possessed more members than the three departments for social sciences and humanities combined.[2] However, the theoretical researchers of the natural sciences never gave up their traditional devotion to fundamental research, and on numerous occasions were reprimanded by Party or governmental officials for straying back to "excessively academic" subjects.[3]

The Call for Reform

Six years after Stalin's death, the most important debate over the administration of science ever witnessed in the Soviet Union broke out. The elevated status given to science and technology in the U.S.S.R. by the success of Soviet rocketry increased the boldness of the scientists' voices in the controversy. At the same time, the ability of the scientists to gain an audience with governmental leaders led to much disagreement among them. In earlier years, when the government often ignored scientists on questions of administration, they had stood together; now divisions and quarrels that had simmered for decades boiled over into public

view. During the peak of the polemics in 1959, four general positions could be clearly discerned: that of the theoreticians of the
natural sciences, that of the engineers, that of the representatives
of the local research institutions, such as the republic academies
of sciences, and that of the university professors.

Nikita Khrushchev indicated as early as February, 1956, that
reforms in the activity of the Academy were needed, but he did
not offer in his first observations any concrete suggestions for
improvement. In his report to the Twentieth Congress of the
CPSU, on February 15, 1956, he remarked:

> The lack of coordination of the work of the scientific institutes
> of the Academy of Sciences, the industrial research institutes,
> and the higher educational establishments is completely intolerable.
> This disconnection and lack of agreement prevent the concentration
> of scientific forces upon the solution of the most important scien-
> tific and technological problems, engender duplication, lead to
> wastefulness, and hamper the introduction of the advances of
> science and technology in the national economy.[4]

Following this speech, a number of articles advocating reform
of the administration of science appeared in Soviet journals and
newspapers. Most of them were quite moderate in tone; the majority concerned the reform of industry and industrial research
rather than of the Academy of Sciences itself. In 1957, the administrative control of industry was dispersed among the approximately 100 local economic councils (sovnarkhozy), and while
this occupied the attention of Party and government officials, the
Academy of Sciences continued its work as before. Then on June
29, 1959, Khrushchev again took up the subject of the Academy,
and this time he advanced definite suggestions:

> The time has come . . . to reorganize the work in the Academy
> of Sciences. . . . I think that a difficult situation has arisen in
> some scientific institutions of the Academy. Some scientists may
> disagree with me, but I consider it unwise for the Academy of
> Sciences to take on questions of metallurgy and coal mining. After
> all, these areas were not within the Academy's domain before.
> But the academicians took into membership Comrade Bardin, the
> splendid engineer and eminent scientist. Understandably, he began
> to ask that an appropriate institute be established for him in
> Moscow. Somewhat the same thing happened to Academician

Sheviakov, the eminent specialist on coal. . . . Let us set up laboratories at plants and factories, establish scientific institutes and other scientific centers under the economic councils, and assign more young people to them, along with experienced and well-known scientists. Think over this problem, comrades, and make suggestions on it. I think this policy will prove correct. . . . We shall ask the U.S.S.R. Academy of Sciences, its presidium, to draft proposals for further improving the activity of the Academy.[5]

Khrushchev's proposal was immediately interpreted by the theoretical scientists as an invitation to submit plans for restoring the status of fundamental research in the Academy of Sciences and eliminating the Stalinist controls on research.

For twenty-five years prior to Khrushchev's speech, a public defense of pure science had been impossible, since the Marxist principle of the unity of theory and practice had been enforced in the Academy to the advantage of the applied sciences. But on August 9, 1959, in an article in *Izvestia*, Nikolai Semenov advanced an outspoken defense of theoretical scientific research.[6] As is customary with controversial articles, the editors appended the notation: "Published for purposes of discussion." Semenov very carefully tied his position to that of the First Secretary of the Communist Party: "Comrade N. S. Khrushchev's speech at the June plenary session of the Central Committee contains a splendid analysis of the role of science and new technology in the building of Communism. . . . In particular, he noted that problems of the metallurgical and coal industries, with which the Academy was not originally concerned, had been incorrectly assigned to it."

Semenov then proceeded to an attack of the Marxist principle that theoretical science, responding to demands placed on it, receives its impetus from industry. He maintained that there was no necessity for engineers in the Academy. Science is not an appendage (*pridatok*) of industry, he argued, but has its own independent assignment, which is "the thorough study of nature and the internal mechanism of phenomena and the mastery on man's behalf of hitherto concealed natural forces." Production does not stimulate theoretical science, he declared, and, to prove his point, referred to several important moments in the history of modern science. Did industry ever hint at the possibility of unleashing atomic energy? On the contrary, atomic energy was the fruit of pure science. The overwhelming evidence is that the value of fundamental research cannot be judged *a priori*, and yet practical administrators continue to hobble research to engineering tasks. "Despite the fact," he wrote, "that for over a century science has constantly surprised mankind by the way its abstract formulas . . . suddenly materialized as turning points in technology, many people are somehow never able to become accustomed to this." No, the needs of industry do not shape the path for science and technology. Rather, science and technology are the moving forces behind the growth and development of industry:

> There are . . . two sources of progress for industry: first, the logical development of technology and production, and second, the logical development of science. To be sure, this breakdown is to a certain extent arbitrary, as both these processes are more or less interconnected: Technology cannot be developed without employing scientific data, and science cannot be developed without taking into account the development of technology. Still this breakdown is roughly legitimate, as is indicated by our use of the two separate words "technology" and "science."

For thirty years, Party ideologists had insisted on the unity of pure and applied science, but Semenov attempted to draw a clear line between them. Furthermore, he believed that responsibility for research in these two areas should be assigned to separate research organizations. In his view, the Academy of Sciences should be primarily responsible for theoretical research, and the engineering institutes, such as the Institute of Metallurgy and the Institute of Mining, should be removed from the Academy and placed under the control of industrial ministries or regional economic councils. Whenever a theoretical problem was solved by the Academy's theoreticians, the results could then be turned over "to the appropriate branch industries."

Semenov also recommended that the Presidium of the Academy abandon its efforts to plan in detail the future course of scientific research. The planning of science, he implied, is essentially different from the planning of industrial production. Semenov noted the absence of successful planning of theoretical research in the past:

If we look at the history of the great scientific discoveries made at the end of the last century and the beginning of the present one, we see that to all intents and purposes there was no conscious planning of these trends in science, at least until the technical possibilities had been brought out with complete clarity. This was a world of elemental forces in which the sole rationale consisted of the intuition of individual men of science who detected the logic in the way science was developing.

Particularly wasteful, the academician continued, was the requirement that scientists in the Academy state in their work plans what supplies they will need to complete their research, since they know that their needs will change in the course of their work. Therefore, to be on the safe side, many scientists order materials to cover all possibilities, despite the additional costs. "When you come down to it," Semenov went on, "it is impossible and irrational to plan the supply system of the Academy of Sciences. The output of the Academy's scientific endeavors is not material processed by machine but scientific truth, which can never be planned in detail."

Semenov's recommendations amounted to a comprehensive reform of the U.S.S.R. Academy of Sciences that would have been the greatest alteration of its structure since the early 1930's. Although he favored a more rational coordination of research, noting the absence of any central planning agency in science, in many respects he wished a return to the administrative position that existed before the Academy's Sovietization. His proposals may be summarized in seven points: (1) remove the narrow engineering institutes; (2) concentrate on fundamental research; (3) reduce the Academy's eight divisions to three; (4) reduce the authority of the Presidium of the Academy; (5) remove geographically remote branches of the Academy from its jurisdiction in the name of efficiency; (6) abandon planning of theoretical research, and (7) give the Academy the undisputed right to retain on its staff the top 10 to 15 per cent of its graduates (instead of letting industry hire them, as so often happened).

Every one of the seven major points made by Semenov can be related to the position of the Academy prior to 1929.* Before that

* For the transformation of the Academy's activities that occurred at the end of the 1920's, see this writer's *The Revolution in Russian Science: The Soviet*

date, the Academy possessed no chairs for engineers, nor was its work planned. It concentrated on basic rather than applied problems, was centered in one or two urban areas, and trained its own personnel. It even was divided into three departments. But it was also fashioned largely on the traditions of the Imperial Academy of Sciences of St. Petersburg. In recommending a return to the old pattern, Semenov exposed himself to the criticism that he preferred the ways of Czarist Russia.

Opposition to the Reform

Academician Ivan Bardin, the head of the Academy's Department of Technical Sciences, and Semenov's colleague in the Academy since its original Soviet reform, answered the chemist's challenge to the engineers in an article in *Izvestia* on August 28, 1959.[7] Bardin flatly accused Semenov of trying to erase the past thirty years and of advocating a return to the Academy of pre-revolutionary times: "Just why must the U.S.S.R. Academy of Sciences, which was awakened to the need for contact with life by V. I. Lenin, constrict the range of its work and retreat to the position of the ill-remembered Imperial Academy of Sciences?" Bardin questioned Semenov's argument that the Academy should not engage in applied research since it had not done so before its Sovietization, and added that such an argument "sounds very strange in our time." Bardin evidently failed to note that Semenov's reference to the Academy's traditional concentration on pure science was almost a direct quotation from Khrushchev's speech of June 29, 1959, to the plenum of the Central Committee.

Bardin's primary aim was to ensure the continued existence of engineering institutes in the Academy and the right of engineers to the title of academician, which carries greater prestige than any other professional title in the Soviet Union. He specifically criticized Semenov for his belief that the Institute of Metallurgy should be removed from the Academy. Metallurgy was, in Bardin's view, a theoretical science, and he suggested that the Institute might properly be called the Institute of the Physics and Chemistry of Metals. But adoption of this name was not wise, he continued, since it would imply a denial of the Party principle of linking science with production.

Bardin was soon joined in his campaign by a number of other distinguished Soviet engineers, who likewise denounced Semenov's attempt to divide science from technology and alleged that he was disrespectful of applied science. As Semenov later caustically remarked, the complaints about his proposals came almost entirely from persons whom he proposed to remove from the Academy.

One of the most outspoken of the engineers to join Bardin was N. V. Lavrov, a professor of engineering sciences, whose views appeared in *Literaturnaya gazeta*.[8] Lavrov suspected Semenov of doubting the validity of the changes that the Soviet Government and the Communist Party had made in the Academy since the Revolution, although Lenin himself, Lavrov declared, was responsible for many of these reforms. Lenin's "Outline Plan of Scientific-Technological Research," composed in April, 1918, contained a clear statement of the close connection of the Academy with industry.[9] According to Lavrov, the post-1929 reform of the Academy was the execution of Lenin's plan for the Academy: "This period in the development of the U.S.S.R. Academy of Sciences, the correctness of which several scientists are now doubting, logically followed from Lenin's 'Outline Plan of Scientific-Technological Research.' "

Lavrov agreed that tremendous progress in the sciences had been made since the late 1920's, but added that although some reorganization of the Academy might be necessary, Semenov's approach was entirely inappropriate: "If one reads the article of Academician N. N. Semenov, one will easily see that the author is little interested in ways of helping the development of the technical sciences, but instead makes only negative suggestions aimed at destroying the Department of Technical Sciences of the U.S.S.R. Academy of Sciences."[10]

A more influential refutation of Semenov's views, also originating among the engineers, came from a group in the Academy's Department of Technical Sciences. Academicians A. Blagonravov, A. Mints, I. Artobolevskii, and B. Stechkin, and Corresponding Member* B. Petrov, addressed Semenov in the

---

* According to the charter of the Academy, a full member (academician) is a person who "has enriched science with works of the first degree of sig-

pages of *Izvestia*.[11] Quoting Semenov's view that the major force behind the development of science is the "logical development," or "self-flow," of theoretical science, they contrasted it with the dictum of Marx and Engels that "pure" science, receiving its stimulus from trade and industry, is thus dependent on the social organization of society. Engels, they pointed out, had once remarked that although "technology depends to a considerable extent on the state of science, science depends to a far greater degree on the state and requirements of technology." And Marx had long ago observed, the engineers continued, that science consists not only of understanding the world but of remaking it; technology, in other words, is the means of remaking the world.

The applied scientists carefully noted that Semenov's proposed organization of the Academy was an expression of his views on the superiority of pure science: "His [Semenov's] reform plan makes no mention of the technical sciences. The reason for this is not at all clear—whether it is because there is no place for them in the Academy of Sciences or because they are not generally regarded as sciences. Such views are sometimes encountered among scientists. The well-known physicist Rutherford went so far as to claim that science is divided into only two classes: physics and stamp collecting." Blagonravov, Artobolevskii, Mints, Stechkin, and Petrov concluded that many of Semenov's errors stemmed from his beliefs "that true science should study the creation of God's hands, and that the study of the works of human hands is something lowly and unworthy of 'lofty science.'"

Other Viewpoints

The contest between the engineers and the fundamental scientists was now fully joined. However, the organizational issue involved was not a simple, two-sided question. Other factions of the scientific and technical intelligentsia submitted their opinions on the role and organization of the Academy of Sciences. The workers in the union-republic academies of sciences and the local research institutes were among the groups most concerned over

---

nificance"; a corresponding member is an "outstanding scientist." At meetings of the Academy, full members cast "decisive" votes, corresponding members cast "advisory" votes.

the proposed reform. These scientists feared that formation of a central planning committee for science and curtailment of administrative control by the U.S.S.R. Academy of Sciences would result in the loss of scientific independence by their institutions.

The local scientists found a spokesman in V. Kirillin, a corresponding member of the U.S.S.R. Academy of Sciences with an interest in the relations of Soviet nationalities. "We must reject the idea that a central organ can plan and coordinate all the scientific work being conducted in the various institutes, laboratories, and higher educational institutions in the Soviet Union," Kirillin wrote. "As a matter of fact, the number of scientific research institutes and higher educational establishments in our country is around 3,000. . . . It is difficult to imagine any sort of single, central institution."[12] Kirillin believed that instead of creating a central coordination agency for science, the government should organize scientific councils (nauchnye sovety) for each area of science and technology. Each council would coordinate research in its area, and institutions doing research in that area would send representatives to the council. Thus, coordination of research would be based on disciplines, and not on geographical or political considerations.

Kirillin's views were immediately supported by B. Paton, an academician (elected President in 1963) of the Ukrainian Academy of Sciences, which has always been sensitive to infringements on its independence. Founded in November, 1918, when the Ukraine was free of Bolsheviks, the Ukrainian Academy of Sciences has been involved in a number of disputes with the central Soviet authorities over alleged nationalism in science.[13] Paton, completely ignoring the idea of a supreme coordinating body for science, stated that the best way to direct research was through "coordination councils" in the most important establishments, or "head institutes" (golovnye instituty).[14]

Yet another voice heard in the discussion was that of the university professors; their criticism of the Academy of Sciences harked back to a rivalry that existed during much of the nineteenth century, when the faculty members of the universities often reprimanded the academicians for their political conservatism and their disregard of pedagogical and industrial concerns. In rebutting Semenov's arguments, Professor A. Kurosh of Moscow State University, Vice-President of the Moscow Mathematics Society, wrote angrily about what he considered was condescension toward the universities:

> Academician N. Semenov's suggestion that the universities—unlike the academies, whose basic task it is to seek out and establish new scientific trends—should regard their main scientific activity as being the development of already extant branches of science gives rise to serious objections. The suggestion may possibly have some sense as concerns those sciences that entail intricate and costly experiments, but in a majority of cases the position is quite otherwise. This is true, in particular, of mathematics. It is precisely the universities that are best adapted to the establishment and development of fundamentally new trends in theoretical mathematics . . . since it is there that the opportunity exists to draw into scientific research young students who are just taking their first steps in science and are therefore better able to grasp new ideas.[15]

Central to Kurosh's rebuttal is his belief that present-day academies of sciences the world over are encumbered by their venerable histories, and that they are therefore not suited to meet the challenges of modern research, as are the universities and industrial research organizations. The U.S.S.R. Academy of Sciences, he declared, has continued to predominate Soviet science in the twentieth century, even while the academies of Western Europe were declining in significance, only because the reforms of the early 1930's, in giving all Soviet society a voice in the Academy's affairs, brought that plodding institution into contact with life. Now Semenov's proposals threatened to make the Academy once again a sanctuary of "academism," or self-absorbed research. Kurosh concluded that the academies of sciences can contribute significantly to the introduction of new scientific ideas only "if they are more decisive in renouncing the 'academic' traditions that have been formed in the course of centuries. What is needed is for the wide scientific community to begin to play a decisive role in the life of the academies, and this includes planning the key orientations in their work."*

* The continuing rivalry between the U.S.S.R. Academy of Sciences and the universities was reflected recently in the proposal of M. Lavrent'ev, Vice-President of the Academy, that several experimental universities be created at which all instruction would be in the Academy's hands. *Izvestia*, July 26, 1966.

Todor Pavlov, President of the Bulgarian Academy of Sciences, came to the support of Semenov's plan in an article in *Izvestia* in which he displayed an understanding of the changes in the Marxist view of science.[16] Pavlov called the view that science flows up from below, rather than down from the top, "nihilistic," since it might lead to the desire to eliminate academies of sciences altogether and to rely only on industrial ministries and factory laboratories for progress in science. Pavlov insisted that although Academician Mints might prefer this arrangement, the academies could not be replaced, and, indeed, had become more important than ever.

The defenders of the Academy emphasized in all their articles that time was working in favor of the academies and the strengthening of theoretical science. A group of fundamental scientists, Academicians A. I. Alikhanov, M. I. Kabachnik, I. E. Tamm, and M. M. Shemiakin, in an article entitled "Times Have Changed," supported Semenov for that reason:

In the first years of Soviet power, when we had practically no scientific institutions other than the U.S.S.R. Academy of Sciences, it was natural to involve it in the solution of even relatively simple technological problems. . . . Now the presence of a number of technological institutes in the U.S.S.R. Academy of Sciences, serving fully developed branches of industry and occupied principally in perfecting extant branches of technology, has become an obvious anachronism.[17]

Semenov himself closed the series of articles on the proposed reform with a rebuttal, under a similarly progressive title, "Get in Step with the Times," which yielded very little to his critics.[18] On the opposition of his friend Bardin, he commented:

The divergence between my views and those of Academician I. P. Bardin . . . is in the specific question of the fate of the Academy's institutes that have a technical, or, as I call it, an industrial, specialization. Academician I. P. Bardin states that the results of physics and chemistry obtained in the institutes of the Academy's Physics and Mathematics Department and Chemistry Department cannot be directly shifted to the industrial institutes and plants. Therefore, there should be institutes of the Technical Sciences Department that act as a bridge between the institutes of the Physics and Mathematics Department or Chemistry Department and the institutes of the various branches of industry. . . . This system is not only cumbersome; it is unrealistic. The technical institutes have never played such a role in the history of the Academy. I do not know of one instance in which the achievements of the Academy's physics and chemistry institutes were introduced in industry with the help of institutes of the Technical Sciences Department.

On the question of the Institute of Metallurgy, Semenov was equally obstinate, refusing to grant it had any right to a place in the Academy:

> The Institute of Metallurgy is indeed working successfully on problems of the physics and chemistry of metals, but only one-third of its personnel is engaged in this. The remaining two-thirds are working on typical industrial problems. Therefore, either the entire institute or these two-thirds should be shifted to industry, while the remaining part is shifted to the Chemistry Department, since the physics and chemistry of metals is one of the tasks of physical chemistry.

Only on the question of the number of departments in the Academy did Semenov make concessions. He withdrew his proposal that the eight departments of the Academy be grouped into three, but he warned that excessive fragmentation of research was harmful, since the most interesting work was being done on the border lines of disciplines, such as in the overlapping areas of chemistry, physics, and biology. Furthermore, mathematics was becoming important in all areas. These factors, said Semenov, should be considered in any reorganization.

The New Needs of Soviet Society

The criticism directed against Semenov by the engineers, the university professors, and the local researchers added up to such a formidable expression of opinion that one could hardly have expected his views to prevail. Furthermore, Semenov's assumptions flew directly in the face of Marxist principles, at least as they had been interpreted during most of the Stalinist period. Yet all the evidence seems to indicate that from the very beginning Semenov's proposals were closer to the inclinations of the Party leadership than were his critics'. He was a member of the Party, an officer in the Presidium of the Academy, and a participant in several important government committees dealing with science and technology. More important, Semenov had taken his cue directly from Khrushchev.

Khrushchev's speech of June 29, 1959, contained the first public suggestion that the engineering institutes, such as the Institute of Metallurgy, be separated from the Academy. In this speech, Khrushchev had even implied that Bardin's election to the Academy had been an unwise move, despite the engineer's unquestioned abilities.[19] Although Khrushchev went on to invite debate on the question of reforming the Academy, he obviously did not occupy a neutral position. Apparently, he viewed the debate merely as a means of measuring the opposition to a policy that he intended to adopt but might modify in details. Semenov not only carefully diagnosed these indications from the leader of the Party, but, as his speeches and articles indicate, he was familiar with the reasons the Party leadership was determined to reverse its policy on the Academy.

What developments between 1930 and the late 1950's led Khrushchev and presumably some of his advisers to consider altering the composition and functions of the prestigious Academy of Sciences? An answer to this question must include a review of the changing goals of Soviet science and the accompanying ideological readjustments.

Prior to World War II, the Soviet Union's major goal was to increase industrial production, whatever the cost, and basic research had to be sacrificed to some extent. In this early phase of industrial expansion, practical needs dictated research objectives, which was in accordance with the Marxist theory of the development of science. Soviet planners of the 1930's believed it was immoral for geologists to study rock strata simply to determine the age of the earth, for oil deposits were desperately needed. Even the humanities had to adhere to pragmatic standards, and so anthropologists studied "Soviet man as a productive force" in the quest for ways to improve the efficiency of the worker or peasant. Men who had been educated as theoretical physicists were allocated to projects that called for mechanical engineers. Often these men performed well at their tasks, as did American theorists assigned to technological problems in World War II.[20] All academicians were required to make frequent trips to factories, in order to lecture workers on the close connection between science and production and to observe at firsthand the engineering problems confronting factory directors. The total number of persons with advanced scientific training was so small that the Party leaders decided they could not afford a sharp division of functions between those scientists engaged in fundamental research and those engaged in engineering research and development. The assignment of theoreticians to engineering tasks was inherently wasteful, but this system of allocation could at least be rationalized with the argument that so long as the Soviet Union remained a backward nation in both industry and science, it could obtain from Western nations the basic knowledge needed for the improvement of its technology.

After World War II, the national goal of Soviet science and technology slowly shifted. The steady rise in the nation's industrial strength contributed to its self-confidence and permitted a longer view at priorities. The growing number of engineering graduates enabled planners to make a more appropriate allocation of engineers and scientists; no longer did theoreticians need to enter directly into the processes of factory manufacture. The industrial plants created their own research and development laboratories and were thus freed of complete dependence on central institutes. Furthermore, as the general level of research in the U.S.S.R. approached that in the rest of the world, the Soviets had to provide more and more of their own basic scientific knowledge. As V. Glushkov, Vice-President of the Ukrainian Academy of Sciences, remarked: "In the future the role of pure science will be constantly growing. As long as we had the task of catching up with the technological development of the capitalist West, we could afford to devote less attention to long-range research, making wide use of the scientific and technological experience accumulated abroad. But those who are marching ahead have no one to learn from."[21]

These, then, were the specific developments that enhanced the idea of reforming the Academy of Sciences and restoring the importance of fundamental science. Moreover, the Marxist views of science had been reinterpreted, and the new theories would allow enactment of the reform without any violation of the Marxist principles that had justified the de-emphasis of fundamental science in the 1930's. Thus, Academician Semenov, more aware of this change in ideology, surprisingly enough, than the engineers who quoted Marx to him, could promote his reform ideas with relatively little fear of being reprimanded by Party ideologists.

The primary ideological issue relating to the reform of the Academy concerned the position of science relative to the productive forces of society. Is scientific research a derivative function of social organization, or is it an independent activity that may, at least on occasion, itself determine the direction of social activity? If Semenov's view that science possessed an "inner logic" or a "self-flow" were correct, science was not a derivative function of productive relationships, and the Academy could therefore justifiably divorce itself from narrow industrial concerns. However, if Bardin and his fellow engineers were correct in saying that pure science received its stimulus from industry, the expulsion of the engineering institutes was unwise, since the theoreticians would then be deprived of motivation in their research.

The Marxist ideologists of the 1930's agreed with the engineers of the 1950's in ascribing a derivative function to scientific research. According to Marxist-Leninist textbooks, the fundamental elements of social life were: (1) the productive forces of society (manpower, machinery, technology, natural resources), (2) the corresponding productive relations (socialist, capitalist, feudal, etc.), which together with the productive forces, form the "economic base," and (3) the ideological superstructure of society (law, morality, religion, art, etc.), which develop not independently but in response to changes in the "economic base." The early Soviet ideologists usually assigned science to the superstructure, believing in the creation not only of a new, class-oriented literature and art, but also of a new science. It was believed that "science is one of the highest, if not the highest of the layers of the superstructure."[22] In the late 1930's and the 1940's, the ideologists continued to include science in the superstructure, following the theories of the linguist N. Ya. Marr, who regarded as a part of the superstructure not only language but also the "highest ideologies," including art, philosophy, and science. If this view had prevailed, a reform of scientific research in the Soviet Union that had as its goal the granting of independence to theoretical research, which was Semenov's chief aim, could hardly have been reconciled with Marxist theory.

The belief that science was a part of the superstructure and therefore a derivative function of society became increasingly awkward, even in the Stalinist period. Marxist theory postulated, for example, that each epoch (feudalism, capitalism, socialism, etc.) had its own superstructure, and emphasized the discontinuities separating these stages. When a new economic base was formed, the old superstructure must fall. But while a Marxist might accept the theory that the Soviet Union needed a complete break with the capitalist superstructure in such fields as philosophy and art, he could hardly hold the same view as regards science. The development of science was obviously additive, and Soviet scientists were beginning where their Czarist predecessors had left off.

Moreover, scientific theory was becoming too independent and potent a force in society to be regarded as a mere reflection of economic relations. In the nineteenth century, there was a certain self-evident persuasiveness to Engels' remark that "if a technical demand appears in a society, then it will move science ahead more than ten universities."[23] By World War II, however, this statement could not be supported by facts. Science no longer served as the minion of industry, merely answering the demands placed on it. Instead, by giving birth to discoveries that shaped technology, it was creating industries that were not anticipated by Marxist economists and modifying social relations in ways not predicted by Marxist theoreticians. Far from being a part of the derivative superstructure, science seemed to be related to the formative economic base.

Late in his life, Stalin initiated an important re-evaluation of the role of science. In his *Letters on Linguistics*, he advanced several new theories, the effects of which in the areas of language and politics, but not in the field of science, are well known abroad.[24] Stalin introduced the concept of social activities that are a part of neither the base nor the superstructure, and stated that science was one of these activities. Discussion of these theories has continued to the present. They were an important issue in the debate over reform of the Academy, since they affected the autonomy of the theoretical sciences.

When Semenov urged the strengthening of theoretical science,

the question of the position of science in the ideological hierarchy
—base or superstructure?—had not yet been resolved. Yet he must
surely have sensed the growing prestige of the fundamental sciences, which led Party ideologists to declare, in the 1961 Party
Program, that "science will become, in the full sense of the word,
a direct productive force."[25] The indications were, then, that in the
near future, science would be considered a major independent
element of the economic base, a motive force which did not depend primarily on social organization or industrial production for
its advancement.

Reforms

Since 1960, the system of science administration in the Soviet
Union has been reformed twice, and the Academy's functions have
been considerably altered.[26] Although the views of no one group
have triumphed, Semenov's program seems to have been followed
more closely than that of any of the other groups. The first reform
was announced on April 12, 1961, the day Yuri Gagarin made the
first circumnavigation of the globe by artificial satellite. This 1961
decree, issued jointly by the Central Committee of the CPSU and
the Council of Ministers of the U.S.S.R., contained the announcement that narrow engineering institutes would be removed from
the Academy and placed under the jurisdiction of the industrial
ministries and state committees. The branches (*filialy*) of the Academy were assigned to the Council of Ministers of the R.S.F.S.R.,
which transferred operational control of them to the regional economic councils. That these changes were designed to permit the
Academy to concentrate upon fundamental research was clearly
indicated in the decree: "The work of the Academy should be
focused primarily on the most important long-run problems of science that are undergoing rapid development."[27]

Since the Academy was released by the reform from many of its
industrial tasks, it could no longer be the coordinating center of all
Soviet science. Therefore, a new organization, superior to the
Academy and in charge of all Soviet science, was established, the
State Committee of the Council of Ministers of the U.S.S.R. for
the Coordination of Scientific Research. The committee was to assign the Academy only the most important scientific problems and

to distribute the others to the industrial research laboratories and the universities.

Although the 1961 reform represented the enactment of many of the proposals made by the theoretical scientists, it failed to provide a rational system for the direction of scientific research. The fundamental scientists of the union-republic academies and the universities, now under the control of the State Committee for the Coordination of Scientific Research, wished to win the freedom of research already gained by the All-Union Academy.[28] The local academies, in an effort to broaden the fields of their research, were duplicating many studies already being conducted in other institutions. As one critic of the republic academies stated: "Each of the local academies modeled itself on the All-Union Academy and hoped to become competent in all fields."

The State Committee for the Coordination of Scientific Research found that the direction of engineering research in industry was considerably easier than the control of theoretical research in the republic and all-union academies. The 1961 reform represented a partial separation of the administration of theoretical research from that of applied research. The logical conclusion of this reform would be to end close governmental supervision also in the remaining theoretical laboratories—those of the republic academies and the universities. And, indeed, by 1963, articles in Party journals indicated that the Party had fully and officially recognized its inability to administer theoretical research. One author commented in the authoritative *Partinaya zhizn:*

> There are institutes and then there are institutes. Consider, for example, the V. I. Lenin All-Union Electro-Chemical Institute. . . . This is an institute with an industrial profile. . . . Party organizations are given the right to control the administration of such institutes. But we have institutes of another type, with so-called academic [theoretical] profiles. Among these, in particular, are the institutes of the U.S.S.R. Academy of Sciences and the union republics. . . . Here the party organizations do not have the right to control the administration.[29]

The second reform, in April, 1963, restored the control of the republic academies to the All-Union Academy, and also gave the head academy the authority to direct research in the universities as well. Thus, the U.S.S.R. Academy of Sciences emerged from the reforms as the supreme coordinator of theoretical research throughout the Soviet Union. Responsibility for control of applied research continued to rest with the State Committee for the Coordination of Scientic Research (transformed on October 2, 1965, into the All-Union State Committee for Science and Technology). The committee's functions were, therefore, somewhat more restricted than had been envisioned by the 1961 reforms. But, to a degree unknown since 1929, fundamental science had been accorded respect and freedom, and the direction of research in this area had been bestowed on scientists of distinction, rather than on political administrators.

The 1963 reform recast the former eight divisions of the Academy into fifteen. At first glance, this alteration seems to bear no similarity to Semenov's proposals. However, the fifteen divisions were assigned to three sections, each of which was to be headed by a vice-president of the Academy and organized along lines similar to, but not identical with, those originally suggested by Semenov, in August, 1959. The chemist later wavered on this particular point, and it is difficult to determine the exact relation between these three sections and Semenov's original proposal.

One of the best indications of the prevalence of Semenov's views over Bardin's was the fate of the Institute of Metallurgy. The retention of this institute in the Academy was one of Bardin's major goals. However, it was among the organizations turned over to industrial agencies. The engineering academicians retained their membership in the Academy, and advanced engineering research is still conducted in the Academy, but this research must promise results of fundamental importance, and not expansion of present knowledge. As Semenov noted, the Academy has always, as a matter of principle, divested itself of functions that can be performed by other organizations. Therefore, the removal of institutes from the Academy's jurisdiction should not be interpreted as a reduction of its status, but as a means of allowing it to concentrate its efforts on the most important areas of theoretical research.

Conclusions

The reforms of the Academy illustrate that the leaders of the Communist Party of the Soviet Union rely on the expert opinion of specialists in making decisions related to specific sectors of cultural and economic activity. But the reforms are an equally clear illustration that the Party does not consider itself neutral in the debates that lead up to decisions. At least under Khrushchev, such debates seemed to be a means of sounding out opposition to Party preferences, or of refining the details of an already formulated Party policy. Consequently, local interest groups may not be able to voice their complaints publicly until the proper signal is sounded by a prominent Party leader. Semenov's belief in the importance of fundamental research had been shared by the theoretical scientists of the Soviet Union for decades, but not until Khrushchev suggested the elimination of the most narrow engineering subjects from the Academy, and the necessary ideological adjustments were being made, could the theorists step out with a bold public espousal of their view. Nevertheless, the latitude in the discussion which then ensued was considerable, and enabled Western observers for the first time in many years to identify clear divisions among groups of Soviet scientists.

The discussions over the Academy were a conscious effort to redefine the national policy on science. Although the Soviet Union has consistently been one of the most energetic countries in the world in its support of science, it has altered both its goals in science and its evaluation of the functions of science. The major goal has been shifted from assisting the growth of heavy industry to attaining world-wide pre-eminence in basic research. At the same time, Soviet planners now believe that theoretical science plays an independent, not a derivative, role. Fundamental science is no longer viewed primarily as a symbol, a cultural and intellectual ornamentation of the Soviet state, although science is still often referred to in that way.

Soviet planners in the 1930's claimed that the socialist state would provide for the welfare of science, a part of the cultural superstructure; they now maintain that science, a part of the economic base, will provide for the welfare of the Communist state. The driving force of progress was previously held to be the socialist organization of society; Soviet leaders now often come close to saying that science will make possible such an organization of society. Of course, Soviet ideologists may reply that the application of Marxist theory to social relations is the genuine source of scientific progress, but in recent years the emphasis has been on science and technology, not on Marxism.

At the pinnacle of the Soviet scientific establishment, the U.S.S.R. Academy of Sciences benefited from the rising prestige of science. The academicians were granted privileges unequaled in the rest of Soviet society: Within certain assigned budgetary and thematic categories, they received authority to work as they wish. A predictable result of this was the shifting of control in research institutes from Party administrators to established senior scientists, a change that has been officially recognized in the Party rules.[30] Furthermore, the Party organizations within the institutes have been made up of distinguished scientists. In the Academy's Institute of Physical Chemistry, for example, eight of the nine members of the Party bureau hold the degree of *kandidat* or *doktor* of sciences, and all of the secretaries of the Party organizations of the individual laboratories within the Institute also hold one of these advanced degrees.

Even in engineering research institutes, where the Party still has administrative authority, Party stalwarts are becoming increasingly hesitant about interfering with researchers. Several recent authors advised Party workers in an electric locomotive research institute: "You cannot influence science and technology by shouting and beating your fist on the table. . . . Before criticizing, let alone making reprimands, you must thoroughly study the situation and be convinced as to why people did not fulfill their assignments. And in any case it is impermissible to punish a Communist scientist for failing to make a discovery or invention at exactly the desired moment."[31]

In the United States, many of the recent discussions concerning science and government have centered on methods of ensuring that scientists have a role in the making of political decisions. New ways are being sought, as Christopher Wright has written, "to build better bridges between the science community and the government."[32] Since World War II, a number of important positions for advisers on scientific affairs have been created in Congress and in the executive branch of the federal government. In the Soviet Union, the desire to bring scientists closer to the government has not been so strong as the desire to formulate national goals in science and to devise a rational means of directing science. This difference between the two countries is not surprising if one remembers that it has been only since World War II (or since the Manhattan Project) that the federal government in the United States has been committed to the promotion of scientific research on a large scale. Because of the centralized nature of the Soviet Union, however, the all-union organs have, since at least the 1924 Constitution, been deeply engaged in the promotion of scientific research and education. And, of course, the Soviet Government has never relied, nor found it necessary to rely, on the advice of local groups to the extent that any democracy must. Therefore, the organizational changes in response to the rise of science are more striking in the United States than in the Soviet Union. The U.S. Government's creation of the National Science Foundation in 1950, to advance fundamental research, elicited no response from the Soviet Union since this function had been performed on the all-union level there for decades.

But there are many indications that the United States has now moved ahead of the Soviet Union in integrating the scientist into governmental decision-making. There are no known equivalents in the Soviet Union to the President's Science Advisory Committee or the Special Assistant for Science and Technology. The irony of this situation becomes clear when it is noted that these positions were created in the United States in response to the challenge of keeping up with the Soviet Union in science and technology after the launching of Sputnik.

Although the Soviet Government may not have called upon the services of its scientists in any new or dramatic way in recent years, it has a long tradition of using science for national policy goals and perhaps does not need to listen to the interesting, but sometimes disrupting, views of its scientists on every possible issue. Soviet scientists are expected to confine their professional opinions to science. Thus, the most important public debate among scientists in the Soviet Union in many years was centered on the question of reorganizing the Academy of Sciences, not on general questions of governmental policy. Furthermore, many Soviet governmental leaders were educated in technical, if not scientific, fields. The Party itself unites the loyal supporters of the regime from all areas, and the scientists on the Central Committee are often called upon to present their views on scientific issues in the press. Within the framework of strict political control by the Party, the Soviet Union has devised a workable, but constantly evolving system for the inclusion of scientific advice in the process of making governmental decisions.

NOTES

1. World War I forced the Academy to turn a part of its attention to applied science. In 1915, the Academy created the Permanent Commission for the Study of the National Productive Resources of Russia (KEPS), a body which seemed at first to be a technological advisory committee for war needs, but which in modified form had a long history after the Revolution. Letter to the author from N. A. Figurovskii, director of the Institute of the History of Natural Sciences and Technology, Academy of Sciences, Moscow, June, 1961; and B. A. Lindener, *Raboty Rossiiskoi Akademii Nauk v oblasti issledovaniya prirodnykh bogatstv Rossii; obzor deyatel'nost' KEPS za 1915–1921 gg.* (Petrograd, 1922).

2. D. A. Senior, "The Organization of Scientific Research," *Survey* (July, 1964), p. 21.

3. In 1938, for example, Sovnarkom, the Council of People's Commissars (Ministers), rejected the Academy's work plan twice because of its "insufficient connection with the demands of economic construction." V. T. Ermakov, "Bor'ba kommunisticheskoi partii za perestroiku raboty nauchnykh uchrezhdenii v gody pervoi piatiletki" (dissertation for degree of Candidate, Department of the History of the Communist Party of the Soviet Union, Moscow State University), pp. 216 ff.

4. *Pravda*, February 14, 1956.

5. *Pravda*, July 2, 1959.

6. N. N. Semenov, "Nauka segodnya i zavtra," *Izvestia*, August 9, 1959. Semenov's article initiated a long series of articles on the same subject (see the following issues of *Izvestia*: August 18, 21, 28; September 2, 6, 27; October 14, 21; November 11; December 16).

7. I. P. Bardin, "Most mezhdu teoriei i praktikoi," *Izvestia*, August 28, 1959.

8. N. V. Lavrov, "O naukakh 'materinskikh' i teknicheskikh," *Literaturnaya gazeta*, September 10, 1959.

9. G. A. Kniazev and A. V. Koltsov, *Kratkii ocherk istorii Akademii Nauk SSSR* (Moscow and Leningrad, 1964), pp. 78–79. Practically every Soviet description of the Academy after the Revolution begins with a citation of this "Outline Plan," but there is little evidence that the Academy itself paid much attention to the plan. Alteration of the Academy's work to suit the Soviet Government did not commence until after 1929.

10. Lavrov, *op. cit.*

11. A. Blagonravov *et al.*, "Izuchat' i peredelyvat' mir," *Izvestia*, September 6, 1959.

12. V. Kirillin, "Nauka i zhizn'," *Pravda*, March 13, 1959.

13. E. Kh. Zankevich, *K istorii sovetizatsii Rossiiskoi Akademii Nauk* (Munich: Institute for the Study of the U.S.S.R, 1957), p. 22.

14. B. Paton, "Za korennoe uluchshenie planirovaniya i koordinatsii nauchnykh issledovanii," *Pravda*, May 10, 1959.

15. A. Kurosh, "Dorogu smelym ideyam," *Izvestia*, August 18, 1959.

16. Todor Pavlov, "Nekotorye aktual'nye problemy nauki i ee organizatsiya," *Izvestia*, November 11, 1959.

17. A. I. Alikhanov, M. I. Kabachnik, I. E. Tamm, and M. M. Shemiakin, "Vremia vremeni—rozn'," *Izvestia*, October 21, 1959.

18. N. N. Semenov, "Idti v nogu so vremenem," *Izvestia*, December 16, 1959.

19. *Pravda*, July 2, 1959.

20. As Robert Oppenheimer once commented, "The great lesson of the last decades has been that men of science who have spent their whole lives in the quest of new knowledge may be among the most gifted practitioners of technology." Quoted in Robert Gilpin and Christopher Wright (eds.), *Scientists and National Policy-Making* (New York and London: Columbia University Press, 1964), p. 9

21. V. Glushkov, "Prokladyvat' tropy v neznaemoe," *Izvestia*, October 19, 1963.

22. S. Volfson, "Nauka i bor'ba klassov," *VARNITSO*, February, 1930, p. 23. In the 1920's, by contrast, there were genuine and open differences of opinion among Soviet philosophers about the position of science in the ideological scheme.

23. K. Marx and F. Engels, *Izbrannye pis'ma* (Moscow, 1947), p. 469.

24. J. Stalin, *Marksizm i voprosy yazykoznaniya* (Moscow, 1950).

25. "Programma Kommunisticheskoi Partii Sovetskogo Soiuza," *Pravda*, July 30, 1961.

26. Academy President A. N. Nesmeyanov was removed from his position on May 19, 1961 (a few months ahead of the expiration of his normal term of office), and replaced by M. S. Keldysh. The reforms of the Academy were announced in "O merakh po uluchsheniyu koordinatsii nauchno-issledovatel'skikh rabot v strane i deyatel'nosti Akademii Nauk SSSR," *Pravda*, April 12, 1961; and in V. M. Keldysh, "O merakh po uluchsheniyu deyatel'nosti Akademii Nauk SSSR i akademii nauk soiuznykh respublik," *Vestnik Akademii Nauk SSSR*, June, 1963, pp. 4–22. For detailed analyses of these reforms, see Nicholas De Witt, "Reorganization of Science and Research in the U.S.S.R.," *Science*, July, 1961; D. A. Senior, *op. cit.*; and James M. Swanson, "Reorganization," *Survey*, July, 1964.

27. "O merakh po uluchsheniyu koordinatsii . . ."

28. From the author's discussions and interviews in Moscow, April and May, 1961, and May, 1963.

29. "Partorganizatsiya nauchno-issledovatel'skogo instituta," *Partinaya zhizn*, No. 16 (1963), p. 33.

30. This interpretation is based on the following statement in the 1961 rules: "Primary Party organizations of industrial enterprises and teaching establishments; state farms, collective farms; and design organizations, drafting offices, and research institutes directly related to production enjoy the right to control the work of the administration." If the research institutes are not directly related to production, i.e., are centers of basic research, the primary party organizations do not control the administration. "Partorganizatsiya nauchno-issledovatel'skogo instituta," p. 33; translation quoted from Jan F. Triska, *Soviet Communism: Programs and Rules* (San Francisco: Chandler Publishing Company, 1962), p. 191.

31. A. Navozov and V. Reut, "Provorot k nauke," *Pravda*, May 25, 1966.

32. Christopher Wright, "Scientists and the Establishment of Science Affairs," in Gilpin and Wright, *op. cit.*, p. 257.

7

The Campaign Against Parasites

Marianne Armstrong

EDITORS' INTRODUCTION

Work in the U.S.S.R. is a duty and a matter of honor for every able-bodied citizen, in accordance with the principle: He who does not work, neither shall he eat.

—Article 12 of the
1936 U.S.S.R. Constitution

In the period immediately after Stalin, Soviet leaders were confident that they could reshape the social fabric of society, by persuasion, by social pressure, and, if need be, by force. The reduction of terror, the amnestying of prisoners, and the general normalization of everyday life, which the leaders believed were steps in the right direction, did, however, encourage some deviant, "anti-social" behavior that the regime was eager to eliminate in its drive to build Communism. Comrades' courts, composed of citizens at work and at their domiciles, were organized to curb drunkenness, lateness, and minor acts of hooliganism. People's Guards, citizens with red armbands, were formed to assist the regular militia in maintaining public order in the streets. To rid itself of idlers, loafers, and shady dealers exhibiting an unsocialist attitude toward labor, the Party in 1957 launched a campaign against parasites. All fifteen union republics promulgated draft decrees against parasitic offenders. The drafts were intended for public discussion, but some proposed as maximum penalty the exiling of an offender to remote areas of the republic for a number of years.

From the account that follows, it is clear that the anti-parasite decrees departed from the regular criminal laws and procedures in two ways. First, they placed most proceedings outside the courts, in meetings of neighbors or fellow workers. Public participation became the order of the day. Second, they permitted the infliction of penalties other than by regular courts, laws, and procedures, thus resurrecting, in less horrible form, the Stalinist short cuts to social control through special boards of the security police and summary court procedures. This opened the door to measures against prostitutes, loafers, suspected speculators, playboys, and drunkards, whom, for one reason or another, the criminal code did not affect. It also permitted the repression of artistic nonconformism and other unwanted behavior not directly punishable under the Law Against State Crimes.

Marianne Armstrong follows the anti-parasite campaign through the experimental decrees in eight smaller republics, the public discussions, the revisions and applications throughout the U.S.S.R., and the further revisions. As in the movement for reform of the family law (see Chapter 2), lawyers and other experts played a large part in the debate. The proposed reform of the family law came upon initiative from below, and was attenuated by the conservatives in the Party. The anti-parasite campaign came upon initiative from above, and was attenuated by both the complaints of lawyers and the unfavorable results of the anti-parasite decrees. Some of the family reforms got through. Some of the anti-parasite campaign survived the years of trial and debate, too. And, finally, both episodes of policy-making were marked by relatively frank public debates that affected the confidential governmental and intra-institutional discussions.

Precedents for anti-parasite legislation existed both in Czarist and in Soviet Russia. The prerevolutionary Code of Criminal Procedure. in addition to regular court practices, provided for "neighborhood investigation" to determine "the kind of occupation, social connection, and way of life of the accused."[1] If found undesirable, the accused was banished from his place of residence. Immediately after the Revolution, the attempt to introduce popular justice led to nonprofessional judges' presiding over cases argued by people's lawyers and people's prosecutors with little, if any, legal training. When this resulted in failure, the regime found itself forced to re-establish traditional practices of law enforcement and procedure. In the early 1920's, new legal codes were promulgated in various branches of law, and the legal system was again in the hands of professionals.

With the Khrushchev era, the concept of popular justice was given new life. Soviet leaders hoped that massive social pressure, rather than mass terror, would reform individuals "who maliciously violate the rules of the socialist community."[2] One device seized upon was the old Czarist practice of banishing undesirable social elements by circumventing the existing court system and legal procedure.

Khrushchev, an early opponent of parasites, was the chief instigator of this move. As early as 1948, as First Secretary of the Ukrainian Communist Party, he had commended general meetings of collective farms "for cracking down on idlers, anti-social, and parasitic elements."[3] In February, 1956, as the leading Party spokesman, he called for mass participation against "people who do not work" in a major speech delivered to the Twentieth Congress of the CPSU.[4] This signaled a comprehensive campaign against parasites that was to reach full force in the spring of 1957. An important forerunner of the campaign was a 1956 decree issued by the U.S.S.R. Supreme Court on the subject of "getting itinerant gypsies to take jobs." The decree provided that "gypsies who are of age and who willfully avoid useful labor and indulge in vagrancy shall be sentenced by people's courts to exile for up to five years with corrective labor."

The Party was seriously disturbed by the non-socialist attitudes toward work that were being expressed by citizens in various walks of life. Many young graduates, preferring to remain in the major cities, would not accept assignments to distant areas where their skills were needed. Secondary-school graduates who were not placed in universities often refused to go to work. In 1955 in Yaroslavl

Oblast (Province), the majority of 2,140 youths who were not accepted by institutions of higher learning did not work because they hoped to be accepted by universities the following year.[5]

Work attitudes on collective farms remained a serious problem. *Sovetskaya Rossiya*, on August 27, 1957, reported that at the peak of the harvest season, when extra workers had to be brought from towns, some collective farmers refused to do any work. Instead, they spent their time loafing and drinking. In Kazakhstan, a Party secretary pointed to fifty farmers on a collective who spent their full time in speculatory activity.[6] Farmers were most often accused of using their horses to transport people and material for private gain, of enlarging their private plots to reap higher profits, and of grazing their cattle, for the same purpose, on the collective pasture.

Other persons scored were the black-market operators who rented out rooms privately at summer resorts, which was against the law, and the middlemen and handicraftsmen who, for their own profit and at the expense of the state, provided speedy and efficient services for scarce consumer items.

To correct the behavior of Soviet citizens "who want to enrich themselves at the expense of society, at the expense of other citizens,"[7] the fifteen union republics, beginning in the spring of 1957, issued drafts of decrees that were intended to curb parasitic behavior. The drafts, varying only slightly from one another, were directed against: "adult able-bodied citizens leading an anti-social, parasitic way of life, maliciously avoiding socially useful labor, and likewise living on unearned income; adult able-bodied citizens occupied in vagrancy or begging, and those beggars and vagrants unable to work or with limited ability to work who maliciously avoid placement in homes for invalids."[8]

A "general meeting" of neighbors was given jurisdiction over all types of parasites except vagrants and beggars.[9] The general meeting was to be formed in towns by either apartment-house committees or street committees and attended by a majority of the residents in that unit. In rural areas, it was to be organized by the village soviet. Only the Tadzhik and Latvian drafts specifically indicated who could initiate a charge of parasitism. (The Tadzhik draft provided that the charge could be made by a citizen or public organization. Latvia made this the prerogative of the militia and apartment-house management in towns, and in rural areas, of the local soviet.) [10]

The sentence, two to five years of exile to specially designated areas, was to be handed down by a voice vote of the majority of those present. Allowance was made for the meeting to limit itself to the issuance of a warning and the establishment of a trial period during which the accused was under obligation to change his mode of behavior. The decision to establish a trial period depended on the accused's promise to reform and on the sincerity of his repentance. The length of the trial period was not specified except in the Uzbek draft, which set a period of up to one year.[11] The executive committees of the district and village soviets were given the responsibility of checking the validity of the public sentence and passing final approval. Some of the drafts set time limits for the passage of final approval, none of which exceeded ten days. The sentence was to be carried out swiftly, but only the Latvian and Tadzhik drafts mentioned that this was the duty of the militia.

The Discussion

Once the draft laws were made public, a nation-wide discussion began. The discussion had a twofold purpose. On the popular level, it created a public awareness that anti-parasite laws would soon go into effect. Numerous meetings at places of work and residence were conducted on the evils of parasitic behavior and its social consequences. Newspaper articles and letters by irate citizens vigorously condemned anti-social elements. Parasites were thrust into the spotlight. One indignant shop-brigade leader from Georgia even went so far as to list the names of his fellow workers who, though working, were apparently not fulfilling the output standards that had been set for them.[12] Special committees, set up to explain the decrees to those who were guilty of avoiding socially useful work, were publicly credited with success in rehabilitating a great number of parasites. Instant rehabilitation was sometimes claimed: "On the collective farm named for Stalin, after becoming acquainted with the draft law, about ten shirkers and idlers expressed a desire to work."[13]

On another level, the discussion gave qualified and interested citizens an opportunity to suggest changes and even oppose specific sections of the proposed legislation. Thus, by permitting the interested parties, within limits, to state their views, the regime was able to draw on expert advice. The participants in the debate fell into two general groups, namely, the lawyers, judges, and procurators who opposed the decrees, and the government officials, political activists, and average workers who were in favor of them.

The critics attacked the vagueness of the definition of parasitism, the setting up of sanctions outside the regular criminal code and criminal procedure, the exclusion of the procuracy, the wide authority given to an extrajudicial body (the general meeting), and the failure to allow the defendant various procedural guarantees provided for under criminal code procedure. Generally speaking, their objections reflected a desire to restrict the investigative and judicial functions that would be assigned to public organizations.

The provisions for personal liability under the new legislation disturbed the critics. G. Sevlikyants, a senior instructor at the Tadzhik State University, expressed the opinion that the phrase "working for appearance' sake, but actually living on unearned income" was subject to broad interpretation and could, for example, result in the prosecution of a person who had a job but who in his spare time raised animals on his private plot and sold them on the open market.[14] Others objected that the anti-parasite laws could be applied to persons who were really liable under the criminal code. G. Anashkin, a leading jurist and Vice-Chairman of the R.S.F.S.R. Supreme Court,* claimed that those living on unearned income, whether working for appearance' sake or not, were usually engaged in "speculation, embezzling of state or public property and the like."[15] Some observed that only criminals such as "speculators, thieves, murderers, and swindlers" could afford to avoid socially useful labor and lead a parasitic way of life for any extensive length of time.[16] It appeared to them that the accepted distinction between a criminal act and a parasitic act was extremely vague.

Other suggestions, offered for the most part by laymen, pertained to enlarging the list of parasitic activities to include enterprise and farm managers whose poor organizational work resulted in the forced idleness of workers, parents who permitted their children to lead idle lives, parents who illegally lived on state support

* He is now head of the Criminal Collegium of the U.S.S.R. Supreme Court.

that their children received, and citizens who were guilty of indulging in "domestic squabbles and gossip and slander."[17] Although the laws as finally adopted did not incorporate any of these suggestions, one cannot say with certainty that the offenders listed here did not at least feel the pressure of the legislation.

The exclusion of the procuracy, the lack of regular judicial procedure, and the authority given to an extrajudicial body drew a critical reaction from M. Naelapea, the Assistant Procurator of Talin. He emphasized that the guilt of the accused must be established beyond any doubt and that only a carefully conducted preliminary investigation under the procurator's supervision could assure that this was done. He argued that the rural soviets and the street and apartment-house committees were not qualified to assume the functions that had been assigned to them.[18]

Anashkin, although opposed to parasitic behavior, believed that "public organizations must not assume the function of judicial investigative agencies." He argued that the failure to observe strict judicial procedure would result in violations of socialist legality; the innocent would be tried as parasites, and criminals could evade prosecution under the criminal code and receive only the penalties provided for by the anti-parasite legislation. He condemned the very method of carrying out the sentence of exile as being contrary to Article 127 of the U.S.S.R. Constitution and to Article 131 of the R.S.F.S.R. Constitution, which guaranteed that "no one may be subject to arrest except by decision of the court or with the sanction of the procurator."[19] Two lawyers in the Kirgiz Republic maintained that unless the accused was allowed to introduce witnesses and documents, the proposed legislation would be in violation of Article 111 of the U.S.S.R. Constitution, which stated that "the accused is guaranteed the right to defense."[20] M. Bolshakov, a consultant in the Tadzhik Ministry of Justice, pointed out that since the right of appeal is "an inalienable principle of socialist democracy," the convicted parasite should be allowed to appeal in a people's court both the public sentence and the approval of the sentence by the executive committee of the village or district soviet.[21] Bolshakov's suggestion was denounced by Yuri Kasatkin, a law professor, as contrary to the main purpose of the legislation, which was "to give the Soviet public broad powers to combat anti-social, parasitic elements." Allowing an appeal to the people's courts would curtail the role of society and shift the major responsibility to the regular judicial agencies.[22]

Anashkin agreed that the public should participate more actively in the struggle against anti-social elements, since this would be in keeping with the view the Party had expressed at the Twentieth Congress: "It is necessary to create such an atmosphere that people who violate the norms of behavior, the principles of Soviet morality, shall feel the condemnation of the whole of society." However, Anashkin questioned the legality of the general meeting on the grounds that the penalty provided for by the legislation was not an expression of social condemnation but a "form of criminal punishment of a judicial nature," which should be inflicted only by a court acting in accordance with established judicial procedure.[23] Another leading jurist, Dr. I. Perlov, accused Anashkin of minimizing the "great moral strength" of the public sentence. Yet Perlov himself had some reservations about the proposed legislation. He suggested that the convicted parasite be allowed to appeal the public sentence to a people's court and that the laws be more detailed with respect to such procedural questions as who would be responsible for the defendant during the trial period, what would be the minimum and maximum length of the trial period, and what would be the procedure if no reform was forthcoming.[24]

Some suggested that hearings be conducted by nonjudiciary bodies but not necessarily at public meetings. Thus an assistant procurator from Kazakhstan wanted the accused to be tried by a street committee in the presence of a deputy from the local soviet and without the attendance of any specific number of citizens. The decision of the street committee would be subject to the final approval of the executive committee of the local soviet.[25] M. Mullaev, a candidate of juridical sciences, said that it would be difficult and at times impossible to gather a majority of the inhabitants living in the territory of an apartment-house committee or street committee. He suggested that cases be examined instead by the apartment-house committee, street committee, or rural soviet, presumably in the presence of those citizens interested enough to attend such meetings.[26] A member of the Kazakh Supreme Court recommended that the local soviet warn persons who were leading parasitic lives and that if no reform took place, the militia should exile the offender after the local executive committee had given its approval.[27]

Various proposals regarding the severity of the sentence were put forward. The more lenient among them contained recommendations for such punishments as one year at corrective labor, with the infliction of exile only if no reform was made by the end of the year. I. Perlov went a step further and proposed that prior release should be allowed for parasites who had reformed during exile. Also suggested was the compulsory placement of parasites in jobs by the executive committees. This suggestion, which was endorsed as a way of dealing with individuals with large families, who would suffer separation otherwise, foreshadowed the 1965 changes in the decrees.

Partisans of greater harshness suggested not only that there be no provision for a trial period but that the term of exile be lengthened to seven years and the parasite not be allowed to return home. One Latvian worker commented that more suitable nomenclature, such as "compulsory moving" or "compulsory resettlement," might be substituted for the word "exile," which was too closely associated with Czarist rule.[28]

The First Anti-Parasite Decrees

Although most suggestions critical of the draft decrees were not immediately adopted, the regime decided, between 1957 and 1959, to test the decrees in eight smaller republics: five in Central Asia, two in the Caucasus region, and one in the Baltic area. People living in the R.S.F.S.R., the Ukraine, and Belorussia, that is, a majority of the population, remained unaffected by anti-parasite legislation until 1961, when the laws were universally adopted—but with significant changes, some of which had been advocated during the debate on the campaign.

The 1957–59 changes were limited to provisions for prior release, in the Azerbaidzhan and Kirgiz republics, and to specified lengths of time for the trial period in the Armenian, Azerbaidzhan, and Uzbek republics. Moreover, the republic governments issued instructions that clarified the procedure to be followed in sentencing parasites.[29]

Despite the adoption of the anti-parasite decrees in eight repub-

lics, the debate continued in 1960. In October, the editors of
Sovetskaya Yustitsiya, the journal of the R.S.F.S.R. Supreme Court,
came out strongly against the suggestion of some readers that parasites be sentenced to compulsory labor terms. This, the editors
wrote, was "completely alien to socialism." They were in favor of
eliminating exile convictions for parasites and replacing them with
economic sanctions that carried such penalties as annulment of
the right to a private plot if unearned income was being derived
from unauthorized construction of homes and dachas (summer
homes); annulment of the right to a private plot if used to raise
products sold at speculative prices on the private market; confisca-
tion of automobiles used to derive unearned income; and exclusion
of parasites from waiting lists for apartments.

A National Policy

The debate over the principles behind the decrees was given new
life when apparently serious practical difficulties arose in the implementation of the 1957–59 decrees in the eight smaller republics.
A group of deputies of the Azerbaidzhan Supreme Soviet complained, for example, that executive committees in their republic
often failed to annul improper decisions of the general meetings.
The deputies pointed out that slack prosecution of parasites
sometimes led to the parasites becoming involved in criminal activities.[30] The Secretary of the Kirgiz Communist Party Central
Committee reported that public (Party, trade-union, Komsomol,
etc.) organizations in the Kirgiz Republic had been slow to expose
able-bodied heads of families who had, he declared, distorted the
"national tradition" of respect for elders by refusing to work and
by spending their time at bazaars and tea rooms.[31]

Failings such as these, plus the criticism voiced by jurists in the
public discussion of the decrees, may have been behind the revisions in 1960/61 that accompanied the extension of the anti-parasite legislation to the entire U.S.S.R. The Georgian anti-parasite
decree of 1960 contained one feature that dominated later revisions. This was a general retreat from "the further extension of Soviet democracy," as enthusiastic ideologues had termed the public's
participation in the anti-parasite campaign through the general
meetings. The 1960 Georgian decree took away from the gen-

eral meeting the power to exile, which it had been granted in the 1957–59 decrees, and provided that it, and public organizations and the militia, could merely recommend to the executive committee of the local soviet the infliction of the sentence of exile. Parasites, moreover, could be paroled after serving only half the term of exile. However, the other liberalizations in the Georgian decree —the milder penalties of from six months' to two years' exile, and the stipulation that exile be within the borders of the republic— were swept aside in the intransigent atmosphere of 1961, the year death sentences were introduced for a range of economic crimes.[32]

In May, 1961, the R.S.F.S.R. finally passed its own version of an anti-parasite decree, which was soon closely copied by all the other union republics, whether or not they already had their own decrees.[33]

The fifteen decrees of 1961, like the short-lived Georgian decree of 1960, reduced the formal role of society by limiting the role of general meetings in these significant ways: (1) The militia and the procuracy were directed to expose those guilty of leading "an antisocial, parasitic way of life" and to investigate each case thoroughly. They could begin an investigation either on the basis of material gathered by them or upon the word of a public organization or citizen. (2) After this investigation, the procurator could send the case to a people's court or to a general meeting at a place of work, where sentence would be passed. (3) The procurator could protest the verdict in a higher court. (4) General meetings of neighbors were eliminated.

Able-bodied citizens not working at all and living on unearned income were subject to exile upon the decision of a district or village people's court. Georgia, during the May, 1961, revisions, made this category of parasites subject to sentence by either a people's court or the executive committee of the district soviet,[34] while Estonia provided that either a general meeting or a people's court could handle such cases.[35]

Parasites allegedly working only for appearance' sake but actually living on unearned income were subject to the jurisdiction of either a people's court or a general meeting at their place of employment. The verdict of the general meeting had to be approved by the executive committee of the local soviet. In practice, the courts took over from the general meeting—the procurators generally exercised their right to decide which body should hear the case in favor of the courts.

Although offenders were still subject to exile for two to five years, warning followed by a trial period became mandatory. Most of the decrees specified that a parasite was to be exiled only if he refused to reform during the trial period established for him. However, if he reformed, he could be released before the completion of his sentence, as under the 1960 Georgian decree.

The new decrees practically omitted mention of begging and vagrancy. Begging was listed as merely one type of parasitic activity among many, and only the Azerbaidzhan decree mentioned vagrancy. Although all the decrees noted that parasitism is often accompanied by drunkenness, only the Estonian and Ukrainian decrees contained articles that dealt specifically with alcoholism.

Unlike the original anti-parasite legislation, the new decrees carefully spelled out what kind of behavior was to be considered parasitic: "occupation in forbidden business, speculation, begging, obtaining unearned income from the exploitation of private cars, the employment of hired labor, obtaining unearned income from dachas and land plots, the construction of homes and dachas with illegally acquired funds and the use of illegally acquired building materials, and other anti-social acts."[36]

Sufficient vagueness remained in this last phrase, "other anti-social acts," however, to save the decree's usefulness as a means of repression through administrative exile. By labeling socially or politically undesirable persons as parasites, local officials could exile them, thus terminating their "anti-social activities." *Nauka i religiya* (*Science and Religion*) has called those studying for a religious life "in reality the same as parasites."[37] Six leaders of clandestine religious sects were exiled under the R.S.F.S.R. decree for working only for appearance' sake while actually living off the contributions of their followers.[38] *Izvestia* suggested that citizens seeking the company of foreigners, the "loafers and hangers-on of foreign embassies," should be exposed to the wrath of the "public" and expelled from the big cities.[39] Anti-parasite decrees provided weapons against nonconformist intellectuals. One of their number, the talented Joseph Brodsky, was convicted as a parasite by a Leningrad people's court and sentenced to a maximum of five years' exile in the harsh Arkhangelsk region despite a strong defense by leading intellectuals and the absence of any anti-Soviet passages in his translations and poetry. (See Chapter 4.)

Implementation Brings Further Changes

No all-union statistics have appeared to tell us how many parasites in the U.S.S.R. have been warned, reformed, or exiled under the 1961 decrees. Harold Berman received a reliable report that in Moscow, during the first year of the R.S.F.S.R. decree, 2,000 persons were exiled and 8,000 more were warned.[40] The declining publicity for anti-parasite procedures indicates the probable falling off of the campaign since then. Berman's data tallied with claims emanating from the U.S.S.R. Supreme Court in 1961 and 1963 to the effect that the majority of parasites reformed after receiving warnings.[41]

A report issued by the U.S.S.R. Supreme Court in September, 1961, was the first comprehensive survey of the results of the anti-parasite measures. The fact that the report was prepared by the highest court in the Soviet Union is further evidence of the metamorphosis of anti-parasitism from a social to a judicial campaign. Although statistics were not published, the Supreme Court painted a grim picture of abuse and inefficiency, listing many "shortcomings" in the struggle against parasites.[42]

A close look at the press reports on the anti-parasite campaign reveals that abuses by officials and evasion by parasites persisted despite the Supreme Court's report. This helps explain why, as we shall see, the anti-parasite laws were further limited after the ouster of the campaign's initiator, Khrushchev. In particular, the warning period was abused by both the officials and the parasites. Some parasites received unrealistically short warning periods of from two to seven days in which to find jobs. In some districts of Moscow, a ten-day period was established, but the people's courts refused to pass sentence on the grounds that this period was inadequate. The confusion arose because the 1961 decrees (for the sake of flexibility, it was said) did not specify the length of the warning period.[43] Anashkin, showing a sustained interest in this area, complained that the trial periods were often set without taking into consideration whether a person was able to go to work outside the limits of his town or district.[44]

Carelessness led to the illegal application of the decrees to persons temporarily employed, to "pensioners, certain classifications of invalids, or those who had temporarily lost their ability to work, to women with minor children, to persons suffering from illnesses which impede their ability at work, and those who need special medical attention."[45]

A people's court sentenced a young woman to three years of exile. The verdict was annulled, however, when the regional procurator established that the girl was incapable of working because of mental deficiency and was being supported by her father. One man received a sentence of three years of exile on the basis of testimony given by three women who had a grudge against him. The sentence was eventually annulled by the Criminal Collegium of the R.S.F.S.R. Supreme Court, which found that he had a good work record and had even been a Party activist. Nevertheless, no action was taken against the women who had given the false testimony.[46]

Abuses occurred on the collective farms, where the authorities attempted to use the decrees to pressure peasants into spending less time on their garden plots. The management on one farm illegally accused a peasant of parasitism because it had decided to exile "not less than four to eight people" in order to improve labor discipline. The militia, the procurator, and the people's court worked in collusion with the farm management. One hundred and eight of the defendant's fellow peasants signed a letter testifying that he was not guilty, but not one of the signers was permitted to testify in court. In fact, they were all expelled from the court room and some of them lost their jobs. Despite the fact that only the farm management had been allowed to speak, the sentence of exile was annulled by the presidium of the regional court.[47]

The observers of this chaos no doubt found little solace in the knowledge that despite the illegal sentencing of innocent persons, the decrees frequently punished the guilty. Apparently, the guilty were often no more than unfortunate derelicts, whom the investigative agencies picked on since they were easier to unmask than parasites who carefully reported to work each day.[48] This was confirmed by information published a few months after the passage of the R.S.F.S.R. decree. It indicated that the majority of exiles did not have a "definite occupation, drifted from one job to another, and before resettlement had not worked for a long period of time and had ignored warnings to go to work." They lived on money obtained from parents and relatives, and most of them were "drunks or hooligans, or engaged in petty speculation." A third of them had prior convictions. S. was described as a typical example. Born in 1938, he was sentenced to ten years for aggravated theft in 1956. He was released in 1960, but chronic drunkenness kept him from holding a job. He managed to live off his winnings from playing cards with juveniles. Eventually, he was sentenced to five years in exile.[49]

Once the parasites had been condemned, taking care of them in exile raised serious problems of its own. Reformed parasites could be paroled. But how was one to parole a parasite if the people's court at the place of exile, seeking approval of the executive committee in his home district, found that he had been so transient before exile that no local government knew him sufficiently to vouch for him? When an exiled parasite became too sick to work, or was impaired by injury, the court had to obtain permission for his release from the procurator who had handled his case back home. The attempt to obtain this permission could be so protracted or fruitless that the court at the place of exile might release the parasite on humanitarian grounds, without the necessary approval.[50]

Many convicted persons continued their parasitism in exile and often went on to commit crimes. The U.S.S.R. Supreme Court officially deplored the lack of proper "working and living conditions" in some exile areas.[51] Plant and farm managers were refusing to hire people who "need nursemaids and watchmen to stand over them"; exiles were being assigned to work in the same groups, with the result that those who wanted to reform were prevented from doing so by the more stubborn offenders;[52] some were being placed in badly working collectives rather than in the superior groups; others had lost all incentive to work because their parents and relatives were sending them parcels and money (one parasite was reported to have received 200 rubles a month from his parents). In sum, the administration of the exile areas was inadequate. Only one militia inspector was in charge of the 150 to 200 parasites who were spread over a huge district in Krasnoyarsk.

By reporting to the inspector once a month, the exiles were virtually free to do what they liked for the rest of the time. Many regularly left the exile area, and their employers did not always bother to report their absences. When they were caught, the punishments were frequently mild, perhaps fifteen days in jail.[53]

Thus, the difficulties arising in the implementation of the 1961 decrees were so great that the Soviet Government was forced to re-examine its policy on parasites.

Under Khrushchev, the U.S.S.R. Supreme Court reacted to these difficulties by ordering that warning periods prior to exile be lengthened in certain cases, that parasites not be tried until all available evidence was carefully gathered, and that this evidence must include "facts concerning the behavior of the accused, his means of support, his record of anti-social offenses, his personal data, such as age, health, family situation, past work record, convictions."

The Supreme Court admonished the people's courts to call all necessary witnesses, and not limit themselves to the explanations of the militia representatives and the defendant; to remind all witnesses of the penalties for giving false testimony; to hear cases in open court with a regular bench, which consisted of a judge and two people's assessors (lay judges); and to allow the accused "to study the case material, to petition for the introduction of additional data, including documents, and to call witnesses" (the regular procedure in criminal cases).

An important directive issued by the Supreme Court in 1963 stated that "in cases in which the procurator participates in the trial or the defendant petitions for legal counsel, the court must admit a defense attorney."[54] This represented a defeat for such hard-liners as the procurator and the scholar who a few months after the adoption of the 1961 R.S.F.S.R. decree had reproved those people's courts which granted defendants the right to petition for counsel and allowed the procurator to take part in the trial (also features of the regular criminal procedure).[55] The Supreme Court's order, then, was a victory for the liberalizers, such as the officials in the Leningrad procuracy who had reproached their fellow procurators for not exercising their right to participate in parasite trials.[56]

By 1963, the professionals and the courts had clearly taken over from the public. General meetings at places of employment heard only 10 per cent of all cases in 1961–63 in Lithuania, and only 2 per cent in the Tatar Autonomous Republic.[57] The Supreme Court implicitly approved this trend, suggesting only that a suitable role for the public might be provided through the use of "visiting sessions" of people's courts. These were, in fact, regular sessions of the people's courts that would be held at places of employment and residence and in clubs, before perhaps hundreds of onlookers.[58]

Further Retrenchment After Khrushchev

On October 6, 1965, exactly a year after Khrushchev's fall, a major revision in the R.S.F.S.R. anti-parasite decree went into effect.[59] It presented a new, limited definition of a parasite—any "able-bodied person stubbornly refusing to engage in honest work, and leading an anti-social, parasitic way of life." No mention was made of persons who work but who actually live on unearned income, that is, who work only for appearance' sake. The role of the public in the form of general meetings at places of employment (the only general meetings then empowered to pass sentence), was completely eliminated. The penalty of exile was abolished in most of the R.S.F.S.R. Upon decision of the local executive committees, parasites could be sent to work "in enterprises located in the district of their permanent place of residence or in locations within the limits of the province, region, or autonomous republic." A decision of the executive committee was not subject to appeal. In Moscow, the province of Moscow, and Leningrad, the people's courts had jurisdiction over all anti-parasite cases. The approval of the procurator was still to be obtained before the militia could send the case to a people's court and the people's courts could still apply the penalty of exile "to specially designated areas" for two to five years with obligation to work. The sentence of the people's court was still not subject to appeal.

No change was made in the provision for prior release from exile after not less than a half of the sentence had been served. The decision to allow such release was now, however, within the jurisdiction of the people's court in the place of exile, a jurisdiction which some courts, as mentioned, had earlier assumed on their own initiative.

These revisions represented the near-demise of one of Khrushchev's favorite policies. The anti-parasite proceedings may still disappear altogether, as did the school reforms of 1958, the Party reorganization of 1962, the regional economic councils, the premature campaign against private farming, and other Khrushchev measures. Khrushchev, it seems, initiated the anti-parasite campaign as a measure of grass-roots social control in line with his efforts to increase public participation in the hope of deprofessionalizing law enforcement and social control. Despite jurists' protests, experimental decrees were enacted in eight of the smaller republics. However, a shift toward participation by judicial agencies appeared in the 1960 and 1961 decrees. Although professional legal opinion had not blocked the campaign, it had finally mitigated the harshness of the decrees. Continuing difficulties in implementing the decrees prompted the courts (presumably with Party approval) to make further revisions, in 1961–63. By 1961, the anti-parasite hearings had moved from general meetings of neighbors and people's courts (1957–61), to people's courts and general meetings at places of employment, to people's courts primarily (1960–61), and finally, in 1965, to people's courts only, with exile a punishment in only a few localities (though assignment to work within the borders of one's province was still a common sentence).

Khrushchev, of course, had increasingly advocated a rational approach to administration. The anti-parasite campaign itself had been considerably transformed while he was still the leader. Although the new regime apparently still considers it correct to force people to work under threat of communal sanctions, one must not forget the willingness of the post-Stalinist regimes to consult, to keep communications open, to allow judicial reinterpretation. These are, perhaps, signs of some political evolution. The Soviet system is not based on the Western principles of parliamentary democracy, privacy, and due process of law, but the professionals, though they have no authorized power, no established rights of expression, do have the power that comes from the dependence of the Party on their expert opinion for the efficient operation of the Soviet system.

NOTES

1. R. Beermann, "The Parasites Law," *Soviet Studies*, XIII, No. 2 (October, 1961), 205.
2. N. S. Khrushchev's speech to the Twentieth Party Congress, in L. Gruliow (ed.), *Current Soviet Policies—II* (New York: Frederick A. Praeger, 1957), p. 54.
3. See A. Boiter, "Comradely Justice: How Durable Is It?" *Problems of Communism*, XIV, No. 2 (March–April, 1965), 87.
4. L. Gruliow, *op. cit.*, p. 54.
5. *Current Digest of the Soviet Press* (hereafter cited as *CDSP*) VIII, No. 26 (August 8, 1956), 25.
6. *Kazakhstanskaya pravda*, May 18, 1957, p. 3.
7. A. Denisov and E. Kirichenko, *Soviet State Law* (Moscow: Foreign Languages Publishing House, 1960), p. 130.
8. From the R.S.F.S.R. Anti-Parasite Draft Decree, in *Sovetskaya Rossiya*, August 21, 1957.
9. Able-bodied vagrants and beggars were to be tried by people's courts and were subject to the penalty of exile with duty to work for two to five years. Vagrants and beggars unable to work were sent to homes for invalids.
10. *Kommunist Tadzhikistan*, May 10, 1957; and *Sovetskaya Latviya*, April 11, 1957.
11. *Pravda Vostoka*, April 26, 1957.
12. *Zarya Vostoka*, August, 24, 1957.
13. *Kommunist Tadzhikistan*, May 26, 1957.
14. *Ibid.*, May 18, 1957.
15. *Sovetskaya Rossiya*, October 12, 1957.
16. *Sovetskaya Estoniya*, October 11, 1957.
17. H. J. Berman, *Materials for Comparison of Soviet and American Law* (Cambridge, Mass.: Harvard Law School, 1958), pp. 368, 370.
18. *Sovetskaya Estoniya*, June 15, 1957.
19. Quoted in G. Anashkin, *Sovetskaya Rossiya*, October 12, 1957.
20. *CDSP*, IX, No. 27 (August 14, 1957), 8.
21. *Kommunist Tadzhikistan*, May 17, 1957.
22. *CDSP*, IX, No. 27, 4.
23. Anashkin, *op. cit.*
24. I. Perlov, *Sovetskaya Rossiya*, October 19, 1957.
25. *CDSP*, IX, No. 27, 7.
26. *Kommunist Tadzhikistan*, May 26, 1957.
27. *CDSP*, IX, No. 27, 5.
28. Berman, *op. cit.*, p. 321.
29. For example, in the Kirgiz Republic the case material was to be examined in the presence of the defendant, who was to be called to account by means of a summons. If the accused failed to report without having sent a valid excuse, the case was tried *in absentio*. At the general meeting, a representative of the district or village executive committee was ordered to be present to assure orderly procedure. The general meeting was to elect a chairman and a presidium of three to five members to conduct the proceedings. The decision of the general meeting was to be immediately

presented to the local executive committee for approval, after which the
executive committee would send its decision to the Ministry of Internal
Affairs, which would implement it. *Sovetskaya Kirgiziya*, February 19,
1959.

30. *Sotsialisticheskaya zakonnost'*, No. 8 (1961), p. 69.
31. *CDSP*, XII, No. 23 (July 6, 1960), 27.
32. *CDSP*, XII, No. 44 (November 30, 1960), 12.
33. *Sovetskaya Rossiya*, May 5, 1961.
34. *Zaria Vostoka*, June 15, 1961.
35. *Sovetskaya Estoniya*, June 11, 1965.
36. *Sovetskaya Rossiya*, May 5, 1961.
37. "Molodezh' i religiya," *Nauka i religiya*, August 8, 1962, p. 4.
38. *CDSP*, XIV, No. 7 (March 14, 1962), 10.
39. *CDSP*, XV, No. 21 (June 19, 1963), 24.
40. H. J. Berman, *Justice in the USSR* (New York: Vintage Books, 1963),
    p. 85.
41. *Byulleten' Verkhovnogo Suda SSSR*, No. 5 (1961), p. 9; and G. Anashkin
    and B. Kolchin, in *Sotsialisticheskaya zakonnost'*, No. 7 (1963), p. 15.
42. *Byulleten' Verkhovnogo Suda SSSR*, No. 5 (1961), for the report.
43. A. S. Shlyapochnikov, "Praktika bor'by s tuneyadstvom," *Sovetskaya
    yustitsiya*, No. 16 (1961), p. 9; P. P. Lukanov, "Praktika bor'by s anti-
    obshchestvennymi elementami," *Sovetskoe gosudarstva i pravo*, No. 3
    (1962), p. 1.
44. Anashkin and Kolchin, *op. cit.*, p. 17.
45. *Byulleten' Verkhovnogo Suda SSSR*, No. 3 (1963), p. 11.
46. For the examples in this paragraph see V. Bolysov and Ya. Gurvich, "I z
    praktiki primeneniya zakonodatel'stvo o tuneiadtsakh," *Sovetskaya yusti-
    tsiya*, No. 18 (1961), p. 10; and A. S. Shlyapochnikov, "Voprosy usi-
    leniya gosudarstvennopravovogo i obshchestvennogo vozdeistviya v bor'ba
    paraziticheskimi elementami," *Sovetskoe gosudarstvo i pravo*, No. 9
    (1963), p. 47.
47. Yu. Georgiev, "Kak ne nado borotsya s tuneyadstvom," *Sovetskaya
    yustitsiya*, No. 6 (1964), p. 20.
48. B. Kim, "Bor'ba s tuneyadstvom," *Sotsialisticheskaya zakonnost'*, No. 3
    (1962), p. 48.
49. A. S. Shlyapochnikov, "Praktika bor'by s tuneyadstvom," p. 8.
50. L. Adushkin, "Zakonodatel'stvo o tuneyadtsakh nuzhdaetsya vo dopolne-
    niyakh," *Sovetskaya yustitsiya*, No. 21 (1962), pp. 12–13.
51. *Byulleten' Verkhovnogo Suda SSSR*, No. 3 (1963), p. 12.
52. *CDSP*, XIV, No. 34 (September 19, 1962), 17.
53. V. Ivanov, "I vot tuneyadtsev, vyselilii . . . ," *Molodoi Kommunist*,
    No. 4 (1964), pp. 99–101.
54. See *Byulleten' Verkhovnogo Suda SSSR*, No. 5 (1961) and No. 3 (1963).
55. V. Bolysov and Ya. Gurvich, *op. cit.*, p. 11.
56. S. Averianov and A. Borodankov, "Organy prokuratura v bor'ba s
    tuneyatsvom," *Sotsialisticheskaya zakonnost'*, No. 10 (1962), p. 50.
57. Anashkin and Kolchin, *op. cit.*, p. 15.
58. *Byulleten' Verkhovnogo Suda SSSR*, No. 5 (1961) and No. 3 (1963);
    and Averianov and Borodankov, *loc. cit.*
59. *Vedomosti Verkhovnogo Soveta RSFSR*, No. 38 (1965), pp. 737–739.

8

America, China, and the Hydra-Headed Opposition

THE DYNAMICS OF SOVIET FOREIGN POLICY

Robert M. Slusser

EDITORS' INTRODUCTION

On October 15, 1964, alert Muscovites noticed the absence of the usual evening edition of Izvestia. They saw workmen taking down huge portraits of the First Secretary of the Communist Party and Chairman of the U.S.S.R. Council of Ministers, Nikita Khrushchev. Some of them guessed what TASS was telling a startled outside world before Soviet citizens were officially notified. Khrushchev was no longer the head of Party and state. On October 16, at the Red Square celebrations in honor of the three-man space flight, Brezhnev and Kosygin took the place of the deposed leader.

Khrushchev's fall is the climax in Robert Slusser's careful reconstruction of the recent influences on Soviet foreign policy. In his study, Soviet relations with the United States are the central issue. He has sought viable reasons for the fluctuations in Soviet-American relations, which have been marked by such milestones as the Middle East and Taiwan Straits crises of 1958, the "spirit of Camp David" in 1959, the alternation of tension and détente over Berlin between 1958 and 1964, the U-2 incident of 1960, the Cuban missile crisis in 1962, and the 1963 treaty banning nuclear tests in the atmosphere, in outer space, and under water.

Interrelated sources of Soviet policy emerge in Slusser's account: domestic problems, especially economic ones; hawk-like and dove-like elements in the formation of policies toward the West; the Sino-Soviet dispute; pressures from within the Soviet East European orbit and from Western Communist parties, notably the Italian Party.

Khrushchev's fate, as this study reiterates, is new proof of the intrigue, punctuated with periods of intense power struggle, that is continually spun behind the façade of monolithic Party unity. Power struggles both influence and reflect the course of Soviet foreign policy.

Despite the official ban on factions, in 1921, the Communist Party has not been immune from them any more than have less disciplined and less powerful parties in other countries. Factions may be defined as groupings in the Party that have their own more or less clearly defined minority platform, and their own more or less permanent organizational ties. Several major factions, in this broad sense, seem to have operated in Stalin's time: (1) the Leningrad group around Andrei Zhdanov, a militant Stalinist who died under mysterious circumstances in 1948; (2) Malenkov and his associates, who decimated the Leningrad group in 1949; (3) Khrushchev with his strong base in the Ukrainian Party appara-tus; and (4) according to Slusser, a loose, not necessarily fully intercommunicating congeries of younger bloods, such as Kozlov, Suslov, and (later) Shelepin, who were scattered in various sec-tions of the apparat, including that in Leningrad, and who had ideological or organizational ties, if only tenuously in some in-stances, with the enigmatic A. N. Poskrebyshev. Poskrebyshev, the most trusted of Stalin's subordinates, headed the personal secretariat through which Stalin ruled all other agencies, includ-ing the Party. At the time of Stalin's death, on March 5, 1953, Poskrebyshev was engrossed in preparations for an apparently great new purge that may well have wiped out all the above-listed group-ings save the last, since the younger hopefuls supported Stalin's and Poskrebyshev's "doctors' plot" frameup.

In 1953, a short-lived triumvirate of Malenkov, Molotov, and Beria took over. Beria and his followers were liquidated in 1953 and 1954, leaving Malenkov apparently supreme, since Molotov had no machine of his own. From outside the original trium-

virate, Khrushchev, his power based on the Party machinery, engineered Malenkov's resignation from the premiership and set Bulganin in his place, in February, 1955. Malenkov joined with Molotov, Kaganovich, and eventually others, such as Bulganin, to form the "anti-Party group," all of them going down to defeat in 1957 and 1958. Khrushchev seemed to many to have attained unassailable power. As First Secretary of the Party, he controlled the Secretariat of the Party and its staff, the center of control over the Party and all other agencies, including the U.S.S.R. Council of Ministers. He presided over the Presidium (Politburo) of the Party, the supreme policy-making body between sessions of the Central Committee. As Chairman of the R.S.F.S.R. Bureau of the Central Committee (abolished in 1966), he supervised Party and government policies in the largest and most important of the fifteen union republics. As Chairman of the U.S.S.R. Council of Ministers, he reinforced his control over the entire governmental apparatus. By virtue of holding four of the most important positions in the Soviet Union (no other individual has held positions in more than two of these organs), Khrushchev appeared to manipulate a welter of agencies at the all-union, republic, provincial, district, city, and village levels, the parallel hierarchies made up of organizations of the Party, ministries, soviets (government councils), police, courts, armed forces, trade unions, and so forth.

Within this structure, with the Beria and "anti-Party group" factions eliminated, the grouping of Khrushchev and his men, most of whom were from the Ukraine, and the loose congeries around Poskrebyshev were the main potential political contenders. At first, apparently, Khrushchev's opponents did not form a faction, in the strict sense of the term. They did not seek to depose him, but opposed him on individual issues of policy. Late in 1959, they began to coalesce gradually into a cooperating faction with the intent of undermining his position. This they managed to do, but only after: (1) Khrushchev's own protégés from the Ukraine, such as Brezhnev and Podgorny, had decided that Khrushchev's style and policies could no longer be tolerated, and (2) the anti-Khrushchev coalition received the support of the military leaders, who had favored him against Malenkov in the 1955–57 struggle, and for approximately the same reason: their dissatisfaction with his defense policy.

Suslov, Kozlov, until incapacitated by his illness in 1963, and, less obviously, Shelepin, Robert Slusser maintains, opposed Khrushchev's foreign policy from genuine disagreement, from rejection of the domestic liberalization to which his foreign policy led, and from a desire to use Khrushchev's setbacks in foreign policy to help bring about his downfall.

Professor Slusser concedes the controversial nature of his "Kremlinological" approach. The editors do not insist any more than he that his account is the final, revealed truth. But the editors believe that Professor Slusser's conclusions about the important role of intra-Party politics and internal problems in the formation of Soviet foreign policy provide valuable hypotheses and pose questions for further study of Soviet politics. Some of the hypotheses are of necessity based on circumstantial evidence, but all are provocative and stimulating in the continuing effort to understand the Soviet Leviathan.

> Treason doth never prosper: what's
> the reason?
> For if it prosper, none dare call it
> treason.
>
> —JOHN HARRINGTON
> Epigrams

> . . . the factionalists were overtaken by the fate that awaits all factionalists. The Party threw them aside, and, without slowing down, is advancing at the head of our glorious people toward its great goal, communism.
>
> —A. N. SHELEPIN
> Twenty-first Congress of the CPSU
> February, 1959

Soviet-American relations during the Khrushchev era became an active, indeed, a crucial area of Soviet decision-making, closely linked with other aspects of foreign policy, with domestic policy, and with the political struggle in the Communist Party of the Soviet Union.

In particular, Soviet policy toward the United States proved to be bound up with the course of the Sino-Soviet dispute. Furthermore, key questions of Soviet-American relations, especially those that concerned the nuclear-arms race and disarmament, directly involved issues of Soviet internal policy. Greater allocation of funds to Soviet agriculture and consumers' goods, for example, meant a reduction in resources available for heavy industry and armaments, with immediate consequences for the Soviet strategic posture. Controversy over precisely these questions of economic policy has continued within the upper echelons of the CPSU throughout the post-Stalin period. Thus, internal policy and foreign policy were directly related. Opposition to the policies of the Party leadership, behind the façade of "monolithic unity," left its mark on such major foreign-policy episodes as the Cuban missile adventure in 1962, the periodic relaxation and heightening of tension over Berlin, and the escalation of the Sino-Soviet dispute.

It may be objected that our knowledge of Soviet affairs is still too limited, and that the significance of what is known is often too ambiguous, to permit the construction of an even reasonably satisfactory working model of Soviet politics in all its complexity. Yet the attempt must be made; the author is profoundly convinced that whatever may prove to be the deficiencies of the present essay, the multidimensional approach is essential to a balanced and adequate understanding of Soviet history and Soviet politics.

From the "Doctors' Plot" to the Defeat of the "Anti-Party Group": 1953–57

The inner course of the struggle for power within the CPSU since Stalin can be understood only against the background of developments in the old tyrant's last years. As Stalin aged, the fight for the succession among his principal lieutenants was waged with ever increasing bitterness and ruthlessness. Amid a climate of growing fear created by selective purges in the Soviet Union and the East European satellites, *Pravda* on January 13, 1953, announced the apprehension of a group of "terrorist doctors," all eminent specialists, the majority Jewish, and collectively responsible for ministering to the Soviet political elite. The doctors were accused of having systematically misprescribed for their high-placed patients, thereby causing the deaths of Party ideologist and Politburo member Andrei Zhdanov and Party military specialist and candidate member of the Politburo A. S. Shcherbakov, and of having plotted other nefarious deeds at the behest of the Jewish Joint Distribution Committee (a non-Soviet charitable organization), working in collaboration with U.S. and British intelligence agencies. These charges, accompanied by a strident campaign in the Soviet press for "vigilance" against foreign and internal enemies, harked back to the 1930's and seemed to presage a renewal of the bloody Great Purge. Stalin's death prevented those behind the plot from carrying their plan to completion, so that there is some degree of uncertainty as to the real purpose of the intrigue, but it is generally agreed that among its principal targets were Georgi M. Malenkov, Politburo member, Secretary of the Central Committee (CC), and Deputy Chairman of the U.S.S.R. Council of Ministers, and Lavrenti P. Beria, also a Politburo member and for many years (though not in the period during which the plot was being prepared) undisputed boss of the Soviet secret police.

The encyclopedically informed Boris Nicolaevsky argued convincingly that the principal planner of the projected purge to which the "doctors' plot" was intended to serve as a prelude was Alexander N. Poskrebyshev, chief of Stalin's personal secretariat, the nerve center in which Stalin's complex system of controls was coordinated.[1] Nicolaevsky also demonstrated the existence of strong ties between Poskrebyshev and Mikhail A. Suslov, leading Party ideologist and specialist in the field of relations between the CPSU and other Communist parties.[2] Among the Party officials who took an active part in the "vigilance" campaign in early 1953, and who can thus be linked with the plot, was Leningrad Party boss Frol R. Kozlov.[3]

The significance of these facts for an understanding of Soviet politics in the Khrushchev era is that these two men, Suslov and Kozlov, although they supported Khrushchev in his showdown with the "anti-Party group" in June, 1957, thereafter opposed many of his innovations in internal policy, identifying themselves consistently as champions of the interests of heavy industry and armaments against those of agriculture and the consumer. Nor did they restrict their activities merely to formal and legitimate opposition; increasingly they took the path of factional politics, establishing territorial bases in the Party and governmental apparatus of the Soviet Union, the multilevel complexities of which lend themselves wonderfully well to political intrigue. We can date their first steps in this direction at least as early as the winter of 1959/60.

The concept of Kozlov and Suslov as oppositionists under Khrushchev has by now gained fairly wide acceptance. To add the name of A. N. Shelepin to this group, however, is bound to evoke surprise. There has been unusual unanimity among analysts that Shelepin was a stanch supporter of Khrushchev. It must be admitted that there appears to be considerable evidence to support this view. During his years as First Secretary of the Komsomol (1952–58), Shelepin threw the weight of that organization behind some of Khrushchev's most important projects, notably the Virgin Land Campaign. In the period immediately preceding the crisis of June, 1957, he kept the Komsomol clear of the struggle between Khrushchev and his opponents, despite valiant efforts by the "anti-Party group" to win it over to their side. At the Twenty-first and Twenty-second Party congresses, he continued the fight against the "anti-Party group," appearing as one of the most irreconcilable antagonists of the defeated faction.

Against this background, Shelepin's appointment to head the Committee of State Security (KGB), in November, 1958, was understandably interpreted at the time as a move by Khrushchev to ensure his personal control over the secret police. Even Shelepin's subsequent accumulation of power—his election to the Secretariat, in October, 1961, and his appointment as Deputy Premier and Chairman of the newly established Committee of Party-State Control, in November, 1962—has not entirely shaken the prevailing conception of him as a Khrushchev man, although some analysts, noting the ominous growth in his power, speculated on whether or not he might eventually threaten Khrushchev's own position. After Khrushchev's fall, of course, it was obvious that at some point Shelepin must have joined the anti-Khrushchev coalition, but there has been no general agreement on how early his opposition is to be dated.

The evidence, indirect but cumulatively significant, indicates that Shelepin's factional activities began at about the same time as those of Kozlov and Suslov, i.e., late 1959–early 1960. At that time, if not earlier, he apparently expanded his base of support (the secret police, the Komsomol, and the central Party apparatus) to include the Belorussian Party, in alliance with Kiril T. Mazurov, Belorussian First Secretary.

Evidence that the Belorussian Party organization during the Khrushchev era differed significantly from those of other union republics can be found in the stenographic record of the Twenty-second Congress of the CPSU, held in October, 1961.[4] A comparative study of the delegations to the Congress from the union republics reveals two peculiarities about the delegation from Belorussia: first, it included a relatively high proportion of the political elite of the republic—the entire upper echelon of the Party hierarchy, down to the level of oblast secretary, and virtually the entire Council of Ministers; and second, it included a small but important group of central Party and government officials having no ostensible connection with Belorussia. Of course, central officials often attend a Party congress from an organization in one of the union republics, and examples of this practice may be found in other union-republic delegations to the Twenty-second Congress. But the non-native contingent in the Belorussian delegation was quantitatively and qualitatively different from similar groups attending the Congress from other union republics. Its members formed a compact group with well-marked policy interests: ideology, foreign policy, specialized defense industry. For example, a prominent Party ideologist and historian, Boris N. Ponomarev, was a member of the delegation, as was one of the Deputy Ministers of Foreign Affairs, G. M. Pushkin (the Minister of Foreign Affairs, Andrei Gromyko, incidentally, is of Belorussian origin). V. D. Kalmykov, Chairman of the State Committee for Radioelectronic Technology, and Marshal K. K. Rokossovsky also attended the Congress from Belorussia.

Another distinguishing characteristic of Belorussia was, and is, its well-marked affinity for the secret police. It has become, for example, the center of the cult of Dzerzhinsky, founder of the Cheka and born on what is now Belorussian territory.[5] In November, 1959, at a time of extensive personnel reassignments in the secret police, the Belorussian KGB chief, Ivan Perepelitsin, was named Deputy Chairman of the All-Union KGB, immediately

subordinate to Shelepin.[6] A further link between Shelepin, the secret police, and Belorussia is provided by the appointment in June,
1960, of A. N. Aksenov, former chief of the Belorussian Komsomol
and for a time Komsomol Secretary under Shelepin, to head the
Belorussian Ministry of Internal Affairs (MVD).

The assumption of a link between Belorussia and Shelepin is
strengthened when one analyzes the careers of the leading group
in the Belorussian Party during the period 1959–61. The core of
the Belorussian Party apparatus, including Mazurov, the First
Secretary, was made up of men who, like Shelepin, had joined
the Party in 1940, immediately after the Great Purge, and had
risen through the ranks during World War II and the late Stalinist period. The common backgrounds and experiences point to a
similarity of ideas and outlook.

For those who insist on documented proof, the evidence linking Shelepin with Belorussia may appear unconvincing. It would
be naïve, however, to expect factionalists in the CPSU to oblige
us with documents pertaining to their activities. The contest in
which they are engaged has the highest stakes, and premature detection means certain failure and disgrace. Under these circumstances, we ought perhaps to be surprised that the evidence for
Shelepin's factional link with Belorussia can be found at all,
rather than that it is not unimpeachably documented. Similarly,
the identification of Shelepin as an oppositionist and factionalist
as early as the end of 1959 cannot be conclusively proven; the
assumption that he was one, however, helps make sense of some
otherwise baffling enigmas in Soviet history during the Khrushchev era, and casts a flood of light on the inner course of Soviet
politics.

Let us assume, then, as a working hypothesis, that Shelepin,
like Kozlov and Suslov, was an oppositionist and factionalist during the greater part of the Khrushchev era. Is there any evidence
for a link between the three? Did they form part of a single opposition group?

As we have seen, the careers of both Kozlov and Suslov provide indications of a link with the "doctors' plot," and thus with
Poskrebyshev. Shelepin, too, has ties with Poskrebyshev. The
clearest evidence is to be found in the circumstances of his appointment to head the KGB, in November, 1958. At that time,

Shelepin held the post of chief of the Department of Party
Organs for the Union Republics in the Party CC, a post to which
he had been appointed only seven months earlier, in April, 1958,
following his release as First Secretary of the Komsomol. The move
from the Department of Party Organs to the post of head of the
secret police has been made in the case of two of Shelepin's
predecessors, N. I. Yezhov (1936–39) and S. D. Ignatiev (1951–
53). In both appointments, the hand of Poskrebyshev can be
detected with a fair degree of certainty. Assuming a regularity in
behavior patterns, we could then make the assumption that
Poskrebyshev had a hand in Shelepin's appointment to head the
KGB. This assumption is strengthened by the facts of Shelepin's
earlier career, particularly his emergence as a picked potential
leader in the central apparatus of the Komsomol in the years
immediately following the Great Purge.

By extension of our hypothesis, we could postulate that it was
Poskrebyshev who provided the common link between the three
principal oppositionist-factionalists of the Khrushchev era. The
evidence suggests, however, not that the three formed a single
organization, but that they operated as individuals, sharing basic
views and policies, cooperating in pursuit of their common goals,
but maintaining no formalized connections. This loose alliance
had the advantage from their point of view that they could not
be attacked as a group; it was necessary for Khrushchev to take
them on one at a time, and his victory over one left the others still
operational. Nevertheless, the presence in the background of Poskrebyshev as strategist and adviser gave the opposition a consistency
of purpose and a resilience that it would otherwise have lacked. To
the factional intrigue he brought his unrivaled experience in
Party politics and his intimate knowledge of how to manipulate
the Party apparatus.

To what extent was Khrushchev aware of these factional opponents and their common base? We can be certain that at some
point he became fully aware of the threat posed by Kozlov, and
that he took definite steps to weaken Kozlov's position. The
evidence with regard to Suslov is less clear-cut, although by the
late summer of 1963 Khrushchev probably was ready to move
against him. His attitude toward Poskrebyshev appears to have
been ambiguous, varying between a willingness to conclude a

temporary alliance and an effort to escape from his influence. Least conclusive of all is the evidence that Khrushchev recognized the threat from Shelepin, or fully realized the significance of Shelepin's link with Poskrebyshev and the other oppositionists. Perhaps, like most Western analysts, he placed reliance on the evidence suggesting that Shelepin was his loyal follower; perhaps he knew or suspected the truth, and put up the best fight he could against steadily mounting odds.

Stalin's death, on March 5, 1953, marked the end of Poskrebyshev's public career, for it meant not only the elimination of his patron and the frustration of his projected purge but the emergence into power of his two most dangerous and irreconcilable enemies, Malenkov and Beria. He managed to escape destruction but had to drop into obscurity, his power apparently irretrievably broken.

Poskrebyshev was saved by the deadly feud that broke out almost at once between Beria and the other members of the post-Stalin "collective leadership," including Malenkov. This struggle brought Beria's brief moment of power and glory to a sudden halt in June, 1953. Before his fall, however, Beria had been able to take action against the immediate organizers of the "doctors' plot"—Ignatiev, the Minister of State Security, was reprimanded and demoted, and his deputy, M. D. Ryumin, was arrested.

It has generally been assumed that Khrushchev was involved in the "doctors' plot," but the evidence does not support this assumption. The intrigue was being prepared in the Ukraine during the 1951–53 period, i.e., when Khrushchev was no longer directly associated with the Ukrainian Party. He may have known about it, but he was neither a participant in it nor one of its principal targets. The continued survival of Poskrebyshev after Stalin's death as a shadowy but still potentially powerful influence in the Party prevented Khrushchev from uncovering the full story of the plot in his "secret speech"; instead he veiled it in ambiguity, implying that Poskrebyshev was no longer a significant figure.

The rise of Khrushchev after September, 1953, and his increasingly intense rivalry with Malenkov led to a major realignment in the upper echelons of the Party. Khrushchev's innovatory policies in internal and foreign policy had the result that by 1957 most of the surviving old-line Stalinists—Molotov, Kaganovich, Bulganin, Voroshilov—were grouped around Malenkov. Poskrebyshev was no less a Stalinist than these men, but his struggle with Malenkov prevented him from throwing his influence to the side of the "anti-Party group" during the showdown of June, 1957.

Another factor behind the support for Khrushchev was the bitter anti-Malenkov feeling that existed in a number of Party organizations, notably those of Leningrad, under Kozlov, which had not forgotten Malenkov's part in the "Leningrad case" of 1949, and Belorussia, under Mazurov, which still retained vivid memories of Malenkov's part in the devastation of the Belorussian Party and government during the Great Purge.

Thus the victorious coalition of June, 1957, included a number of Party functionaries who were anti-Malenkov rather than enthusiastically pro-Khrushchev. It was primarily out of these anti-Malenkov forces that the internal opposition of the Khrushchev era was formed.

Khrushchev Ascendant: June, 1957–December, 1959

Khrushchev followed up his victory in June, 1957, with sweeping organizational changes in the leading organs of the Party—the Presidium and the Secretariat. The ousted members of the "anti-Party group" were replaced by loyal Khrushchev followers and by those who had supported him. At CC plenums in October and December, 1957, Khrushchev consolidated his gains, establishing a clear predominance that lasted, with only minor readjustments, until December, 1959.

Organizationally, Khrushchev had an impressive lead over the opposition, yet he was never able to achieve a full and conclusive victory. Suslov was impregnably entrenched in the Presidium and Secretariat. Kozlov, who had been named to the Presidium after the June, 1957, plenum, suffered some loss of power in the reorganization of December, 1957, but was able to recoup by building a new center of strength in the governmental apparatus of the R.S.F.S.R. and the U.S.S.R., so that by the summer of 1959 he was being semi-officially identified as second in line to Khrushchev in the Party and government.

An important accession of strength for Khrushchev in these

years was the creative intelligentsia, which saw in his attack on Stalin's "cult of personality" the charter for greater relaxation of Party controls in the cultural field.

But Shelepin's appointment to head the KGB (November, 1958) caused a shift in the balance of power. Far from strengthening Khrushchev's control over the secret police, this move placed control of a vital organization in the hands of a potential oppositionist, whose loyalty was to the Party organization and ideology rather than to Khrushchev personally. Shelepin's predecessor, General I. A. Serov, was a veteran secret police official who had worked closely with Khrushchev in the Ukraine in the early 1940's; he was put in charge of the GRU (military intelligence, with an extensive espionage apparatus abroad). During the year following Shelepin's appointment, extensive changes were made in the upper echelons of the KGB.

In the field of internal policy, the 1957–59 period was marked by continuous activity initiated by Khrushchev: the dissolution of the Machine Tractor Stations, proposed at the CC plenum of February, 1958; the education reform, introduced at a Komsomol congress in April, 1958; the abolition of compulsory deliveries by the collective farms, proposed at the CC plenum of June, 1958; the drafting of the Seven-Year Plan, which was presented at the November, 1958, CC plenum; the revising of the plan, which was finally adopted at the Twenty-first Party Congress, in January–February, 1959; and the campaign for grass-roots social controls through anti-parasite decrees, volunteer People's Guards, and comrades' courts (see Chapter 7).

This was a period also of important Soviet technological achievements. In August, 1957, the Soviets successfully fired their first intercontinental ballistic missile; in October, they launched the world's first artificial satellite. These triumphs greatly strengthened Khrushchev's position and contributed to a feeling of buoyant optimism within the Soviet leadership. It appeared that the balance of strategic power, which had favored the United States since 1945, had finally shifted to the Soviet Union's side. Soviet spokesmen made confident predictions of the effect these developments would have in advancing Soviet foreign policy.

Khrushchev was strongly tempted to use the new weapons, if not actually, then at least as a means of exerting pressure on the

West, particularly the United States. In the major international confrontations of 1958—the Middle East crisis of July and the clash in the Taiwan Straits in September—it turned out, however, that the United States had not been intimidated by Soviet claims of strategic superiority; instead, it acted without apparent concern over possible Soviet counteractions. Meanwhile, the United States was systematically strengthening its global position by a series of bilateral military agreements providing for the stationing of U.S. medium-range ballistic missiles on overseas bases.

From these developments Khrushchev evidently drew the conclusion that further effort was needed to speed up the pace of Soviet armament if it was to be used effectively in Soviet foreign policy. Shortly after the Taiwan Straits crisis, the Soviet Union launched a new series of nuclear tests, and on November 27, 1958, Khrushchev proclaimed a six-month deadline for the settlement of the Berlin problem on Soviet terms. Once again, however, success eluded him. The date of the announced deadline came and went, in May, 1959, with no signs of Western concessions, and in June the Soviet Government somewhat lamely offered the Western powers a one-year extension of their rights in Berlin.

Concurrently with his efforts to force concessions from the West by threats and pressure, Khrushchev was exploring the possibility of reaching limited agreements with the United States. The inconsistency reflected not merely the usual "dialectical" character of Soviet foreign policy but the genuine ambiguities and inconsistencies of Khrushchev's own attitudes. A complete materialist in his values, Khrushchev could not help envying America's material prosperity and technological power, although as a Soviet patriot and a Marxist-Leninist, he was convinced that what capitalism had achieved could and would be surpassed by Communism. He had a naïve but powerful faith that the Communist system, freed of Stalinist constraints and animated by the desire of its citizens for the good things of the material life, could attain a level of well-being higher than could be reached under capitalism.

To maximize material incentives, however, it would be necessary to allocate a greater share of the national resources to agriculture and consumers' goods, at the expense of heavy industry, ferrous metallurgy, and armaments, the traditional top-priority categories in the Soviet budget. This meant that acceptance of Khrushchev's internal policies depended on his proving to his colleagues that it would be not merely desirable but safe to reduce Soviet military expenditures. His attempts to provide this proof were inconsistent but complementary: on the one hand, he used Soviet weapons as a means of pressure on the United States to force it to make major concessions in foreign policy, and thus, symbolically at least, to acknowledge Soviet strategic predominance; and on the other, he sought areas of limited Soviet-American agreement that might ultimately lead to a general reduction of international tension and thus justify a cut in Soviet military expenditures. Both policies, at least in the beginning, were based primarily on internal considerations.

Of the two policies, intimidation and conciliation, it was the latter that by early 1959 appeared to offer the greater hope for success. A Soviet-American cultural-exchange agreement had been signed in January, 1958; a year later Mikoyan made a highly successful trip to the United States, which was followed by other official visits—Kozlov in July, a return visit by Nixon in August, and finally a formal trip by Khrushchev himself in September–October. When the cultural-exchange agreement expired in October, it was renewed for two years. In the final weeks of 1959, agreement was reached between the Soviet Union and the Western powers for a four-power summit meeting to be held in Paris in May, 1960.

While the Khrushchev regime's relations with the United States were moving in the direction of cooperation and *détente*, those with China were rapidly deteriorating. Khrushchev's policies toward the United States contributed to the worsening of Sino-Soviet relations. The Communist Party of China (CPC) had at first been even more sanguine than the CPSU about the influence on the international strategic balance of the Soviet technological advances of August–October, 1957. The Chinese had confidently looked to the Soviet Union not only for help in building their own atomic weapons, in accordance with a secret agreement of October, 1957, but for diplomatic support in their disputes with the United States. On both counts the year 1958 brought them sharp disappointments.

During the first half of 1958, the Chinese endeavored with some success to force Khrushchev to show greater militance in foreign policy and less willingness to break away from Stalinist rigidity in internal policy. The Chinese had come to regard the policies of Tito's Yugoslavia as a touchstone and as the embodiment of everything they most disliked. They condemned Tito's internal policies as "revisionism" of basic Marxist-Leninist principles, and they opposed any efforts by Khrushchev to effect a rapprochement with Tito.

Chinese efforts to influence Khrushchev in the formation of Soviet foreign policy reached their peak, both in intensity and in degree of success, during May and June, 1958. The Chinese Party's May 5 condemnation of the new Yugoslav Party program, which had been adopted at the Ljubljana Congress in April, was followed by a similar but somewhat less vigorous Soviet stand (*Pravda*, May 9). On May 27, the Soviet Union canceled credits granted earlier to Yugoslavia. Speaking in Bulgaria (June 1 and 3), Khrushchev sounded an uncharacteristically harsh anti-Yugo-slav note. Since Soviet policy toward Hungary, after the unsuc-cessful revolt of 1956, had become a particularly sensitive area both in Sino-Soviet and Soviet-satellite relations, the announce-ment on June 16 of the trial and execution of the deposed Hungarian Premier, Imre Nagy, can be taken as the high point of Chinese influence and of the efforts by Khrushchev to appease them; the Chinese made no secret of their satisfaction over the outcome of the trial.

While Chinese pressure was mounting, the struggle for power in the CPSU was also sharpening. *Pravda* on April 24 reported a speech by Kozlov in which he uncompromisingly championed the priority of heavy industry as "the cornerstone of all branches of our economy." Speaking to Western correspondents at a reception in Warsaw the next day, Mme. E. A. Furtseva, one of Khru-shchev's most loyal supporters, assured her listeners that "Yugo-slavia and we have been friends and will remain friendly."[7] A move by Khrushchev to discredit the conservative opposition and to strengthen his popularity with the creative intellectuals was the adoption of a CC resolution on May 28 "correcting" the resolution on music of February 10, 1948, which had further restricted the freedom of Soviet composers, and in which Suslov had had a significant part.

At the CC plenum of June 17/18, Khrushchev achieved an unqualified success. Not only did the plenum accept his proposals for the abolition of compulsory delivery of agricultural products and the substitution of cash transactions between the RTS's (Technical Repair Stations) and the kolkhozes, but it named two of his followers, N. V. Podgorny and D. S. Polyansky, as candidate members of the Presidium.

Strengthened in his position and with his internal policies approved, Khrushchev was ready to throw off the tutelage which the Chinese were trying to exert over Soviet foreign policy. At the height of the Middle East crisis of July, 1958, he omitted China from his proposal for a summit meeting to settle the crisis, and named India instead as the principal Asian power concerned. In August, when he paid a visit to Peking, feelings were tense; the Chinese had by this time rejected Soviet proposals for closer coordination of the armed forces of the two nations, and they now announced that they would achieve their goal of Communism by their own unaided efforts, taking the shortcuts of forced industrialization (the "Great Leap Forward") and the people's communes. Khrushchev expressed skepticism over the prospects of these methods. Of greater concern to him than the Chinese attitude of independence, however, was the claim to doctrinal priority within the world Communist movement which their policies represented. Henceforth, a major motivating factor in Khrushchev's policies was the urge to demonstrate that he, not Mao Tse-tung, was the real heir of Marx and Lenin in defining and developing Communist ideology.

To substantiate their claim that the United States was a "paper tiger," and to force the Soviets to support them in a clash with America, the Chinese began bombarding the offshore islands Quemoy and Matsu in June. At the height of the resulting international tension, in September, the United States stood firm while the Soviet Union gave only verbal support to the Chinese, limiting itself to a threat of retaliation with nuclear weapons in case the United States should attack China.

As Soviet-American relations took a turn for the better during the first half of 1959, Sino-Soviet relations continued to deteriorate. On June 20, the Soviet Government formally but secretly abrogated the secret atomic-aid agreement of October,

1957.[8] In July and August, at a plenum of the Chinese Party CC, Mao crushed an internal challenge to his power by a factional group evidently supported by Khrushchev.[9] In September, on the eve of Khrushchev's departure for the United States, the Soviet Government proclaimed its neutrality in the Chinese-Indian border clash.

For the Chinese the point of no return was Khrushchev's visit to the United States, which culminated in his talks with President Eisenhower at Camp David and the issuing of a joint Soviet-American communiqué that called for the settlement of "all outstanding international questions, not by the application of force but by peaceful means through negotiation."[10] Nor did the Chinese find anything pleasing to them in the program for general and complete disarmament which Khrushchev presented to the U.N. General Assembly on September 18.

In an effort to convince the Chinese leaders of the value of his U.S. policy, and to patch up the ominously widening rift in Sino-Soviet relations, Khrushchev made a hurried trip to Peking immediately after his return from Washington (an earlier delegation, headed by Suslov, was already in the Chinese capital). The visit, however, merely confirmed the Chinese in their antagonism to Khrushchev's policies and deepened their dislike of him personally.

The Opposition on the Offensive: December, 1959–May, 1961

Against this background we can better understand why it was at this moment that the first signs appeared of definite factional activities by Khrushchev's opponents. All three of the principal oppositionists engaged in these activities, but Kozlov's words and actions provide the clearest indications of the opposition's motives.

By 1959, Kozlov had defined his position on the principal issues of internal policy and had identified himself as a spokesman for the interests of heavy industry, metallurgy, and armaments. His trip to the United States in July, 1959, provided an opportunity for him to show that in foreign policy, too, he did not see eye to eye with Khrushchev. Whereas Khrushchev returned from his September–October visit with a changed attitude and a new sense of the opportunities open to Soviet-American collaboration in international affairs, Kozlov's trip left him with his views unaltered, as he explicitly stated on his departure.[11] He viewed America through the lenses of a dogmatic Communist ideology and believed implicitly in Soviet misinterpretations of the history of Soviet-American relations.

At the CC plenum of December 21–25, 1959, Khrushchev encountered unexpectedly strong opposition from Kozlov and Suslov to his proposals for changes in agricultural policy, and not only failed to reach agreement but lost ground organizationally: A. I. Kirichenko and N. I. Belyaev, two of his followers in the Presidium, were subjected to criticism for policy failures in Kazakhstan and, in January, 1960, were reassigned to less important posts. The part played by the opposition in these changes was revealed by the fact that a key post in the reorganized Kazakh Party following Belyaev's ouster was assigned to a follower of Kozlov.[12]

The innovations introduced by Khrushchev in 1959, particularly his policy of rapprochement with the United States, broadened the area of intraparty conflict and introduced new opportunities for linking internal disputes with disagreements over foreign policy. In the first months of 1960, the emerging opposition began to take advantage of developments that could be used to discredit Khrushchev's foreign-policy innovations and thus open the way for organizational defeats and increased pressure on questions of internal policy. (Khrushchev, of course, had taught the opposition to link disputes over foreign and internal policy by demonstrating the direct causal connection between his policies in the two fields.)

In a speech to the Supreme Soviet on January 14, 1960, Khrushchev announced a cut of 1.2 million men in the Soviet armed forces, justifying the reduction on the grounds that development of the missile arm had rendered obsolete not only large standing armies but aircraft and surface vessels. Henceforth, he said, the strength of a great power would be measured not by the number of men it maintained under arms but by the amount of fire power it could employ.[13] To underline his point, the Soviets held a series of missile tests in the Central Pacific from January 15 to February 15, for the announced purpose of developing "a more powerful rocket to launch heavy earth satellites and undertake space flights to planets of the solar system."[14] And in his speech to the Supreme Soviet, Khrushchev boasted that Soviet scientists had developed an "incredible" superweapon, "even more perfect and even more formidable" than the existing Soviet atomic and hydrogen weapons.[15]

Khrushchev supplemented his rocket-rattling and troop reductions with new proposals for comprehensive disarmament measures and with an emphasis on the possibility of better understanding between the Soviet Union and the United States. He announced that President Eisenhower would visit the Soviet Union in June, and said that "the Soviet Government hopes that the noble cause of creating trust in relations between the Soviet Union and the U.S.A., to which we devoted our efforts at Camp David, will be successfully continued in Moscow."[16]

This speech reflected Khrushchev's espousal of the parallel but scarcely compatible policies of (1) strengthening the Soviet missile forces and (2) working for a better understanding with the United States. Both policies activated internal opposition, the former primarily among military service chiefs, the latter among political leaders, with the distinct possibility that links might develop or be forged between the two opposition groups.

During the early months of 1960, Khrushchev spent much time on the road: from February 10 to March 5 he visited a number of states in Asia and the Middle East, and from March 22 to April 3 he was in France to confer with de Gaulle.

The month of April proved to be a turning point in the internal political struggle, and it is instructive to note the sequence of events, each of which contributed to the final outcome. On April 1, France exploded its second atomic bomb (the first had been set off on February 13); on the following day, Khrushchev concluded his talks with President de Gaulle, having failed to reach any important agreements. On April 9, a U.S. spy plane, the high-altitude U-2, made an unopposed but not unobserved flight over Soviet territory. On April 18, Molotov submitted an article to *Kommunist* for the ninetieth anniversary of Lenin's birth, which reportedly paralleled closely the Chinese position on international Communist strategy.[17] The next day, the Chinese launched a major ideological campaign with an editorial entitled "Long Live Leninism!"—a militant statement of their doctrinal position on the issues over which they disagreed with Khrushchev, and a clear bid for ideological leadership in the international Communist movement.[18] On April 22, Kuusinen, whose behavior marks him as a consistent supporter of Khrushchev, maintained in a speech to commemorate the Lenin anniversary that Lenin had differentiated between militant diehards and possible partners for peaceful co-existence among the "imperialists."[19] On April 27, an issue of *Questions of the History of the CPSU* was sent to press with an article that warned: "One cannot but reckon with the possibility of the development of relapses into anti-Party actions by certain elements, especially at moments of a sharp turn of course."[20] On April 29, *Pravda* published a poem repenting the adulation of Stalin, written by Alexander Tvardovsky, editor of *Novy mir* and one of the liberal writers who had welcomed Khrushchev's policies of curbing Stalinist controls in Soviet cultural life. (This appears to be Khrushchev's first direct use of the liberal writers in the power struggle. See Chapter 4.)

The denouement came in the first week of May. On May 1, another U-2 flight over Soviet territory took place, but this time the plane was brought down by the Soviets and its pilot, Francis Gary Powers, was captured. Three days later at an unannounced plenum of the CC, Khrushchev suffered a severe organizational defeat. Kirichenko and Belyaev, whose positions had already been weakened, were ousted from the Presidium. The most significant shift, however, took place in the Secretariat. No fewer than five Khrushchev supporters—Kirichenko, A. V. Aristov, P. N. Pospelov, N. G. Ignatov, and Mme. Furtseva—were dropped (a sixth, Brezhnev, was to follow in July). At the same time, Kozlov moved in, turning over his post as First Deputy Premier of the U.S.S.R. to Kosygin, who moved up from candidate to full member of the Presidium.[21] Prior to these changes, Khrushchev had enjoyed a commanding majority in the Secretariat—ten Khrushchevites (including himself) to one lone oppositionist, Suslov. With the addition of Kozlov, the strength of the opposition was doubled, while the losses suffered by Khrushchev left him with only two supporters, Kuusinen and Mukhitdinov, and reduced his majority to a mere 3 to 2.

At the abortive summit conference which followed this organizational defeat, Khrushchev tried unsuccessfully to salvage something out of the wreckage of the Camp David diplomacy by pressing Eisenhower for an apology, but the President's candid admission of responsibility for the U-2 flights and his refusal to apologize gave Khrushchev no alternative but to end the conference in a sputter of verbal fireworks. Frustrated in his attempt to reach an agreement with the Western powers at the summit conference, Khrushchev moved to achieve his goal of *détente* by another route. On June 2, the Soviet Government announced a revised plan for general and complete disarmament, incorporated in a draft treaty which the Soviet delegation at Geneva submitted on June 7.[22]

The collapse of Khrushchev's hopes for a summit agreement with the Western powers was duly noted by the Chinese, who found in it striking confirmation of their own evaluation of Western policy. They were also, as usual, unimpressed by the Soviet plan for disarmament. Chinese criticism of Khrushchev's handling of Soviet foreign policy was given vigorous expression at a meeting of the World Federation of Trade Unions held in Peking in early June, which was noteworthy as the first occasion on which the Sino-Soviet dispute, hitherto confined to ideology, assumed the aspect of an organizational struggle between the two parties for allies in the international Communist movement.[23] Of particular importance for the future was the fact that the Chinese at the WFTU meeting made special efforts to win the support of the Albanians (since none of the other European parties could be wooed away from the Soviets), an effort crowned by success even though the Albanian delegation at the meeting included several strongly pro-Soviet members.

The Chinese bid to undermine Soviet hegemony was a challenge Khrushchev could not afford to ignore. At the next suitable occasion, which was provided by a meeting of Communist delegations to the Third Congress of the Rumanian Workers' Party at Bucharest in late June, Khrushchev launched an attack on the Chinese the vigor of which took them by surprise and made a solution of the differences between the two parties incomparably more difficult.[24] It was Kozlov, however, even though he had not been present at the Bucharest meeting, who reported on it to the CC plenum that met July 13–16, 1960.[25] (It was at this plenum, incidentally, that Brezhnev was dropped from the Secretariat.) Kozlov's speech has not been published, but it was evidently militantly anti-American, to judge by the resolution the plenum adopted on the subject.[26] At the Bucharest meeting, Suslov was named chairman of a commission, representing twenty-six CP's, which was charged with drafting a statement for submission to the international Communist conference scheduled to be held later that year.

During the summer of 1960, it was not only Kozlov who took an anti-American line: Khrushchev at this time also swung over toward a more militant posture, as, for example, in a speech on July 9 in which he promised Soviet military support to Cuba, including rockets if necessary.[27] A few days later, he asserted that "the Monroe Doctrine has outlived its time" and "has died a natural death," although he denied that the U.S.S.R. wanted or needed missile bases in Cuba.[28]

Seen in perspective, Khrushchev's swing to anti-Americanism in the summer of 1960 can be recognized as a tactical maneuver, a temporary accommodation with the opposition designed to enable him to weather the storm until more favorable conditions permitted him to resume his search for a Soviet-American *détente*. It must therefore be clearly distinguished from that of the opposition, e.g., Ponomarev, who stated in an article on "peaceful co-existence" that President Eisenhower and Secretary of State Herter were "pursuing a provocational aggressive policy."[29] And the secret police under Shelepin made its contribution to the anti-American campaign at this time with a show trial of Francis G. Powers.

The shift to a harder line toward the United States was accompanied by efforts to reverse the downward course of Sino-Soviet relations—a coincidence of policies that was to recur at other periods of oppositional insurgency during the Khrushchev era. In August, the Yugoslav politician and political theorist Edvard Kardelj published a series of articles under the title *Socialism and War*, which sought to provide a rationale and strategy for the Soviet policy of "peaceful co-existence" vis-à-vis the West, and which condemned the militant Chinese stance.[30] Chinese dislike for the Yugoslavs, as mentioned, was well known, and it was therefore widely accepted as a distinctly pro-Chinese move when *Pravda* on September 2 published a review of Kardelj's book which charged that the Yugoslav politician was in effect helping "U.S. imperialism" by "repeating the slander spread by the

U.S. imperialists about the 'aggressiveness' of the People's Republic of China."[31]

Eight days later, in a long public letter to the CPSU, the Chinese replied to the Soviet attack at the Bucharest meeting and set forth a program to overcome the differences between the two parties.[32] Of particular importance was the proposal that the CPSU should "draw a clear line of demarcation between the enemy and ourselves," i.e., not place China and the United States on the same level in Soviet foreign policy. This letter was followed by a conference between representatives of the two parties; it failed, however, to resolve any of the basic difficulties.[33]

One of the most striking features about the Sino-Soviet dispute has been the evident failure of the Chinese to find real allies within the Soviet leadership. An explanation of this failure should probably be sought primarily in the Chinese assertions of doctrinal superiority, since no Soviet leader was willing to recognize these claims. We can deduce that the Chinese position found some support within the Soviet leadership, however, from the fact that by the end of September, Molotov, the principal ideological spokesman of the unreconstructed "Stalinists" in the CPSU, had lost his post as Ambassador to the Mongolian People's Republic.[34]

Khrushchev, ever the master of the varied approach, now attempted to further his foreign policies in the U.N. Speaking before the General Assembly on September 24, he proposed the replacement of the position of Secretary General by a three-man board on which the Soviet Union would have one permanent member, and reiterated his 1959 proposals for general and complete disarmament.

The Chinese Party's letter of September 10, though it failed in its immediate purpose of swaying the Soviet leadership toward a more pro-Chinese attitude, did help prepare the way for the international conference of Communist and workers' parties which met in Moscow in November and December, 1960. At this meeting the dispute between the two parties not only continued but was widened as an increasing number of the other parties took sides. The final statement issued by the conference satisfied neither side but could be interpreted in accordance with the views of either side.[35]

Even this much show of unity was too much for Khrushchev,

however; at the banquet for the departing delegates, on December 2, he offered a toast to Yugoslavia as a "socialist country," a gesture certain to infuriate the Chinese since, in their eyes, it "violat[ed] what the fraternal parties had agreed on."[36]

A new phase in Soviet-American relations opened with the inauguration of John F. Kennedy as President of the United States, on January 4, 1961. Khrushchev lost no time in sounding out the new administration. At a New Year's reception in the Kremlin he said, "We would like to forget this unfortunate incident [the U-2 overflights]," and reminded his listeners that President Kennedy had earlier stated that "if he were President he would express his regret to the Soviet Government over the U-2 plane flight."[37] In an important policy statement on January 6, Khrushchev defined Soviet policy with regard to various kinds of war, stating that the Soviet Union not only would work to prevent the outbreak of a general nuclear war but was also opposed to local wars that might develop into general nuclear wars. He made an exception only in the case of "liberation wars," e.g., the armed struggles in Cuba and Algeria; such wars, he said, were "sacred" and would be supported by the Soviet Union. The danger of war between the "imperialists" and the Soviet Union, he said, could be avoided by a policy of peaceful co-existence and disarmament. Taking sharp issue with the Chinese point of view, he stated that a world victory of Communism could best be achieved not by force but by "intense economic, political, and ideological struggle" carried on within the general framework of peaceful co-existence.[38]

At the CC plenum of January 10–18, 1961, Khrushchev pushed hard for larger allocations to agriculture as a means of improving the well-being of the population; Kozlov and Suslov championed the interests of heavy industry. Personnel changes made by the plenum left the balance of power in the Presidium substantially unchanged.[39]

It was announced at the plenum that the Twenty-second Party Congress would be convened in October, 1961. This was to be a "regular" Congress, i.e., one empowered to elect a new Central Committee. Khrushchev was designated to prepare and present a new Party program (the first since 1919, and only the third in the Party's history), and Kozlov was to report on new Party statutes. The division of labor was significant: Khrushchev was staking out a claim as a major theorist, partly to offset Chinese claims to doctrinal priority, partly to strengthen his internal prestige, while Kozlov was concentrating on the Party machinery.

The decision to convoke a regular Congress was the signal for an intensified struggle within the Party leadership to acquire or retain control of Party organizations in the union republics. On December 28, 1960, Kozlov took part in a plenum of the Armenian Party CC at which a new First Secretary was installed; at the following plenum, on February 10, 1961, this First Secretary presided over sweeping changes in the Buro (the top decision-making body of the CC) and the Secretariat.[40] On April 11 and 12, Kozlov attended a plenum of the Tadzhik Party CC, at which both the First Secretary and the Second Secretary were replaced.[41] This action, however, marked the end of his factional activities for the time being; when he failed to appear at the May Day festivities in Moscow, it was explained that he had suffered a heart attack.

Khrushchev had meanwhile been continuing his friendly overtures to the new administration in Washington. Shortly after the January plenum, he held a private meeting with U.S. Ambassador Llewellyn Thompson at which the possibility was discussed of releasing two U.S. airmen who had been held in Soviet jails ever since their plane was shot down over Soviet territory on July 1, 1960. The formal announcement of their release on January 25 was accompanied by a Soviet statement that President Kennedy had issued an order forbidding U.S. aircraft to violate Soviet airspace, which was promptly confirmed by the White House.[42]

Exploratory negotiations were continued at the foreign-minister level. On March 18, a joint Soviet-American communiqué stated that "frank conversations on various questions of common interest" had been held by Secretary of State Rusk and Soviet Foreign Minister Gromyko.[43] In April, however, prospects for an improvement in Soviet-American relations received a rude jolt with the abortive Bay of Pigs invasion of Cuba. Khrushchev sent a series of sharp messages to President Kennedy, charging the United States with responsibility for the attempted invasion and warning that the Soviet Union would render Cuba "all necessary assistance" in case of an armed attack by the United States.[44]

Sino-Soviet relations in the early months of 1961 were relatively quiet. At talks held in Moscow between governmental delegations of the two powers in early February, the Chinese explained that their decision to curtail economic ties with the Soviet Union was motivated by the belief that they could now carry forward their industrialization program without outside assistance, and by a desire to lighten the aid burden of the Soviets.[45] Beneath the surface, however, the process of alienation between the two parties continued unchecked, although it now centered around the developing feud between Albania and the Soviet Union, or rather between the Albanian Party leaders and Khrushchev. Albania's break with Khrushchev had complex origins, reaching back at least as far as the period following the Twentieth Congress. Fear of Yugoslavia, determination to prevent it from dominating or absorbing Albania, and unrelenting opposition to any Soviet moves toward closer ties with the Yugoslavs appear to have been the principal causes of the Albanian leaders' decision to defy Khrushchev.[46]

The alliance between the Albanians and the Chinese, as we have seen, received its impetus mainly at the Peking session of the WFTU in June, 1960. By early 1961, it had hardened into a full-fledged ideological alliance directed not only against Khrushchev but increasingly against the Soviet regime as such; by this time the Albanian leadership had successfully rid itself of the Party officials who had favored a continuation of the traditional pro-Soviet line. A landmark in the escalation of the Soviet-Albanian and Sino-Soviet disputes was the Fourth Congress of the Albanian Party of Labor, which convened in Tirana, February 13–20, 1961.[47]

Khrushchev Moves to Regain the Initiative: May–October, 1961

Kozlov's illness in April, 1961, was followed by a surge of organizational activity on the part of Khrushchev. At the May 8/9 plenum of the Kirgiz Party CC, V. N. Titov, acting on Khrushchev's behalf, pushed through a reorganization of the Party apparatus, including the removal of a follower of Kozlov who had been installed in February, 1960.[48] Titov continued his organizational work at a plenum of the Moldavian Party CC on May 29, at which major personnel changes were carried through.[49]

The organizational drive was accompanied by a diplomatic offensive. On May 19, it was announced that Khrushchev and President Kennedy would meet in Vienna for two days, June 3/4. At this meeting, Khrushchev presented two documents: a note threatening unilateral action to cut off the Western powers from Berlin at the end of six months if Soviet conditions for a German settlement were not met, and a policy statement setting forth the Soviet position on disarmament.[50] In reply, Kennedy affirmed the legal rights of the Western powers in Berlin and stated that the United States was determined to maintain these rights "at any risk." In a radio and television report to the Soviet people after the conference, Khrushchev repeated his ultimatum, stating that "conclusion of a peace treaty with Germany cannot be postponed any longer. A peaceful settlement in Europe must be attained this year."[51]

Unknown to Khrushchev, however, Colonel Oleg Penkovsky, a member of the Soviet military intelligence organization (GRU), had established contact with American and British officials in late April and had begun to provide them with information on Soviet intentions and capabilities, thus weakening Khrushchev's hand in the approaching struggle over Berlin.[52] It cannot be demonstrated, of course, that information provided by Penkovsky was a crucial factor in stiffening President Kennedy's determination to defend the Western powers' position in Berlin during the crisis of August, 1961, but it may well have made a substantial contribution toward that end.

Late in August, after the failure of Khrushchev's Berlin offensive had become obvious, the Soviet Government announced that it would resume atomic testing, justifying its action by citing alleged aggressive threats by the United States and its allies. The test series, starting on September 1, was the largest ever conducted above ground, culminating in a colossal blast of over fifty megatons on October 30. On September 9, while the tests were in progress, Khrushchev rejected a British-American proposal for a three-power agreement to ban nuclear tests in the atmosphere, stating that "the Soviet Union cannot and will not accede to such a deal."[53]

The test series tended to overshadow the Twenty-second Party Congress, which Khrushchev had planned as a showcase for his new Party program, a blueprint for the building of full Communism in the Soviet Union within twenty years. In other ways, too, the Congress failed to develop along the lines called for in the Khrushchevian script. The downgrading of Stalin's character and policies, initiated at the Twentieth Congress, in 1956, was somewhat unexpectedly renewed, and with it an attack on internal and foreign "neo-Stalinists," meaning primarily the "anti-Party group" and the Albanians, who here served as a polite cover term for the Chinese. This action contributed new fuel to the smoldering Sino-Soviet dispute; the Chinese demonstratively came to the defense of the Albanians.

The significance of these developments with relation to the struggle in the Party has been obscured by the fact that several members of the covert opposition, including Shelepin and Mazurov, lent a vigorous hand to the renewed attack on the "anti-Party group," and thus appeared to be supporting Khrushchev's offensive against the "cult of personality" and the "neo-Stalinists."[54] It is noteworthy, however, that the principal target of Shelepin and Mazurov was Malenkov, not Stalin, and that all the speakers at the Congress who participated in the renewed attack on the "cult of personality" confined their remarks to the period of the 1930 purges, leaving entirely unmentioned the abortive purge of the early 1950's. Khrushchev's reference in his "secret speech" to the "doctors' plot" and Poskrebyshev's part in it was to be the first and—so far—the last occasion on which these matters were officially brought to the fore at a Party Congress.

"Anti-Stalinism," it should be noted, has served as a deceptively simple cover for what is in reality a highly complex phenomenon. It would be desirable to specify *whose* policies (Beria's, Malenkov's, Poskrebyshev's), during *which* period (the Great Purge, the late 1940's, the early 1950's), were being attacked in any given manifestation of "anti-Stalinism." It was the last-named variant (Poskrebyshev, in the early 1950's) that was conspicuous by its absence from the speeches delivered at the Twenty-second Congress, a fact that reflects the difference in relative strength between Khrushchev and the Poskrebyshev group at the congresses of 1956 and 1961.

In introducing the new Party statutes at the Congress, Kozlov claimed that "never yet has there been such firm and unshakable Leninist unity of the Party ranks as in our days."[55] The question naturally arose—Kozlov explicitly stated that it had been raised

during the pre-Congress discussion of the draft statutes—whether
it was still necessary to include in the statutes organizational procedures designed to prevent the formation of factional groupings.
Kozlov's answer to this question, not surprisingly, was a firm
"yes": the case of the "anti-Party group," he said (credit for whose
routing he assigned personally to Khrushchev), showed the possibility of new attempts to shake the unity of the Party. Moreover,
he continued, "the sources for ideological waverings of individual
persons or groups are still not completely eliminated"; some Party
members might fall prey to bourgeois influence from abroad, while
others might fail to keep pace with the dialectical development of
society and remain wedded to outmoded dogmas.[56]

Kozlov's praise of Party unity and his condemnation of factionalism, together with his tribute to Khrushchev's part in preserving
Party unity, should not be allowed to obscure the fact that the
new statutes which he presented to the Congress opened wider an
already existing door to the formation of factional territorial bases
in the Party. The new Party statutes quietly eliminated a provision
in the former statutes (Article 42) under which appointment of
secretaries of oblast and krai committees, as well as the secretaries
of the CC's of the Party organizations in the union republics, was
subject to confirmation by the All-Union CC.[57] Thus the new
statutes made it easier for a member of the Secretariat to influence
the selection of key officials in the territorial and republic parties,
for the purpose of building up a factional organization, without
supervision or interference by the CC.

The significance of the Twenty-second Congress in terms of the
factional struggle becomes even clearer when one turns from the
speeches and resolutions to the personnel changes effected by it.
Organizationally, the Congress was a defeat for Khrushchev. At
the first plenum of the newly elected CC held after the Congress,
he lost five supporters in the Presidium—Mme. Furtseva, Ignatov,
Kirilenko, Mukhitdinov, and Pospelov.[58] Even with these losses, it
is true, he still retained control of the Presidium. Far more serious
from his standpoint was the reorganization of the Secretariat. The
faithful Mukhitdinov was dropped, while of the five new members
—Demichev, Ilyichev, Ponomarev, Spiridonov, and Shelepin—
only two, Demichev and Ilyichev, were dependable Khrushchev
supporters. Ponomarev (who attended the Congress, as we have

seen, from Belorussia) was closely linked with Suslov, while Spiridonov was a follower of Kozlov in the Leningrad Party organization. For the first time since 1957, therefore, Khrushchev and his
followers were outnumbered in the Secretariat.

In mid-November, Shelepin turned over the KGB to his former
colleague in the Komsomol, V. Ye. Semichastny. This step not
only enabled Shelepin to devote full time to his work in the Secretariat but also freed him from the onus of too close association
with the secret police, a crippling handicap in a bid for supreme
power, as Beria's fate sufficiently indicates.

Semichastny's career seems like a deliberate but simplified imita-
tion of Shelepin's. Like Shelepin, he served for a time as First Secretary of the Komsomol (1958/59); like him, he moved on to head
the CC Department of Party Organs for the Union Republics;
like him, he became head of the KGB. He reached the latter post,
however, only after a detour: in the summer of 1959, he turned
over his Komsomol post to Sergei Pavlov and was elected Second
Secretary of the Azerbaidzhan Party, which had just undergone a
purge of "nationalist" elements under Mukhitdinov's supervision.[59]
Semichastny remained in his Azerbaidzhan post until his appointment to head the KGB. This sequence of events, together with the
fact that Semichastny's earlier career was closely identified with
the Ukrainian Komsomol, has been generally interpreted as evidence that he was a member of Khrushchev's "Ukrainian machine" and that his appointment to head the KGB represented the
continuation of Khrushchev's policy of ensuring the close personal
control of the secret police which he supposedly inaugurated with
the appointment of Shelepin to that post in 1958. Khrushchev
may, in fact, have regarded Semichastny as a loyal follower in November, 1961, but the evidence is ambiguous; the assignment to
Azerbaidzhan can also be interpreted as a deliberate interruption in
what had been planned as the orderly sequence of moves whereby
Semichastny would follow in Shelepin's footsteps in the Komso-
mol-CC-KGB sequence. Whatever Khrushchev's views were, the
evidence links Semichastny with the opposition rather than with
Khrushchev. It will be sufficient to note his long, intimate working
relationship with Shelepin in the Komsomol; his well-defined views
on foreign policy—anti-U.S., anti-Yugoslav, pro-Chinese; his vocif-
erous antiliberalism in Soviet cultural affairs; and his promotion

from candidate to full membership in the CC at the first plenum held following Khrushchev's fall, to make clear his position with regard to the internal struggle.[60]

Khrushchev and the Opposition Deadlocked: November, 1961–October, 1962

The reorganization carried out by the Twenty-second Congress and the first post-Congress plenum left the contestants for control of the Party almost evenly matched. Khrushchev still dominated the Presidium but was outnumbered in the Secretariat. In addition to its gains in the Secretariat, the opposition had maintained its grip on the secret police. Under these circumstances it is not surprising that Soviet foreign policy in early 1962 was hesitant and inconsistent. Khrushchev and the opposition were like two wrestlers circling around one another, waiting for an opening they could turn to their advantage. In the early months of 1962, Khrushchev moved to improve relations with the United States, while the opposition explored the possibility of healing the breach with China.

On February 10, 1962, the downed U-2 pilot Francis G. Powers was returned to the United States in exchange for a convicted Soviet spy, Colonel Rudolf Abel, and on February 21, Khrushchev in a message to Kennedy proposed a pooling of U.S. and Soviet space efforts.[61]

On February 22, the All-Union CC sent a letter to the Chinese proposing "an end to needless controversy over issues on which we have differing views," and the "avoidance of public speeches containing statements that cannot smooth over our differences but can only aggravate them."[62] Shortly afterward, a mission headed by Ponomarev stopped off in Peking on its way home from North Vietnam; among those present to greet it on its return to Moscow in early March was Shelepin, thus providing one of the rare occasions during the Khrushchev era on which Shelepin permitted himself to appear in public in open association with a member of the opposition.[63] Although nothing has been published concerning the negotiations, it has been noted that toward the end of March there was a virtual cessation of Soviet-Albanian polemics, which had reached a climax in December, 1961, with the formal rupture of diplomatic relations between the two, and that a lull in the Sino-Soviet dispute set in at about the same time.[64]

Khrushchev's efforts to improve relations with the United States were meanwhile encountering serious obstacles. On March 2, Kennedy announced that the United States would resume atomic testing in the air, with the obvious purpose of overcoming the advance gained by the Soviets in their test series in the autumn of 1961.

The CC plenum that met from March 5 to March 9, 1962, to discuss investment priorities, was something less than an unqualified success for Khrushchev, and he was forced to acknowledge explicitly the continuing need for priority allocation of funds to defense, "the bedrock of the existence of our socialist state, of its development and successes."[65]

While the plenum was meeting, on March 7, Kennedy proposed a broad program of Soviet-American space cooperation, but the effect of this gesture was substantially nullified not only by the new U.S. test series but also by Stewart Alsop's article in a late March issue of the Saturday Evening Post, in which he attributed to Kennedy the view that "under certain circumstances it is possible we shall take the initiative in nuclear conflict with the Soviet Union."[66] Soviet commentators were quick to pick up the implications of the Alsop article: on March 31 Pravda carried an article by "Commentator" entitled "Whom Do Such Speeches Benefit, Mr. Kennedy?" The view attributed to the President, which he did not deny, proved a godsend to the opposition, for it strengthened their argument that U.S. policy was avowedly aggressive and that the Soviet Union could not afford to reduce allocations to heavy industry and armaments.

During April and early May, after nearly a year, Khrushchev renewed his organizational offensive to weaken Kozlov's position. A CC decree of April 10 accused the Leningrad City Party Committee of failure to draw proper conclusions from earlier criticism of its agricultural practices.[67] Two weeks later, Spiridonov lost his position as First Secretary of the Leningrad Party and was promoted to the titular job of Chairman of the Council of the Union of the Supreme Soviet.[68] That his transfer represented a demotion was spelled out in unmistakable terms at a plenum of the Leningrad Oblast Party Committee on May 3, when Khrushchev presided in person over his removal as First Secretary of the province as well.[69] Spiridonov's ouster erased the opposition's lead in the Secretariat. The plenum of April 26 saw another Khrushchev triumph: Kirilenko was brought back as a full member of the Presidium, and two days later it was announced that he had been appointed Deputy Chairman of the CC Bureau for the R.S.F.S.R.[70]

At the same time, Khrushchev took steps to strengthen his claims as chief ideological spokesman in world Communism. On April 5, a third, unscheduled volume of the *Chrestomathy on Marxist-Leninist Philosophy* was sent to the press, consisting almost entirely of Khrushchevian materials, including speeches and the CPSU program adopted at the Twenty-second Party Congress of which he had been publicly identified as the principal author.[71] To legitimize the policy of "peaceful co-existence," an article by three scholars was published in *Izvestia* on April 18 which alleged (without documentary proof) that Lenin was the true originator of this policy.[72]

The Chinese reply to the CPSU letter of February 22, sent on April 7, called for a new international conference of Communist parties, as proposed by a number of CP's (including the pro-Chinese parties of Indonesia, Vietnam, and New Zealand), and urged the CPSU to initiate active steps to resolve its differences with the Albanian Party of Labor.[73] Instead, Khrushchev moved toward friendlier relations with Albania's archenemy, Yugoslavia. In the latter part of April, Soviet Foreign Minister Gromyko paid a five-day official visit to Yugoslavia that concluded with the publication of a joint communiqué in which it was stated that the visit had "confirmed the identity or similarity of views [of both parties] on basic international questions."[74]

About this time, border incidents and alleged Soviet meddling in Sinkiang (Chinese Turkistan) added fuel to the Sino-Soviet dispute. According to a later Chinese statement: "In April and May, 1962, the leaders of the CPSU used their organs and personnel in Sinkiang, China, to carry out large-scale subversive activities in the Ili region of Sinkiang and enticed and coerced several tens of thousands of Chinese citizens into going to the Soviet Union."[75]

Khrushchev's organizational gains of April and early May continued or were offset—the significance of the event is open to either interpretation—by the appointment, on May 11, of A. A. Yepishev (who had been serving as Soviet Ambassador to Yugoslavia) to head the Main Political Administration of the Armed Forces (PRU). Yepishev replaced F. I. Golikov, who retired for reasons of health.[76] This appointment has been generally interpreted in the West as a move by Khrushchev to strengthen his control of the armed forces, on the assumption that Yepishev, who had held Party posts in the Ukraine under Khrushchev, was his loyal follower.[77] Yepishev's career, however, particularly his service as Deputy Minister of State Security in 1951–53, identifies him as a close associate of Poskrebyshev. It appears that Yepishev was called on to play one of the most delicate and important roles in the factional struggle against Khrushchev: as chief of the PRU, his mission was to extend the opposition's influence in the armed forces without alerting Khrushchev to what was transpiring. Yepishev carried out this responsible assignment brilliantly, and was rewarded by promotion to full membership in the CC at the first post-Khrushchev plenum, in November, 1964.

As Ambassador to Yugoslavia, Yepishev had contributed effectively to the task of improving Soviet-Yugoslav relations; on the eve of his departure from Belgrade, he was awarded a Yugoslav state decoration "for services in connection with the development and strengthening of peaceful cooperation and friendly relations between the two countries."[78] Thus Khrushchev had reason to regard him, as virtually every Western analyst has done, as a loyal Khrushchevite, and to consider his appointment a move by Khrushchev to tighten his control of the armed forces.

The opposition made effective use of President Kennedy's tacit acceptance of the principle that under certain unspecified circumstances the United States might initiate a nuclear conflict. Khrushchev attempted to draw the sting from Kennedy's position by stating that he would not reciprocate in kind (speech in Sofia, May 19),[79] but the opposition hammered the point home, and on June 1 their tactics bore fruit in the form of an official announcement of a price increase in consumers' goods, which was justified on the grounds that the "international reaction led by the U.S.A. is at present furiously rattling the saber, pursuing a feverish arms race, and hatching plans for a surprise nuclear-rocket attack on the U.S.S.R. and the socialist countries."[80] Kennedy's position as set forth in the Alsop article was prominently featured in support of this assertion. On the same day, a decree of the Presidium of the Supreme Soviet lowered the draft age from eighteen to seventeen, thereby ensuring the maintenance of the strength of the Soviet armed forces at a high level, another reversal of Khrushchev's policies in the military field.[81]

Three days after the announcement of the price increase, the Soviet Government issued a formal statement condemning the current U.S. nuclear test series and linking it with the Kennedy-Alsop statement as proof of aggressive intentions on the part of the United States.[82] During June, Khrushchev and other Soviet spokesmen came back again and again to the Kennedy position, an indication of the importance it had assumed in the internal struggle for power.[83]

In early July, the United States stepped up the pace of the nuclear-arms race. A massive U.S. underground test on July 6 was followed the next day by a smaller test, which was, however, the first U.S. test in the atmosphere since 1958. On July 9, a nuclear device was set off in the stratosphere over the Pacific, temporarily disrupting radio communications in the area.

The Kennedy Administration had meanwhile been engaged in a reassessment of comparative U.S. and Soviet capabilities, and had reached the conclusion that in reality there had been no "missile gap" favoring the Soviet Union, and that the United States was ahead and had been all the time. In a speech on July 10, Khrushchev sharply disputed this view, citing in support the superblasts of the Soviet 1961 test series and claiming possession of weapons that the United States could not match, including an antimissile missile.[84] On the following day, however, the State Department issued a statement affirming the U.S. nuclear lead, which the Soviet press, in a TASS statement published on July 13, promptly challenged as "from beginning to end a gross misrepresentation of the facts."[85] But the TASS statement implicitly conceded the U.S. claim to superiority by maintaining that the Soviet Union, as the power that had been forced to catch up to the original U.S. nuclear lead, had a moral right to "test last," an argument obviously meant to justify a new series of Soviet tests. On July 22, accordingly, the Soviet Government announced its decision to resume nuclear testing, justifying the step on the basis of not only the recent U.S. series but also the "aggressive designs" of those "who threaten us and our allies with preventive war" (a clear reference to the Kennedy-Alsop statement).[86]

It was within this context—a sharply heightened arms race with the United States, accompanied by U.S. claims of nuclear superiority and an implied strategy not barring a pre-emptive strike, while Khrushchev had been forced onto the defensive in internal policy by the opposition's effective use of the issue of alleged U.S. aggressiveness—that the decision was taken to install medium-range ballistic missiles in Cuba. The exact date of the decision is unknown, but it must have been before mid-July. According to available evidence, the Soviet rocket buildup began in the second half of the month, and the decision may have been reached during the visit to Moscow in early July of a Cuban trade mission headed by Raúl Castro.

As to the identity of the initiator of the venture, there can be little doubt that it was Khrushchev. The pattern of his actions over a period of years makes that a reasonable assumption, and all available evidence tends to confirm it. His motive was again, as in the Berlin crises of 1958/59 and 1961, to gain a symbolic but nonetheless decisive diplomatic-military triumph over the United States, which would buttress his internal position. The idea of using Cuba as a Soviet missile base was not new; we have noted Khrushchev's denial of a year earlier that the Soviet Union needed such a base, coupled with his assertion that the Monroe Doctrine was dead.

It is highly unlikely, however, that Khrushchev acted alone in deciding on the missile venture. Had he done so, the failure of the move would certainly have resulted in organizational defeats for him in the Party comparable to those of the May, 1960, plenum. On the contrary, the first post-crisis plenum, as we shall see, appeared to be an organizational victory for Khrushchev. Not only for Khrushchev, however: at the November plenum, Shelepin was to take a long step forward, and it is reasonably clear that the agenda for the November plenum was fixed while the missile venture was still being carried out, i.e., while Khrushchev might have been confidently expecting the gamble to be successful.

A bargain between Khrushchev and Shelepin thus underlay the organizational changes of the November plenum. This analysis helps to explain why there were no open recriminations by the opposition against Khrushchev following his retreat in Cuba and why a member of the opposition, Ponomarev, published an article on the eve of the November plenum defending the missile gamble.[87]

The temporary lull in the Sino-Soviet dispute which had begun in late March continued into the summer, with each side maintaining its position but without bitter invective. The brief period in February and March during which the opposition had been able to influence Soviet policy toward China had passed, and when the CPSU replied on May 31 to the Chinese letter of April 7 (in which the Chinese had proposed an international Communist conference), its apparent acceptance of the proposal was accompanied by a condition—the ideological submission of Albania to the CPSU —which the Chinese were certain to reject.[88]

Despite the heightened arms race and the clandestine Soviet preparation of missile bases in Cuba, some progress was made during the summer of 1962 toward more cordial Soviet-American relations, which further exacerbated the Sino-Soviet dispute. During August, the Kennedy Administration, feeling secure in its nuclear superiority, took several steps in the direction of a limitation of the nuclear-arms race. On August 1, the President announced the United States' willingness to accept national monitoring of an international test-ban treaty, a concession to the Soviet position.

Soviet confidence at this time was strengthened by a number of technological advances. A new Soviet test series opened on August 5; six days later, Soviet space scientists scored a significant triumph with the first twin orbital flight.

On August 25, the Soviet Government informed the Chinese that Secretary of State Rusk had proposed the conclusion of an agreement among the nuclear powers to prevent proliferation of atomic weapons, and stated that it had given an affirmative answer to this proposal, thus reiterating its denial of nuclear aid to the Chinese.[89] On August 27, the British and U.S. delegations at the Eighteen-Nation Conference on Disarmament submitted a draft treaty on a partial test ban (excluding all but underground tests). On August 28, V. V. Kuznetsov, head of the Soviet delegation to the conference, criticized the proposal as favoring the Western powers, but nevertheless offered to accept a partial ban accompanied by a moratorium on underground testing, an offer the

Western delegations held unacceptable, since it did not include any provisions for verification.[90]

It is not necessary to follow here the development of the Cuban missile crisis in detail; what is significant in the present context is the evidence pointing to a sudden sharpening of the factional struggle as the crisis approached its denouement. On October 20, the Chinese launched a massive attack along the Indian border, claiming that India was preparing to attack them. Later, they said that Khrushchev had known of their plans a week in advance and had acknowledged the validity of the evidence they had cited as proof that India was making preparations for an attack.[91] The next day, while Khrushchev still had reason to be confident of victory, *Pravda* published an anti-Stalinist poem by Yevtushenko, "Stalin's Heirs."[92] On the following day, Penkovsky was seized "redhanded," according to the later official indictment.[93] Once again, as in August, 1961, Penkovsky's intelligence reports to the West had helped to undermine Khrushchev's bluff and had increased the United States' confidence in its position. On October 24, China presented a three-point proposal for settlement of its dispute with India; a day later, both *Pravda* and *Izvestia* hailed the proposal as an "acceptable" and "constructive" basis for negotiations to end the conflict.

The turning point in the crisis came on October 28, when Khrushchev, appalled by the evidence of U.S. determination to force withdrawal of the missiles from Cuba, sent Kennedy a letter that signified Soviet capitulation.[94]

Renewed Offensive by the Opposition and the Elimination of Kozlov: November, 1962–April, 1963

From the immediate aftermath of the Cuban missile crisis to Kozlov's second and more serious heart attack in April, 1963, is a period in which the opposition gradually extended its offensive to all major policy fronts, internal as well as foreign, and in which the struggle for power was broadened to include the Communist parties of a number of European states. At first glance this is surprising, since it would appear that Khrushchev was able during this period to overcome the deadlock in the ruling bodies of the Party and re-establish his predominance.

The CC plenum of November 19–22, 1962, made a number of important decisions, the most striking of which was the reorganization of the Party into agricultural and industrial sectors.[95] Khrushchev's memoranda for the period September–October, 1962, make it clear that he had personally sponsored this plan; its adoption, therefore, was a victory for him.[96] He also registered a gain in the reorganization of the Secretariat, where four new secretaries—A. P. Rudakov, I. Ye. Polyakov, Ya. V. Andropov, and V. N. Titov—were added, bringing the total membership to twelve. It is reasonable to assume that at this period these men were Khrushchevites. Khrushchev was thus in a position to congratulate himself on having brought to a successful conclusion his assault on the opposition's stronghold in the Secretariat, which he had begun with the ouster of Spiridonov.

Another organizational change initiated by Khrushchev was the establishment by the plenum of the Central Asian Bureau of the CC.[97] The idea of coordinating the economies of the four Central Asian republics had occurred to Khrushchev during his tour of the area in September and October, and at the plenum he presented the proposal to establish the bureau without having consulted his colleagues in advance. This highhanded procedure has been interpreted as a sign of Khrushchev's unchallenged power at the time,[98] yet it can now be recognized as one of those mistakes that were to cost him heavily at a later time. Significantly, he did not immediately succeed in his further purpose of establishing an administrative organ to rationalize and coordinate the Central Asian economy. It was not until February 5, 1963, that a Central Asian Council of the National Economy was established, replacing the planning and administrative organs of the Kirgiz, Uzbek, Tadzhik, and Kazakh republics.[99] That the move aroused opposition in these republics, and that the opposition was effectively employed in the grand strategy of Khrushchev's overthrow, can be confidently inferred from the fact that this council was one of the first of Khrushchev's organizational innovations to be abolished after his fall.[100]

Khrushchev's gains at the plenum can be seen in retrospect to have been offset by the establishment of a formidable new center of power in the Party and government which he did not directly control and which constituted an ominous challenge to his dominance. This was the Committee of Party-State Control, which was to function under the CC and the Council of Ministers.[101] On November 23, immediately after the plenum, Shelepin was appointed to head the new committee. In effect, the plenum had re-established the old Commissariat of Workers' and Peasants' Inspectorate (Rabkrin), which had served as one of Stalin's principal bases in his drive for power in the 1920's. Like Khrushchev's reorganization of the Party apparatus, the resurrection of the commissariat had been prepared by a campaign in earlier months, but one in which Khrushchev had taken comparatively little part.[102]

The opposition mounted its offensive first in the policy area of relations between Party ideology and the creative intelligentsia. At the November plenum, a group of conservative critics, artists, and Party ideologists reportedly petitioned the CC to halt the growing movement toward relaxation of controls in literature and the arts,[103] a movement that had been effectively used by Khrushchev to enlist support among the intellectuals for his policy innovations. It was a gain for the opposition, therefore, when on December 1, Khrushchev was maneuvered into a direct condemnation of experimentation in the visual arts at an exhibition of works of painting and sculpture by a group of Moscow artists known as "the Belyutin circle."[104] The exhibit had been shown privately during November, with a minimum of publicity; the decision to transfer it to larger quarters and to place it squarely in the center of the Party leadership's attention was a master stroke in the factional struggle. (See Chapter 4.)

The conservatives were quick to take advantage of the breach that opened between Khrushchev and the creative intelligentsia. They forced the liberals onto the defensive at a meeting, on December 7, between various Party leaders and a group of writers, artists, and other intellectuals. At this meeting, Galina Serebryakova, a writer of Stalinist views despite her personal history (she was not only a veteran of the labor camps but had lost two husbands in them), startled her audience by the disclosure that Poskrebyshev was living near Moscow and—what was even more sensational—was writing his memoirs.[105] Mme. Serebryakova's disclosure, which may have been intended to intimidate not merely the intellectuals but Khrushchev as well, came close to public identification of the underlying tensions in the Soviet leadership during the Khrushchev era.

From December, 1962, to late March, 1963, the conservatives continued to press the attack on the cultural sector, while Khrushchev and his principal ideological spokesman, Ilyichev, assumed the role of defenders of strict Party control in literature and the arts, partly because Khrushchev sincerely believed in the necessity for control (an indication that his alliance with the liberal intelligentsia was more a matter of tactics than the result of sincere conviction), but mainly because this was the only way in which he could ride out the attack. (His behavior in this episode was thus similar to that which he had followed with regard to Soviet-American relations in the summer of 1960.)

During the period November, 1962–January, 1963, congresses were held by several European Communist parties: Bulgaria, November 5–14; Hungary, November 20–24; Italy, December 2–8; Czechoslovakia, December 4–8; and East Germany, January 15–21, 1963. Each congress was attended by a delegation from the CPSU headed by a member of the Presidium: Suslov in Sofia, Kuusinen in Budapest, Kozlov in Rome, Brezhnev in Prague, and Khrushchev himself in East Berlin. Thus the two most openly identified members of the opposition, Suslov and Kozlov, took part in the congresses along with Khrushchev and two of his most dependable supporters in the Presidium.

These congresses provided an opportunity for the acceleration of the principal processes at work in the international Communist movement: the internal struggle for power in the CPSU, which now included a competition for control of the other parties, and the contest between the Soviets and the Chinese for ideological and organizational hegemony. In Western analyses of these congresses, the latter process has received most attention, and it has been generally assumed that each of the five CPSU delegations at their respective congresses was following a single operational plan, aimed at sharpening the split with the Chinese. The proceedings of the congresses, however, show marked differences both in the behavior of the CPSU delegations and in the subsequent actions of the parties concerned, differences which in some cases were to play crucial roles in the struggle for power in the CPSU, as well as in the international Communist movement.

The most important congresses from this point of view were those held in Italy and Czechoslovakia, though all of the congresses made their contribution to the general trend.

At the earliest of the congresses, that in Bulgaria, Suslov supervised an extensive purge of "Stalinists"; subsequent events proved, however, that the Bulgarian Party had been in no significant way "liberalized" by this purge, nor brought into line with the Khrushchevian concept of "de-Stalinization."[106] The Hungarian Congress produced no developments of general significance, as was to be expected from the encounter between the most pro-Khrushchev of the East European regimes (Kadar's) and the most pro-Khrushchev member of the Presidium (Kuusinen).

By contrast, the Italian Congress was the meeting ground of a Party that had enthusiastically welcomed Khrushchev's policy innovations at the Twentieth Party Congress and of a leading oppositionist, Kozlov. This combination produced the ambiguous developments that have puzzled Western analysts, particularly the evident turn on the part of the Communist Party of Italy (CPI) from its previous close adherence to Khrushchev's line in foreign policy.[107] During the Congress, Italian and Soviet spokesmen presented wide-ranging criticisms of the Albanian and Chinese ideological positions, to which the Chinese replied in kind. In the final resolution adopted by the Congress, however, criticism of the Albanians was considerably muted, while the Chinese were not directly identified at all. Furthermore, during the Congress, the Italians invited the Chinese to take part in bilateral talks to eliminate the differences between the two parties (an invitation which the Chinese ignored). In his speech to the Congress, Kozlov defended Soviet policy during the Cuban missile crisis but failed to assign any credit to Khrushchev for the peaceful solution of the crisis.[108]

The Congress marked a turning point in the Party's history. While Palmiro Togliatti and the CPI were subsequently no less stanch than formerly in their support of Khrushchev's policy of internal liberalization and his concept of decentralization in the international Communist movement, they quietly but firmly broke with his tactic of pushing the split with the Chinese to an open break.

Of Togliatti at an earlier period it has been said that "he had come to realize that the prospects for any Communist were strictly dependent upon his support of the winning side among the warring factions inside the Russian Bolshevik Party."[109] The evidence of the December Congress indicates that Togliatti was still guided by this principle, and that he was sufficiently impressed by Kozlov's presentation of the case for the anti-Khrushchev opposition to switch his loyalty from Khrushchev to the opposition. This shift was to have momentous consequences not only for the course of the Sino-Soviet dispute but also for Khrushchev and Togliatti personally.

In Rome, a pro-Khrushchev Party had been visited and influenced by a leading oppositionist; in Prague, a stubbornly unreconstructed Stalinist Party was host to a Khrushchevian emissary who was able to achieve only part of his mission. To understand fully the significance of the Czechoslovak Party Congress in relation to the struggle for power in the CPSU, it is necessary to review some earlier developments in the history of the Czechoslovak Party.

In 1956, shortly after the Twentieth Congress of the CPSU, the Czechoslovak Party conducted an inconclusive investigation of the 1952 trial of Rudolf Slanský and others, which formed the penultimate act in the drama of purge in the satellites that ended in the January, 1953, announcement of the "doctors' plot."[110] In February, 1961, Rudolf Bárák, who had headed the 1956 investigating commission, led a Czechoslovak delegation to the Fourth Congress of the Albanian Party, where his behavior led the Albanians to identify him as a Khrushchev supporter.[111] Four months later, he was ousted as Czechoslovak Minister of Internal Affairs.[112]

Despite the renewal of the anti-Stalin campaign at the Twenty-second Congress of the CPSU, in October, 1961, the Czechoslovak Party firmly refused to reopen its investigation of the Slanský trial. Bárák's 1956 investigation, however, had put him in possession of facts which not only proved the trial to have been a judicial frame-up but also constituted a serious threat to the position of the Party leadership, including First Secretary Novotný. Early in February, 1962, Bárák was ousted from the Czechoslovak Presidium (a move enthusiastically applauded by the Albanians), and two weeks later, Novotný announced his arrest on charges ranging from embezzlement of state funds to an attempt to seize power.[113] Two months later, Bárák was convicted and sentenced to fifteen years' imprisonment.[114]

At the December, 1962, Congress, the Czechoslovak Party leadership thus had reason to be confident of its ability to resist Khrushchevian pressure for renewed measures of "de-Stalinization." By now, however, there was a mounting demand in the Party itself for a reinvestigation of the 1952 trials, and Novotný somewhat reluctantly returned to the subject. Although he placed the blame for the inconclusive character of the 1956 investigation on Bárák, and assured the Congress that victims of unjust imprisonment had been freed, he announced that a new commission had been appointed to investigate the political trials of 1949–54. It was to report its findings in four months.[115]

Subsequent events confirmed the existence of a direct link between the slow process of "de-Stalinization" in Czechoslovakia and the struggle for power in the CPSU. When the opposition appeared to be in the ascendant, token gestures were all that the Czechoslovak Party felt called on to make; it was only after Khrushchev had clearly won an internal victory that the Czechoslovak Party began seriously to purge its Stalinists and rehabilitate the victims of Stalinism.

The outcome of the Cuban missile crisis had left Khrushchev with the difficult problem of justifying Soviet actions, first in moving the missiles into Cuba, then in moving them out under pressure from the United States. In a speech to the Supreme Soviet on December 12, he addressed himself to this delicate task.[116] His defense of Soviet policy centered around the argument that the Soviet purpose in moving the missiles into Cuba had been to prevent an attack by the United States on the island, that this goal was achieved when Kennedy pledged that there would be no invasion if the missiles and other offensive weapons were withdrawn (Khrushchev failed to mention the vital U.S. stipulation that the withdrawal must be supervised by U.N. observers), and that the outcome of the crisis was therefore neither a defeat nor a victory for either side but a reasonable compromise in which each side made concessions in the interests of world peace.

Khrushchev's argument thus included an explicit recognition of the U.S. leaders' soberness and sense of responsibility, and of their trustworthiness in carrying out their pledged word, which was in the sharpest possible contrast to the Chinese characterization of the U.S. leaders as "imperialists" whose only motive was aggression and whose promises were worthless. Khrushchev added insult to injury, as far as the Chinese were concerned, by alluding to their "failure" to "liberate" Macao and Hong Kong, and by labeling as "Trotskyite" the position of the Albanians and other unnamed critics of Soviet behavior. Moreover, he once again explicitly recognized Yugoslavia as a "socialist" country (in a tribute to Tito, who was then on a state visit to the Soviet Union).

The Chinese responded promptly and vigorously to these calculated affronts. On December 15, the CPC published a theoretical article justifying its efforts to line up support for its position among other Communist parties, [117] and followed this with a series of programmatic articles analyzing its principal policy differences with Khrushchev.[118] Taking advantage of the forum provided by the November–December congresses of the European Communist parties, the Chinese had already been seeking converts to their views. A serious clash occurred at the January, 1963, Congress of the East German Socialist Unity Party (SED) in East Berlin. A speech to the Congress by Khrushchev on the sixteenth, though it contained gestures toward reconciliation with the Chinese, included also an unrestrained assault on their views.[119] On January 18, Wu Hsiu-chüan, head of the CPC delegation to the Congress, delivered a slashing reply, attacking not only "American imperialism" and the Yugoslav "revisionists," but Khrushchev's policies in Cuba and elsewhere.[120]

The increased boldness of the opposition in early 1963 led to a renewal of their factional activities. During February, Kozlov toured the Central Asian republics. In his visit to Kazakhstan from February 20 to 23, he supervised significant personnel changes in this previously Khrushchevian territory.[121]

The general offensive of the opposition was accompanied by signs of insubordination to Khrushchev within the Soviet armed forces. The Soviet military leaders had long been restive under his dominance. They had been critical of his manpower cuts in the armed forces and of his emphasis on missiles and nuclear weapons at the expense of traditional doctrine. The Soviet retreat in Cuba was followed by increased tension in relations between the Party and the armed forces, and by February an unmistakable note of hostility to Khrushchev could be detected in statements by military leaders. Characteristic was an article that Marshal Malinovsky wrote to mark the anniversary of the battle of Stalingrad, in which he minimized the part played by Khrushchev in planning the strategy of the battle, and compounded this act of disrespect by including a favorable reference to Marshal Zhukov, whose name had been systematically de-emphasized in Soviet military history ever since his ouster from the Presidium in October, 1957.[122]

In the early months of 1963, the Communist regime in Rumania was added to the list of trouble spots for Khrushchev. Like Czechoslovakia, Rumania had undergone a political purge in 1952, when plans were being launched in the Soviet Union for a new purge. Between 1953 and 1960, the post of Soviet Ambassador to Rumania had been held successively by two men—Melnikov and Yepishev—who had been implicated in the "doctors' plot." These facts may help to explain why the Rumanian Workers' Party, under First Secretary Gheorghiu-Dej, had been even more successful than the Czechoslovak Party in resisting all efforts to "de-Stalinize" and to reopen the 1952 trials.

In April, 1962, the Rumanians pushed to completion their collectivization program for agriculture, in preparation for launching a program of industrialization. At a meeting of the Council of Mutual Economic Aid (CMEA) in June, 1962, they clearly stated their intention of building up Rumanian industry, in obvious disharmony with Khrushchev's plans for a division and rationalization of labor among the members of CMEA, in which Rumania was to play the role of principal purveyor of agricultural foodstuffs and raw materials for the more highly industrialized member states.[123] When the CMEA Executive Council met in Moscow on February 15–21, 1963, Rumanian intransigence was even more marked, and, more serious for Khrushchev, it now included an increasingly independent line in foreign policy.[124] Taking advantage of the opportunity for maneuver provided by the Sino-Soviet dispute, the Rumanians sent their ambassador back to the Albanian capital (from which all Soviet-bloc diplomatic missions had been withdrawn following the Soviet-Albanian diplomatic break in December, 1961). In early March, they concluded a trade agreement with Albania, and in April, one with China.

Henceforth, Rumania was to pursue its way in open disregard of Khrushchev's wishes, in the evident conviction that his position was too insecure to make adherence to his policies obligatory.

As in other periods of heightened offensive by the opposition, so at this time new efforts were made in the CPSU to settle the differences with the Chinese. On February 21, the CPSU sent a letter to the CPC which deplored the damage to the international Communist movement that had resulted from "the open and increasingly sharp polemics" between the two parties and which called for "immediate, concrete practical steps aimed at improving the atmosphere in relations among all fraternal parties."[125] As a step in this direction, the CPSU proposed a meeting of representatives of the two parties "at a high level," the attention of which would be focused on "the common tasks to be accomplished in the struggle against imperialism and its aggressive plans, for the further broadening of the people's liberation struggle, for the solidification and all-round development of the world socialist commonwealth and intensification of its influence all over the world, and for strengthening the unity of the Communist movement"—a formulation clearly designed to conciliate the Chinese by accepting their priority scale on the agenda for the proposed conference.

In the negotiations that followed, each party tried to maneuver the other into conceding its past errors by sending its leader to the proposed meeting. Khrushchev, perhaps foreseeing the likelihood of a Chinese invitation to him to visit Peking, had already canceled a projected visit to Southeast Asia. In an interview with the Soviet Ambassador on February 23, Mao Tse-tung blandly ignored this fact (assuming it was known to him) and, while politely declining to go to Moscow himself, suggested that Khrushchev might stop off in Peking on his way home from Cambodia. This suggestion was incorporated in the formal CPC reply (dated March 9) to the Soviet letter of February 21.[126] The CPC letter was conciliatory in tone; it not only welcomed the proposal for bilateral negotiations but promised to observe a temporary moratorium on public replies to direct attacks on the CPC by members of the CPSU and other parties. Behind this elaborate display of cordiality, however, lay a stratagem: the Chinese were testing the CPSU's sincerity by forcing Khrushchev either to make the trip to

Peking, thereby in effect admitting that he had been in the wrong and that the CPC was the legitimately aggrieved participant in the dispute, or to assume the responsibility personally of refusing. The letter was successful in achieving this purpose, as will presently be made apparent.

Problems of resource allocation—the focal point of the policy dispute within the Soviet leadership—were discussed by Khrushchev with unusual frankness in a pre-election speech on February 28, 1963. He drew a direct connection between the need for high military expenditures and the slow pace of improvement in Soviet living standards. "If the international situation were better," he said, "if we could achieve an understanding and shake off the burden of arms, this would multiply the possibilities for a further upsurge of the economy and increase the well-being of the people."[127]

Khrushchev's opponents now ventured to make the clearest overt expression of internal opposition during any period prior to Khrushchev's fall. The conservative attack on the cultural front continued at a meeting in the Kremlin on March 7–8 between top Party and government leaders and prominent artists and writers. At the meeting, Khrushchev and Ilyichev stressed the need for strong Party controls in literature and the arts, thus, as before, bending with the wind and doing the work of the conservatives.

On March 13, Khrushchev presided over a joint session of the Presidium and the Council of Ministers which carried through an extensive administrative reorganization of the Soviet economy, centralizing defense and armament production under a newly established Supreme Council of the National Economy and thus partially reversing his earlier moves to overcome excessive centralization in the administration of the Soviet economy. Shortly thereafter, he left Moscow for the south, making inspection stops along the way as he traveled to his vacation retreat at Gagra, on the Black Sea. There he remained for the rest of March and the first half of April.

On April 5, a decree was adopted by the Supreme Council of the National Economy which provided for an investment during 1963 of 1 billion rubles above the planned level in consumers' goods; the decree was not published, however, until April 21, under

circumstances that indicated it had encountered strenuous opposition in the Presidium.

During Khrushchev's absence from Moscow, the opposition was
given an opportunity to show its style in the conduct of Soviet internal and foreign policy. A virulent anti-American campaign was
mounted;[128] the conservative attack on the cultural and intellectual liberals was vigorously pushed; and Kozlov extended his
factional activities in Central Asia, adding Turkmenistan to the
republics in which he had supervised major personnel changes.[129]

The anti-American campaign got under way, on March 12, with
a Soviet note protesting alleged firing by U.S. warships on a Soviet
trawler, an action which the note characterized as "a gross violation of generally recognized norms of international law and of
the principles of freedom of navigation on the high seas, an act of
undisguised arrogance capable of leading to grave consequences."[130]
On March 22, a protest was made against the United States' attempt to block the sale of steel pipes to the U.S.S.R. by Japan
and West Germany.[131] On March 23, a TASS statement called
the French nuclear explosion of March 18 "a challenge to the
peoples" and linked it with the U.S. atomic armament program.[132]
On March 27, a note protested an incident of March 17 involving
a Soviet commercial vessel,[133] and on the same day, the Soviet
Foreign Ministry rejected as unfounded a U.S. protest of March
15 concerning an alleged violation of U.S. airspace over Alaska by
a Soviet plane.[134] On March 29, a Soviet note demanded that the
United States pay for damages sustained by a Soviet freighter in an
alleged attack by anti-Castro Cuban émigrés.[135]

This flurry of diplomatic protests was accompanied by a series
of stridently anti-American articles in the Soviet press. On March
17, *Pravda* stigmatized the forthcoming trial of the U.S. Communist Party under the McCarran Act as "one of the most dis-
graceful acts [ever perpetrated] against the elementary rights and
freedoms of the American people," and maintained that "reaction
is trampling underfoot the Bill of Rights and the Constitution,
which the defenders of the 'American way of life' so shrilly ad-
vertise."[136] On March 27, Yuri Zhukov, in an article in *Pravda* on
U.S. policy in South Vietnam, wrote: "Look here, people! Here is
your American freedom and democracy in action. This is a page
from the life of the cannibals of our time."[137] The secret police con-

tributed to the anti-American campaign with a long article on the Penkovsky case in *Izvestia* (March 12/13), which identified him as "an American spy," linked him exclusively with American diplomats, and neglected to mention that it was a *British* businessman, G. M. Wynne, who had been his principal Western contact.[138]

In the latter part of March, Khrushchev began to reassert his policy-making powers. Systematically, he counterattacked on one front after another, gradually recapturing the initiative and in the process eliminating one of his most dangerous opponents.

On March 30, the CPSU sent a lengthy reply to the CPC letter of March 9.[139] In sharp contrast to the CPSU letter of February 21, the March 30 letter represented Khrushchev's point of view, providing an extensive review of his position on the principal ideological issues in dispute between the two parties. The letter took up such problems as the nature of imperialism, the reduced likelihood of major wars, the need for peaceful coexistence, and the nonexportability of revolutions. Despite its polite tone, its formulations were certain to infuriate the Chinese, especially the again-repeated statement with regard to Yugoslavia: "We believe it to be a socialist country." This statement, incidentally, provides strong evidence that the March 30 letter expressed the views of Khrushchev, since the question of Yugoslavia's status had by this time become an important point of dispute not only between Moscow and Peking but also within the Soviet leadership. Khrushchev had hinted at the existence of differences of opinion on the subject in his above-mentioned speech to the Supreme Soviet of December 12, 1962, when he said: "Some claim that Yugoslavia is not a socialist country. [However,] if one proceeds from objective laws, from the teaching of Marxism-Leninism, it is impossible to deny that Yugoslavia is a socialist country."[140] The events that now transpired, in early April, 1963, revealed that the Chinese were not the only ones who denied to Yugoslavia the right to be called "socialist."

On April 8, *Pravda* published the annual list of slogans for May Day. Two were of special interest, numbers 18 and 29:

18. Fraternal greetings to the working people of the People's Republic of Albania, who are building socialism! Hail to the eternal, indestructible friendship and cooperation between the Soviet and Albanian peoples! . . .

29. Fraternal greetings to the working people of the Federal People's Republic of Yugoslavia! May the friendship and cooperation between the Soviet and Yugoslav peoples develop and grow stronger in the interests of the struggle for peace and socialism!

Coming as it did immediately after the characterization of Yugoslavia as a "socialist" country in the CPSU letter of March 30, this formulation constituted both a concession to the Chinese and a direct challenge to Khrushchev. The challenge was not permitted to pass unopposed.

On April 9, *Pravda* published a factual summary of the newly adopted Yugoslav constitution (which the Chinese were later to denounce as "the embodiment of the out-and-out revisionist program of the Tito clique"). Kozlov's last public appearance for a number of months, and his last active participation in Soviet politics, took place on April 10, when he attended the Second All-Union Congress of Artists. On the same day, *Pravda* announced that a plenum of the CC would convene on May 28, at which Ilyichev would present a report on ideology. On April 11, *Pravda* published a short but unprecedented announcement "correcting" the May Day slogan on Yugoslavia to read:

29. Fraternal greetings to the working people of the Socialist Federal Republic of Yugoslavia, *who are building socialism* [italics added]. Hail to the eternal, indestructible friendship and cooperation between the Soviet and Yugoslav peoples!

These developments were accompanied by a sudden renewal of the Soviet-American dialogue. On April 8, agreement was reached by the two powers on the establishment of a direct telephone connection between Moscow and Washington,[141] and on the same day, a note was sent to the United States urging joint measures to halt the further spread of nuclear weapons.[142] On April 11, *Izvestia* reported a statement by a group of U.S. physicists advocating conclusion of a ban on nuclear testing, the first Soviet comment on what was to become a dominant theme in Soviet foreign policy in the following months, while *Pravda* carried a translation of the statement itself. When the Soviet press announced on April 18 that the KGB had completed its investigation of the Penkovsky case, there was no reference to U.S. implication.[143]

Khrushchev returned to Moscow in triumph on April 20, "sunburned, smiling, and at the top of his form," according to an American observer,[144] and plunged at once into the tasks of administration. The next day, the Soviet press carried a belated account of the consumer-oriented decree of April 5.[145] From April 22 to April 24, Khrushchev presided over an R.S.F.S.R. conference on Party leadership in industry and construction, concerning which *Pravda* reported that his "brilliant speech was listened to with huge attention, and more than once was interrupted with warm applause." The speech emphasized a number of Khrushchev's favorite themes in economic policy: the importance of greater attention to the chemical industry, the possibility of economies in armament production by improved administration, and the economic advantages that would accrue from all-union division of labor in industrial production. He touched briefly on the role of the creative intelligentsia, and despite his reassertion of the need for Party ideological controls, was much less categorical in his formulation than he had been at the March 7/8 meeting.

The setback to the opposition was unmistakable, but Khrushchev's victory was still incomplete. On May 3, it was announced that the plenum of ideology would be postponed until June 18.[146] On the following day, exactly three years from the date of Kozlov's appointment to the Secretariat, his illness was announced, but in a way which indicated that he retained his position on the Presidium and Secretariat.[147]

The announcement of Kozlov's illness was immediately followed by signs of renewed confidence on the part of the liberal writers. On May 5, the April issue of the liberal journal *Novy mir*, publication of which had been delayed, was released to go to press; its lead article, by Tvardovsky, the editor, was a reaffirmation of the journal's editorial policies and an attack on Party hacks in literature.[148] At about the same time, Tvardovsky gave an interview to UPI correspondent Henry Shapiro, stressing in it the same themes and linking Khrushchev directly with the policy of increased cultural liberalism.[149]

These internal events, though important, were speedily overshadowed by developments in the field of foreign affairs. A distinctly perceptible acceleration now took place in the pace of events in both Soviet-American and Sino-Soviet relations: with

America, steady progress to the conclusion of an agreement to ban nuclear tests above ground; with China, an equally steady advance to the brink of an open, irrevocable split.

Khrushchev Triumphant: May, 1963–July, 1964

Following the incapacitation of Kozlov, Soviet politics came under the domination of Khrushchev, all opposition either eliminated, won over, or temporarily silenced. The high point of Khrushchev's unchallenged dominance extended from the June, 1963, plenum to mid-October, when signs appeared of renewed opposition, internal and external. Late autumn, 1963, to early spring, 1964, was a period of unstable equilibrium, which was followed by a new upturn in Khrushchev's fortunes, more apparent, however, than real; thereafter the curve was downward, reaching a major turning point late in July, 1964.

During these fourteen months, the main themes of Soviet internal and foreign policy and related developments in the international Communist movement recurred in ever new variations and combinations, so that the history of the period resembles an enormously complex four-dimensional jigsaw puzzle. Even more clearly than before, problems of Soviet relations with the United States and China now tended to overshadow all other foreign-policy considerations.

On May 9, 1963, Chinese Premier Chou En-lai informed the Soviet Ambassador at Peking that the CPC had selected a delegation to the forthcoming bilateral talks in Moscow. Mao, of course, would not come; the two chiefs of the delegation, Teng Hsiao-ping and Peng Chen, were known for their hostility to the Soviet leadership. The Chinese proposed that the date for the conference be postponed until mid-June; a formal reply to the CPSU letter of March 30, Chou said ominously, would be sent later.[150] The Soviets replied on May 11, thanking the Chinese for agreeing to the conference, accepting the proposal for its postponement, but objecting that June was inconvenient for them, since it was "overloaded with previously planned activities, including some of an international character."[151] They suggested July 5 as the commencement date for the meeting, a proposal the Chinese accepted on May 14. In the sparring for advantage in which the two parties had been engaged since February, the Soviets had scored every point: The Chinese would come to the Soviet capital, at a date chosen by the Soviets to convenience themselves. But there was a price to be paid for these triumphs, in Chinese resentment, and it was to flare out during June. The immediate cause of Chinese bitterness was the direction that Soviet policy toward the United States now took.

The Penkovsky case, in preparation since late October, 1962, reached the court in early May, 1963. The trial lasted from May 7 to May 11 and ended with the conviction of Penkovsky and his British contact, Wynne. Penkovsky was sentenced to be shot, Wynne to be imprisoned for eight years (he was later returned to Great Britain in exchange for a convicted Soviet spy). The trial necessarily generated a considerable volume of anti-American propaganda: the prosecution stressed the danger to Soviet security represented by Western, especially American, espionage, but attempted to minimize the damage done by Penkovsky to Soviet security. The most important internal result of the case was the subsequent shakeup in Soviet military intelligence: Serov lost his post as chief of the GRU, and with him fell many of the senior military intelligence officials abroad;[152] their posts were available for staffing by the victorious KGB.

The Penkovsky trial was not the only evidence of anti-Americanism in Soviet policy at this time; on May 20, the Soviet Government protested the presence of U.S. nuclear submarines in the Mediterranean, and proposed that the Mediterranean area be declared a nuclear-free zone, i.e., not only free of submarines but of U.S. rocket bases in Italy, Greece, and Turkey.[153]

At this point, however, a distinct shift in Soviet policy toward the United States became perceptible, as persistent probing by the Kennedy Administration finally elicited a favorable response from Khrushchev. On May 21, a Soviet-American memorandum on collaboration in the field of atomic energy during 1963–65 was signed in Moscow.[154] A week later, *Pravda* reported that a group of prominent U.S. intellectual leaders had urged President Kennedy to place the question of a treaty on banning nuclear tests before the American people. On May 29, Secretary of State Rusk publicly supported a proposal by a group of U.S. senators for a partial ban on testing, arguing that it would be in the interests of both powers;

a few days later, the Soviet press picked up the story.[155] Alarmed, the Chinese warned the Soviet Government on June 3 that the C.P.R. would "not let pass unnoticed" a Soviet-American agreement aimed at preventing China from sharing in the control of atomic weapons.[156] The Soviets replied reassuringly on June 9: the position of the Western powers on a test ban, they stated, provided no basis for an agreement.[157]

Then, on June 10, President Kennedy delivered his speech at American University: "The Strategy of Peace." The United States and the Soviet Union, Kennedy said, had certain common interests, and he announced that high-level talks on a test-ban agreement would commence shortly in Moscow. A TASS report on June 11 stated that President Kennedy and British Prime Minister Macmillan had agreed to send representatives to Moscow for talks in mid-July.[158]

On June 14, the Chinese produced their long-deferred reply to the CPSU letter of March 30. It was a scathing attack on Khrushchev's entire position, an open appeal from his policies to those of Lenin and Stalin, and an unconcealed bid for hegemony in the international Communist movement.[159] Not content with firing this verbal broadside, the Chinese took prompt steps to have it widely distributed in the Soviet Union, knowing from experience that the Soviets could not be expected to reprint it in their press.

In an interview published on June 15, Khrushchev called Kennedy's American University speech "a forward step toward a realistic appraisal of international conditions," and added that if the President's words were followed by "practical deeds, the American Government will encounter the understanding and support of the Soviet Government."[160]

In this altered situation, the postponed CC plenum, when it finally assembled (June 18–21), devoted a greater share of its attention to the Sino-Soviet dispute than to the announced agenda topic—ideology in relation to literature and the arts. On this subject, to which both Ilyichev and Khrushchev addressed themselves, the plenum represented a distinct shift away from the ideological militancy of the March 7/8 meeting. On the more urgent problem of relations with the Chinese, the plenum was an undiluted triumph for Khrushchev. The resolution adopted on the subject stated that the plenum "fully and unanimously approves the political activity of the Presidium of the CPSU Central Committee and Comrade Nikita Sergeyevich Khrushchev . . . in further consolidating the forces of the world Communist movement, as well as all the specific actions and measures undertaken by the Presidium of the CPSU Central Committee in its relations to the Central Committee of the Communist Party of China."[161]

Organizationally, too, the June plenum was a success for Khrushchev. Although Kozlov, who was still out of action, was not removed from the Secretariat or Presidium, his duties in the Secretariat were divided between two Khrushchev supporters, Brezhnev (who had been dropped from the Secretariat in July, 1960) and Podgorny, First Secretary of the Ukrainian Party.

By a historical irony whose symbolism was not lost on any of the participants, the bilateral Sino-Soviet talks in Moscow, which began on July 5 and were broken off inconclusively at the request of the Chinese on July 20, overlapped the test-ban negotiations, which commenced on July 15 and moved rapidly to their successful conclusion ten days later with the initialing of a three-power agreement. The day before the negotiations opened, the CPSU published an "open letter" replying to the CPC letter of June 14 and at the same time (reversing its originally announced decision not to publish the Chinese letter) giving its full text in translation.[162] In this way the Soviet public was provided with its first extensive account of the Sino-Soviet dispute from an official source. The CPSU letter included a lengthy exposition of the Soviet stand in the dispute and a justification of Khrushchev's policies, both internal and foreign. While stressing that Communism was the implacable foe of capitalism, the letter defended the Khrushchevian theory and practice of "peaceful coexistence." "One gets the impression," it stated, "that the leaders of the CPC think it to their advantage to maintain and intensify international tension, especially in the relations between the U.S.S.R. and the U.S.A."[163]

During this period of initiatives by Khrushchev, the opposition continued its activities circumspectly. At the July 5 plenum of the Moldavian Party CC, Shelepin delivered what the local press called "a long speech"; a week later he addressed Moldavian Party economic administrators.[164] True to his customary caution, he refrained from making any immediate organizational changes, but at the following plenum, on October 16, 1963, drastic changes were made in the assignment of Moldavian Party officials charged with the administration of industry.[165] Another sign of continuing oppositional activity was the press report on July 11 that Kozlov, who was described as "convalescing," had received a visit from Hungarian Premier and Party First Secretary Janos Kadar.[166]

While the test-ban negotiations were approaching their successful culmination, the secret police introduced a sour note by producing a defector from the United States who, in a letter published in *Izvestia* on July 23, denounced U.S. intelligence activities, declaring, "I want everyone to know the truth about the U.S.A., with its vaunted American way of life."

For Khrushchev the initialing of the test-ban agreement was only the first step in a broad campaign to solve "the fundamental international problems." In an interview published on July 27, he listed half a dozen further steps he hoped to see taken,[167] and a few days later, in a talk with a delegation of visiting U.S. agricultural specialists, he outlined the corresponding internal policies that he advocated—a substantial increase in allocations for chemical fertilizers, with the cost of the program to be met in part by savings from a cutback in military expenditures.[168]

With the test-ban treaty signed, to the accompaniment of a massive Soviet press campaign aimed at justifying Soviet adherence to the treaty and refuting Chinese criticism of it, Khrushchev took off for a vacation at Gagra. There, on August 13, he presided over an informal get-together of writers, both Western and Soviet, who had been attending a meeting of the Council of the European Association of Writers in Leningrad. The high point of the occasion was the first public reading of a new poem by Tvardovsky, "Terkin in the Underworld," a devastating satire on Stalinism, which had been circulating in manuscript. This event, rather than the inconclusive plenum of June, 1963, marked the real end of the conservative offensive on the cultural front which had opened in December, 1962. Two days after the Gagra meeting, the full text of Tvardovsky's poem was published in *Izvestia*, preceded by a laudatory introduction by Adzhubei, the editor and Khrushchev's son-in-law.[169]

The restoration of Khrushchev's authority during the late spring and summer of 1963 was accompanied by an easing of pressure from two sources of trouble that had plagued him previously, the military and the Czechoslovak Party. Military grumbling subsided: a conference of service personnel held in Moscow early in May reached the unequivocal verdict that "military doctrine is developed and determined by the political leadership of the state."[170] In Prague, the long-delayed process of de-Stalinization got under way on May 14, when Karol Bacilek, who had been Minister of National Security at the time of the Slanský trial, was ousted from the Czechoslovak Party Presidium and from his post as First Secretary of the Slovak Party.[171] On August 23, three days after Khrushchev began a state visit to Yugoslavia, TASS reported that the Czechoslovak Supreme Court, having reviewed the political trials of 1949–54, "fully absolved" Slanský and the other principal defendants on charges of "anti-state conspiratorial" activity, although it found evidence that Slanský and others had "crudely violated Party statutes and the principles of Party work." Two army officers who had served as Deputy Ministers of Internal Affairs during the trial were sentenced to prison terms.[172] On September 20, the Stalinist V. Siroky lost his posts as Premier and Presidium member, along with Vice Premier Dolansky and others.[173] Yet the purge of the purgers was incomplete: Novotný and the inner core of the Party *apparatchiki* around him retained their grip on power.

Khrushchev also made progress toward easing, if not fully solving, the Rumanian problem. In late June, the Rumanians had demonstrated their stubborn intransigence by publishing a summary of the June 14 CPC letter (an example followed by no other satellite regime), and they had boycotted the seventieth birthday celebration for Walter Ulbricht in East Berlin at the end of June (it was at this gathering, incidentally, that Khrushchev had first announced Soviet willingness to sign a partial test ban with the Western powers).[174] At the end of July, however, a compromise with the Rumanians was reached: For agreeing to sign the test ban—an action which soon came to be regarded as a basic test of loyalties in the contest between Moscow and Peking for allies in the world Communist movement—they received official Soviet sanction for their policy of industrializing their economy.[175]

It was at this moment, in the late summer of 1963, just at the height of Khrushchev's prestige and power, that a rift appeared in one of the basic elements of his political strategy. As mentioned, Khrushchev believed that Communism, if suitably administered and effectively organized, would prove superior to capitalism as an economic system capable of producing material abundance for the masses. An essential element in this concept was that substantial improvements would be made in the performance of Soviet agriculture, long the ailing partner in Soviet economic life. It was a hard blow to Khrushchev, therefore, when 1963 proved to be a disastrous year for Soviet agriculture.[176] By the late summer, it was obvious that grain procurements would be far below estimates and that a serious shortage of basic foodstuffs threatened the Soviet Union.

To meet the immediate crisis, Khrushchev negotiated for purchases of wheat abroad on an unprecedented scale; to solve the underlying problem, he intensified earlier plans for a re-allocation of investment funds to the chemical industry (which would provide fertilizers for agriculture). In late August, he announced that a CC plenum would be held toward the end of the year to discuss the problem.[177] These measures failed, however, to remedy the damage to Khrushchev's prestige and that of his policies caused by the agricultural failure. By resorting to foreign grain purchases, moreover, he had admitted the superiority of capitalist agriculture. Thus the crop failure of 1963 must be included among the basic causes of the loss of faith in Khrushchev's policies that contributed to his eventual downfall.

During August and September, the Chinese stepped up the pace of their attack on Khrushchev and his policies, and with some reluctance the Soviets replied in kind. It is primarily to the accounts of the background and development of the dispute, which both sides now published (in an effort to prove the ideological soundness of their positions), that the world is indebted for its detailed knowledge of the history of the dispute.

The abortive Sino-Soviet talks in July had been intended to prepare the way for an eventual international Communist conference similar to those of 1957 and 1960; the failure of the talks might thus have been expected to result in the indefinite postponement of the general conference. Instead, in mid-September, the Soviet press began systematically calling for the convocation of a general conference *without* first holding mutually satisfactory Sino-Soviet talks. The campaign opened with the publication in *Pravda* on September 17 of an excerpt from a resolution adopted three days earlier by the moderately pro-Soviet British Communist Party, tendentiously edited so as to suggest that the British Party supported the Soviet demand for a conference.[178]

The date on which this campaign got under way is noteworthy: it followed by one day the conclusion of an agreement with Canada for a $500-million purchase of wheat, and it coincided with the last occasion on which Suslov's name was mentioned in the Soviet press until early 1964.[179] That there was high-level opposition to some of Khrushchev's policies at this time can be inferred also from indications in the Soviet press, shortly after this date, of attempts to undermine Mikoyan's position by downgrading his role in earlier Soviet history.[180]

The Soviet press campaign to generate support for an international Communist conference to condemn the Chinese continued through late September and early October, taking the form of the reprinting in *Pravda* of pro-conference resolutions by the miniscule Portuguese and Paraguayan Communist parties (both wholly dependent on Soviet subsidies)[181] and a joint resolution by the Dutch and Italian parties, also edited in such a way as to give the misleading impression of support for the Soviet position.[182] The Chinese meanwhile kept up a steady barrage of articles attacking Soviet policies, searching out particularly vulnerable spots and devoting particular attention to Khrushchev himself. The high point of the Soviet counterattack came on October 18, with a conference on scientific methodology at the Academy of Sciences which formally condemned the philosophical foundations of the Chinese position,[183] and an issue of *Kommunist* which included a number of articles containing the most uncompromising Soviet attacks on the Chinese thus far published.[184] At this point, however, the Soviet campaign to force the calling of an international Communist conference faltered and lost impetus. A note of conciliation and of fundamental Sino-Soviet solidarity can be detected in certain Chinese statements of mid-October.[185] Several moderate Communist parties, led by the Italians, had meanwhile indicated their opposition to the Soviet demand for a conference.[186]

There was also evidence at this time that Khrushchev was facing a strong opposition effort to undermine his policies and his leadership. In a speech at Krasnodar on September 26, he admitted publicly for the first time the extent of the 1963 crop failure and the purchase of wheat abroad; publication of the speech was delayed, however, until October 2.[187] In an interview published on October 25, he defended his agricultural policies, including the grain purchase and the emphasis on development of the chemical industry, but in a defensive way that indicated some backtracking; increased allocation of funds to chemistry, he said, would not result in any cut in Soviet military spending.[188] At the same time, he deplored the recent exacerbation of Sino-Soviet polemics, disclaimed on behalf of the CPSU any responsibility for the situation, and said that the CPSU would do everything it could to bring the dispute to an end.

The turn in Soviet policy away from further sharpening of the dispute with China coincided with the appearance of new difficulties in Soviet-American relations. As had frequently happened before, the source of the difficulties was Berlin. In mid-October, a tieup occurred on the Berlin Autobahn. The American press and State Department minimized the difficulty as the result of a local misunderstanding; between November 4 and November 6, however, there was a recurrence of the trouble, and this time the State Department lodged an official protest.

Direct action by the secret police aimed at embroiling Soviet-American relations took place simultaneously. On October 30, Professor Frederick C. Barghoorn of Yale University, who was concluding a trip to the Soviet Union to conduct sociological research, was arrested on the charge of espionage; his arrest was not announced, however, until November 14.[189]

At about this time, the Soviet press carried a number of unusually belligerent articles by Soviet military men. Writing in *Izvestia* on November 17, Soviet rocket chief Marshal Krylov claimed that "the relative invulnerability of the United States has come to an end."[190] On November 20, Radio Moscow broadcast a talk by Colonel General Tolubko, another rocket specialist, in which he threatened that Soviet rockets would "completely wipe out the countries that have allowed their soil to be used for American war bases."[191] The next day, the Ministry of Foreign Affairs rejected as groundless the U.S. protest against the Berlin Autobahn tieup.[192]

It was against this background of sharply heightened Soviet-American tension that the world learned on November 22 of the assassination of President Kennedy in Dallas. According to the findings of the Warren Commission, the assassin was Lee Harvey Oswald, an American who had lived in the U.S.S.R. from 1959 to 1962, spending most of that time in the Belorussian Republic, and bringing back with him to the United States a Soviet wife, Marina (whose uncle was a colonel in the Soviet secret police). Soviet and Communist press and propaganda media went into action immediately on receipt of the news from Dallas, charging that responsibility for the crime rested with a right-wing conspiracy of Texas oil millionaires and political reactionaries.[193]

Less than a week after the assassination, the CPSU undertook new measures to heal the breach with the Chinese and their ideological allies. On November 26, the CPSU sent an appeal for reconciliation to the pro-Peking Japanese Communist Party; three days later, the CPSU addressed the CPC with a proposal to halt open polemics, and advanced a program of concrete measures aimed at the normalization of relations between the two parties, in order to create conditions under which an international conference would "lead not to a split in the world Communist movement but to the real unity and solidarity of all the fraternal parties, of all the forces of peace and socialism."[194] For its part, the CPSU promised to observe a voluntary moratorium on the further publication of polemical material. A *Pravda* editorial of December 6 renewed the appeal for an end to Sino-Soviet polemics, and cited the assassination of President Kennedy as evidence of the increased activity of reactionaries.[195] There is some evidence that the Chinese leaders were swayed by this campaign. Speaking in Cairo on December 20, Chou En-lai declared: "If anything unusual happens, the Soviet Union and China will stand shoulder to shoulder and arm to arm."[196]

For Khrushchev personally, the assassination of President Kennedy was a setback from which he never fully recovered. In his message of condolence to President Johnson he called it "a hard blow" to world peace and Soviet-American collaboration,[197] and the words expressed more than mere rhetoric. Through a painful process of trial and error, he and the late President had tested each other out and had learned to place a kind of rough trust in one another. Thanks largely to American forbearance, the Cuban missile crisis had served paradoxically to emphasize the common interest of the two superpowers in preserving world peace, a fact which Khrushchev had explicitly acknowledged in his speech of December 12, 1962, and which had paved the way for conclusion of the test-ban treaty, in July, 1963.

It was not merely that the death of Kennedy broke the personal relationship which had been built up between the two leaders; more serious were the implications of Soviet commentaries on the crime. By depicting the assassination as proof of the power of American right-wing extremists to impose their brutal veto on the policies of the President, the Soviet media damaged the concept of the American leadership as sober and responsible, and seriously undermined the possibility of future Soviet-American collaboration in the interests of a stable peace. The assassination, then, worked in favor of the political objectives of those opposing Khrushchev at that time.

Khrushchev tried to secure the continuation of his policy of limited *détente* with the United States amid the uncertainties of the new administration in Washington. Speaking at the CC plenum of December 9–13, he said: "I would like to believe that the same forces in the U.S.A.—those who think realistically and understand the responsibility their country bears for the fate of the world—will make known their will and find the means to restrain the aggressive militarist circles, the 'madmen,' in order to prevent a dangerous development of events into which both the United States and other countries would inevitably be drawn."[198] Citing a statement by Secretary of State Rusk on December 10, in which Rusk had called for "security in our entire environment," Khrushchev remarked: "Well said. One might only wish that there were more such opinions, and, more important, that such statements were backed up by appropriate action."[199]

At the plenum, Khrushchev maintained that the task of building up Soviet heavy industry had now been substantially completed and that increased investment in the chemical industry was therefore feasible.[200] He also projected further cuts in Soviet military manpower, a suggestion which was received with silence or outright hostility by leading military spokesmen.[201]

Khrushchev's efforts at improving Soviet-American relations found support at this time in articles by representatives of a number of Soviet interest groupings—military, scientific, and journalistic.[202] Strikingly out of key, however, was a contribution by the secret police to the worsening of relations between the two countries—the trial in Sofia of a Bulgarian diplomat accused of spying for the United States. His case, said *Pravda*, was evidence that "the dark forces of reaction do not balk at the foulest means to cause damage to the socialist countries and to counteract the relaxation of international tension."[203]

At the end of the year, Khrushchev granted an interview to a foreign correspondent. On December 31, *Pravda* and *Izvestia* published his replies to questions by UPI correspondent Henry Shapiro (the man to whom Tvardovsky had granted the interview of May, 1963, which signaled the turning point in the conservative offensive on the literary front). "We want," said Khrushchev, "new relations of peaceful collaboration, neighborliness and friendship to develop between the peoples of the United States and the Soviet Union in the new year. . . . We believe that the American people do not want war, either. . . . We responded with satisfaction to the statement of the new U.S. President, L. B. Johnson, that he intends to continue in foreign policy the line of peaceful settlement of international problems, improving relations with the Soviet Union and discontinuing the 'cold war.'" Khrushchev then went on to list the standard items on his list of steps to be taken to reduce tension between the Soviet Union and the Western powers.[204]

Efforts by both sides to improve Soviet-American relations continued in early 1964. On January 21, the Johnson Administration submitted a five-point proposal to the Geneva disarmament conference which called for the renunciation of force in international disputes, a freeze on production of missiles, a halt in the production of fissionable materials for military use, the establishment of observation posts to monitor a comprehensive test ban, and an agreement to halt the proliferation of atomic weapons. On January 29, *Pravda* published a Soviet Government memorandum set-

ting forth "measures aimed at an easing of the arms race and a
relaxation of international tension." Although most of the measures listed were those already familiar from Khrushchev's earlier
proposals, there was one which coincided significantly with the
U.S. proposals—prevention of the further spread of nuclear weapons. Since this point, on which the two superpowers were in tacit
agreement, was clearly aimed at preventing China, among other
nations, from obtaining nuclear weapons, it is not at all surprising
that there was an immediate crescendo of Chinese attacks on the
CPSU and Soviet policy. On February 4, editorials in both *People's Daily* and *Red Flag* accused the CPSU of being "in collusion
with imperialism," and of "betraying the cause of the socialist
revolution."[205] It warned that as a result of Soviet policies, an open
split in the world Communist movement was inevitable.

The renewed Chinese attacks produced a significant shift in the
balance of forces in the Soviet leadership. After his long eclipse,
Suslov reappeared in the Soviet press in January, 1964; at the end
of the month he headed a CPSU delegation that conducted negotiations in Moscow with representatives of the Vietnamese Workers' Party. The renewed Chinese polemics completed a process
that evidently had been under way for some time; Suslov now resolved to speak out forcefully in condemnation of the Chinese
position, even though this meant expressing approval for Khrushchev's handling of the Sino-Soviet dispute.

The CC plenum of February 10–15, 1964, was convened for the
publicly stated purpose of discussing "the intensification of agricultural production on the basis of broad application of fertilizers,
development of irrigation and comprehensive mechanization, and
introduction of the achievements of science and advanced experience for the most rapid increase in production of agricultural products." The most significant report at the plenum, however, was
delivered not by U.S.S.R. Minister of Agriculture Volovchenko, the
chief speaker on the publicly announced agenda topic, but by Suslov, who at a closed session on February 14 read his report "On the
Struggle of the CPSU for the Solidarity of the International Communist Movement."[206]

Suslov's report was an exhaustive analysis of the ideological principles at issue in the Sino-Soviet dispute, and a closely reasoned
demolition of the doctrinal foundations of the Chinese position.

Of great significance in regard to the internal struggle in the CPSU was the fact that he championed the very policies of Khrushchev that had been most unacceptable to the Chinese—peaceful coexistence, limited agreement with the United States, recognition of Yugoslavia as a socialist country, and so forth. He characterized the Chinese position in terms of the utmost scorn—"a rehash of Trotskyism"—and denied to the CPC the right to claim that its policies were Marxist-Leninist: "The facts indicate that nationalism is gaining increased ascendancy in the entire policy of the Chinese leadership and is becoming a mainspring of their activities."[207]

Finally, and most gratifying to Khrushchev, Suslov rejected the CPC's attacks on Khrushchev personally and affirmed that "our Central Committee, headed by that true Leninist, Nikita Sergeyevich Khrushchev, is united and monolithic as never before, and the Chinese leaders—and not they alone—should make up their minds to that." Suslov continued with warm words of praise for Khrushchev: "Comrade N. S. Khrushchev, with his inexhaustible energy, his truly Bolshevik ardor and adherence to principle, is the recognized leader of our Party and people. He expresses the most cherished thoughts and aspirations of the Soviet people. The Leninist line pursued by our Party cannot be divorced from the Central Committee, from Nikita Sergeyevich Khrushchev. . . ."

Although Suslov's speech was not published in the Soviet press at the time of the February plenum, its substance was undoubtedly known to the Chinese. They knew that on February 12 the CPSU had circulated a letter among other Communist parties calling for "collective measures" against the CPC in order to "rebuff" them.[208] On February 20, the CPC warned the CPSU that it intended to publish the texts of the correspondence between the two parties since November 29, 1963.[209] Seven days later, it proposed that the two parties conclude an agreement that "each side will, on the basis of parity, publish in its press, together with the documents, articles, and materials of its own side that criticize the other side, the documents, articles, and materials from the other side that answer the criticism, both those that have already been published and those that will be published."[210] The CPC continued its attack on February 29 with a formal reply to the CPSU letter of November 29, 1963.[211] The Chinese proposed that bilateral talks be held in the autumn of 1964, to be followed by a meeting of seventeen parties in preparation for an eventual world conference of Communist parties, which would be "an assembly of solidarity on the basis of the revolutionary principles of Marxism-Leninism" —in other words, which would endorse the Chinese position in the dispute.

The focal point in the dispute had now clearly come to be the proposal to hold an international Communist conference to consider the dispute and search for ways to overcome it. Each side strove to ensure that the conference, when convened, would be held under conditions in which it would have the advantage, and that the other side would bear the blame for the failure to convene a conference, or for its unsuccessful outcome if convened.

On March 7, the CPSU proposed that bilateral talks be held in May, to be followed in June or July by a preparatory conference, leading finally to a full-scale meeting in the autumn.[212] The Chinese, however, were determined not to be forced into a general meeting at which they would be outvoted; they therefore advocated a delay, meanwhile seeking to win support for their position among other parties. Their formal reply to the March 7 letter was not sent until May 7, but their rejection of the CPSU proposal was amply indicated earlier by articles in the Chinese press. A particularly violent verbal onslaught appeared on March 31, defining armed struggle as "the universal law of the proletarian revolution" and calling for the "re-examination and correction" of the 1957 declaration and the 1960 statement adopted at the Moscow conferences of Communist parties.[213]

The Soviet Union was in the meantime making persistent efforts to improve its relations with the United States. During the first three months of 1964, there were a number of incidents involving alleged overflights of Soviet territory by U.S. planes, but Soviet protests differed markedly in tone from those sent in similar incidents during the ascendancy of the opposition a year earlier. Particularly striking was the conciliatory tone of a TASS report on March 27 concerning a flight by U.S. planes over East Germany on March 10: "In view of the regret expressed by the government of the U.S.A. concerning this violation and its assurance that strict instructions have been issued to American authorities to prevent similar violations in the future, it has been recognized as possible, upon consultation between competent authorities of the G.D.R. and the Soviet Union, to make an exception in this particular case and merely to expel the crew members of the RB-66 from the G.D.R."[214]

The bitter Chinese attack of March 31 produced an immediate response in the Soviet Union. On April 3, *Pravda* published the text of Suslov's February 14 speech to the plenum, and accompanied it by the hitherto unpublished resolution adopted by the plenum on the subject, as well as by an editorial, "Fidelity to the Principles of Marxism-Leninism."

The emergence of Suslov as the Party's most outspoken and uncompromising critic of the CPC's ideological position must have appeared to Khrushchev to signify that he had finally overcome the threat to his position represented by the conservative opposition. Kozlov had been eliminated in April, 1963; a year later, so it must have seemed to Khrushchev, Suslov had been forced to recognize the soundness of his handling of the Sino-Soviet dispute, and to testify to his leadership abilities.

Khrushchev's euphoria, his sense of having finally overcome his most dangerous internal opponents, was significantly heightened between April 17 and April 22, 1964, when his seventieth birthday was celebrated with elaborate ceremony. When a new Order of Lenin, with a Gold Star, was presented to him by Brezhnev, Khrushchev replied: "With satisfaction I want to say that at present we have complete unity of the Party and the people."[215] Mikoyan presented a testimonial signed by all the members of the Presidium and Secretariat which said: "With all our hearts we wish you, Nikita Sergeyevich, good health, many years of life, and new successes in your tremendous and wonderful activity." The glow of approbation that surrounded Khrushchev in April, 1964, was nevertheless deceptive; it was the glow of sunset rather than dawn.

It was painfully obvious that the show of monolithic unity with which the CPSU greeted Khrushchev on his birthday was not matched in the international Communist movement. The Japanese Party sent an unprecedentedly curt telegram for the occasion: "We congratulate you on your seventieth birthday."[216] Gheorghiu-Dej failed to attend the birthday festivities in Moscow. Much more damaging to Khrushchev was the action of the Italian Party.

In a report to the Italian Central Committee which *L'Unità* published on April 23, Togliatti voiced his serious objections to the kind of international Communist conference for which Khrushchev had been calling and recommended measures aimed at the scaling down of the Sino-Soviet conflict.

During early April, most of May, and the second half of June, Khrushchev was away from Moscow on extended trips: April 3–12, in Hungary; May 9–23, in Egypt; and June 16–July 4, in the Scandinavian countries. As on similar occasions in the past, he acted with an apparent confidence in his position, but there was a note of frenetic striving for new successes which suggested recognition that his internal position was no longer as secure as formerly. As he traveled he handed out awards with a lavish hand: Kadar received the Order of Lenin, and Nasser was awarded the title "Hero of the Soviet Union."

Efforts to maintain improved relations with the Johnson Administration continued. On April 21, *Pravda* published a statement by Khrushchev in which he maintained that recent events, particularly the test-ban treaty, had "contributed to a definite strengthening of trust in relations among states and the creation of more favorable conditions for the adoption of further measures that would lead to the cessation of the arms race and the solution of the main problem, the problem of disarmament." The statement continued with the announcement of a Soviet cutback in the production of fissionable materials for military purposes and the assurance that similar statements would shortly be issued in the United States and Great Britain.

The three-power tacit agreement on a slowdown in production of fissionable materials for military purposes fell short of being a real triumph for Khrushchev. More valuable to him as evidence of the continuing possibility of Soviet-American collaboration was the signing on June 1 of a consular treaty, the first in the history of Soviet-American relations. In a report on the event, Soviet Foreign Minister Gromyko called it "a positive step in the matter of normalizing and improving relations between the U.S.S.R. and the U.S.A.," and held out the prospect of "still greater tangible results if the two sides multiply their efforts and in the same spirit turn to the solution of still larger and more complex international problems."[217] Gromyko's hopes, and those of Khrushchev, were destined to remain unfulfilled, however; the consular treaty, still unratified by the United States as of mid-1966, was the last major effort by Khrushchev to shape Soviet policy toward better relations with the United States.

At this time, a new obstacle appeared in the path of improved Soviet-American understanding: the increasingly cordial relations between the United States and West Germany, and the U.S. proposal to arm NATO with nuclear weapons and to extend to West Germany, as a member of NATO, a limited right of access to their control. Speaking at Budapest on April 3, Khrushchev warned that "the chief source of the threat of war in Europe—renascent West German militarism—still remains."[218] On June 12, the Soviet Government concluded a twenty-year friendship pact with the G.D.R. At the Soviet–G.D.R. friendship rally in the Kremlin held to mark the signing, Khrushchev stated: "The facts show that the policy of the West German ruling circles is today the most aggressive and adventuristic in Europe." On June 25, the Soviet Government protested the Western-sponsored plan to hold elections for the Federal Republic of Germany in West Berlin on July 1, 1964, calling it "one of the manifestations of the dangerous policy of the revanchist circles of the F.R.G. aimed at the revision of the results of World War II." "It is difficult to suppose," the Soviet note continued, "that the U.S. Government does not understand the meaning of these actions."[219]

The Chinese reply to the CPSU letter of March 7 was sent on May 7. It dismissed the Soviet proposals for an international Communist meeting in the autumn of 1964 as "double-dealing," and charged that the CPSU was "striving with every fiber of [its] being for an alliance with American imperialism, the common enemy of all peoples."[220] "To judge by the present state of affairs," the letter stated, "a meeting of CPC and CPSU representatives is not only impossible in May but would even be premature in October of this year." The CPC proposed postponing the bilateral negotiations until May, 1965, and suggested that "if at that time either side, the CPC or the CPSU, thinks that the time for such a meeting is still not ripe, it might be postponed again." The letter went on to warn that, in the absence of any "international organization like the Comintern, [when] there is no permanent agency that would have the right to call an international conference as was done under the Third International," it would be "impermissible" for a single party to make a "unilateral" decision to hold an international Communist conference. "Do you want to go this far? Do you want to get into such a blind alley?" the Chinese asked, adding, "Do not say later on that we did not warn you."

The CPSU reply on June 15 characterized the CPC's objections to the proposed conference as "completely groundless," and suggested that the real reason for the CPC desire to postpone the meeting was "to free [its] hands for carrying out factionalist, splitting activity."[221]

Khrushchev on the Road to Oblivion: July–October, 1964

The decision to oust Khrushchev which crystallized within the Soviet leadership during the summer of 1964 was not the result of shifts in the ruling bodies of the CPSU. The elevation of Brezhnev and Podgorny to the Secretariat in June, 1963, was the last major organizational change in these bodies before Khrushchev's fall; Kuusinen's death on May 17, 1964, affected the balance of power by removing a consistent and reliable supporter of Khrushchev's policies, but was not enough in itself to explain why a majority against him emerged later in the year. The explanation must therefore be sought in a consideration of policies, both internal and foreign, which finally prompted supporters and protégés of Khrushchev to join the long-standing opposition. As before, the main problems of Soviet foreign policy at the time were those concerning relations with China and the United States. By the summer of 1964, Khrushchev had come to the end of his ability to improvise new variations on the basic themes of his foreign policy. He was still capable of forcing through important decisions—e.g., the consular treaty with the United States, the international Communist conference to condemn the Chinese—but only at the cost of increasing still further the mounting odds against him. The course of events, which at one time had seemed to provide support for his policies, now demonstrated their bankruptcy.

The CPSU had sent the Japanese Party a letter on April 18 pleading for "a joint struggle against imperialism" and presenting a lengthy justification of the Soviet position on the use of atomic weapons. The letter went unanswered, and on July 11 the CPSU wrote again, this time with the intention of bringing the affair to the attention of all Party members; both letters were published in the issue of *Partiinaya zhizn* which was sent to the press shortly after July 14.[222] On that date, the Chinese published another in their long series of slashing attacks on the CPSU;[223] it charged that the Soviet Party had departed from the true principles of Marxism-Leninism and claimed that its apostasy was the result of the survival of "bourgeois elements" in Soviet society, against which a determined struggle would have to be waged—an open call for the formation of an internal opposition to Khrushchev.

Khrushchev's last major victory in the formulation of policy toward the Chinese came in the decision announced in *Pravda*, on August 10, that a preparatory conference of representatives of twenty-six Communist parties would be called on December 15, to be followed in mid-1965 by a full-scale world Communist conference. Nothing was said about further bilateral Sino-Soviet talks.

It was not only in the CPSU leadership that grave doubts existed as to the wisdom of this policy. In July, Togliatti flew to the Crimea to confer with the Soviet leadership and present the objections to the convocation of a general conference which the CPI had already voiced on a number of earlier occasions. Finding that his advice was ignored, he prepared a lengthy statement setting forth his views and then, three days after *Pravda* announced the convocation of the conference, suffered a crippling heart attack (a month earlier a similar occurrence had finished off the veteran French Communist Party leader Maurice Thorez, who was also visiting the Soviet Union). Togliatti's death on August 21 did not, therefore, completely silence this most dangerous, because most reasonable and moderate, opponent of the plan to call a general conference; on September 4 *L'Unità* published the full text of his "Testament." The sensation it caused made it impossible for the CPSU to ignore it; on September 10, *Pravda* reprinted it in full.

While his policies toward China were thus encountering strenuous opposition, Khrushchev's policies toward the United States were undergoing a radical transformation. In a speech to graduates of Soviet military academies on July 8, he had specified a number of steps taken recently to reduce Soviet-American tension, and, while rejecting U.S. claims of strategic superiority, had affirmed that the Soviet Union would never launch an attack.[224] Thereafter, the trend shifted toward increased Soviet-American hostility. The U.S. Presidential campaign raised anxieties concerning the possible future course of American foreign policy. Soviet commentators paid particularly close attention to the Republican Party convention, which met in San Francisco. The nomination of Senator Goldwater and the adoption of a platform which indicated that if elected he would end the efforts by previous administrations to reach limited agreements with the Soviet Union constituted a threat to one of Khrushchev's most important long-term foreign-policy objectives. Speaking in Warsaw on July 21, Khrushchev characterized the policy of the Republican Party as "a course that endangers the entire world, including the people of the U.S.A."[225]

On July 25 (the anniversary of the initialing of the test-ban treaty), *Pravda* and *Izvestia* published a TASS statement commenting on a U.S. announcement of an agreement whereby NATO forces, including those of West Germany, would be provided with information relating to atomic weapons. By this step, said the statement, the United States "is preparing [its allies] for the possession of nuclear weapons and for the use of them in a very short time and at a moment suitable to itself." The signing of the agreement, the statement charged, "is explained first of all by the demands of West Germany."

On the same day, *Pravda* reported that on the preceding day a meeting of the Presidium of the Council of Ministers of the U.S.S.R. had been held under the chairmanship of Khrushchev, at which basic economic trends were discussed in preparation for drafting plans for 1966–70. No previous case has been noted of a reported meeting of the Presidium of the Council of Ministers. By identifying Khrushchev solely in his governmental capacity, was the announcement intended to convey to alert readers the information that Khrushchev no longer enjoyed the support of the Party apparatus?

What appears to be a significant counterpart to the July 25 announcement was a decision taken by the Supreme Soviet on July 15 to release Brezhnev from his duties as Chairman of the Presidium of the Supreme Soviet (to which post Mikoyan was appointed), in order to free him for full-time work as Party Secretary.[226] The same Supreme Soviet session named Boris Ponomarev Chairman of the Commission for Foreign Affairs of the Soviet of Nationalities. It is symptomatic of the increasingly unceremonious way in which Party ideologists were treating Khrushchev at this time that in an article published in the *World Marxist Review* in August, Ponomarev completely ignored Khrushchev's efforts in his negotiations with Nasser in May to bring the Egyptian regime within the sphere of the world Communist movement.[227]

Further hints of a shift in Party allegiance followed. On July 29, *Pravda* juxtaposed two brief news items: in Moscow, Foreign Minister Gromyko had received his East German counterpart, Lothar Bolz, and in Bonn, Khrushchev's son-in-law, Adzhubei, had been received by West German Chancellor Erhard. Unmistakably tendentious was a *Pravda* report of August 1 concerning a press conference held by David Rockefeller, president of the Chase Manhattan Bank, following a conference with Khrushchev. The meeting, Mr. Rockefeller was quoted as saying, "proceeded in a very unrestrained and friendly atmosphere." The implication to be drawn from this sequence of reports was reasonably clear: Khrushchev, having ceased to act as leader of the CPSU, was preparing a new agreement with the United States, probably involving concessions to West Germany in regard to the control of nuclear weapons.

The harsher tone toward the United States was intensified in August. On August 3, the Soviet Foreign Ministry delivered a protest against a series of alleged U.S. violations of Soviet rights on the high seas between June 18 and July 25, warning that these "intolerable actions violate the freedom of the seas in international waters" and "may have grave consequences."[228] Fuel for the growing blaze was contributed by the United States. On August 2, American planes replied to North Vietnam attacks on U.S. warships in the Gulf of Tonkin by air raids on the North Vietnam mainland, the first such action in the Vietnamese war, and at about the same time the State Department brushed aside tentative secret feelers from the North Vietnamese regime for the initiation of peace negotiations.[229]

A number of articles in the Soviet press contributed to the anti-U.S. campaign. Writing in *Izvestia* on August 9, Yepishev argued that notwithstanding U.S. claims of superiority in military equipment, the Soviet Union would emerge victorious from a war against the United States because its soldiers possessed a higher morale than those of America, founded on their belief in the ideology of Marxism-Leninism. On August 12, *Pravda* published an article by G. Frantsov, Dean of the Academy of Social Sciences under the Party CC, which depicted America as moving rapidly toward fascism, with the Goldwater candidacy interpreted as a sign that the internal U.S. political crisis was approaching its climax.

While all this was taking place, Khrushchev was engaged in a tour of rural installations, gathering material, as he explained, for the forthcoming November plenum of the CC at which he was scheduled to deliver a report on agriculture. At the outset of his tour, Khrushchev was still endeavoring to keep alive the possibility of collaboration with the United States; on August 5, the anniversary of the signing of the test-ban treaty, *Pravda* published his answers to questions by the editors of *Pravda* and *Izvestia* in which he maintained that the signing of the treaty had "contributed to the relaxation of international tension," and in which he specified three further steps that should be taken in the same direction: a peace settlement with Germany, general and complete disarmament, and an international agreement on the renunciation of the use of force to solve territorial disputes and border questions. "It is especially important," Khrushchev said, "to guard this store of trust [between the Soviet Union and the United States] and to strengthen and expand it in every way."

The growing strife in Vietnam, however, wrought a sharp change in Khrushchev's public statements on relations with the United States. Speaking in Ordzhonikidze on August 8, he condemned recent U.S. bombing raids as "a new attempt to employ in relations between states arbitrariness and piratical methods that have been denounced by the peoples."[230] "If the imperialists dare to unleash war," he warned, "then this war, although it will cause much loss of life and suffering among the peoples of the world, will end in the complete rout of capitalism." Even stronger in tone was a speech delivered in Prague on August 27.[231] "We decisively condemn," he said, "the aggressive actions of the American imperialists, which are fraught with the most serious consequences to the cause of peace and the safety of the peoples." He still manifested some restraint, however, by adding: "It is not at all my intention to intimidate anybody. I am only observing, by way of preventive medicine, so to speak, that he who encroaches on the national independence of the peoples, on their right to decide their destiny independently, risks receiving a decisive rebuff." And in the same speech he lashed out against China: Chinese policy, he said, proved that "we are faced with a frankly great-power chauvinist line, for the sake of which the Peking leaders are prepared to destroy the socialist commonwealth."[232]

Time was running out for Khrushchev. At the beginning of September, an ominous new note was sounded with the opening of a campaign of self-assertion on the part of the secret police. Articles commemorating the ninetieth anniversary of the birth of V. R. Menzhinsky, head of the OGPU from 1926 to 1934, appeared in a number of newspapers on September 1, which emphasized his role in strengthening the principle of Party control over the secret police.[233] On September 4, the first of a series of articles appeared on Richard Sorge, the Soviet Union's most important and successful spy, whose exploits in Japan before World War II were now for the first time officially revealed to the Soviet public.[234]

The heightened activity of the secret police was not limited to newspaper articles; on September 12, a bizarre episode took place at a monastery near Moscow, where a West German diplomat was subjected to a mustard gas attack. The motive of the attack was fairly obvious: to embroil relations between the Soviet Union and West Germany, thereby erecting an insuperable obstacle in the path of Khrushchev's suspected efforts to establish better relations with Bonn. The openness with which the secret police showed its opposition to the policies of its nominal master, the First Secretary of the Party, was an unmistakable indication that his days in power were numbered.

The reasons Khrushchev's supporters within the Presidium joined the oppositionists in removing him from power have not yet been fully revealed. Their common concern over his arbitrary handling of foreign and domestic problems undoubtedly was a major factor.

On September 30, Khrushchev left Moscow for what was to be his last vacation at Gagra, having first sent to the Secretariat a plan for "the industrialization of agriculture" and a proposal to name Adzhubei as a CC Secretary charged with special responsibility for agriculture.[235] Recalled from his vacation, Khrushchev faced the *fait accompli* of hostile majorities in the Party Presidium and CC. The world learned late on October 15 and Soviet citizens the next day that Khrushchev had resigned from his leading Party and government posts on October 14.

In the period immediately following Khrushchev's fall, some members of the anti-Khrushchev coalition received promotions. At the emergency plenum of October 14, Brezhnev, who had been "concentrating on his Party duties" since mid-July, took Khrushchev's place as First Secretary. The Supreme Soviet Presidium formally appointed Alexei Kosygin as Premier on October 15. At the November, 1964, plenum, Shelepin joined the Presidium as a full member. Semichastny (representing the secret police) and Yepishev (for the armed forces) were raised to full CC membership. In March, 1965, Mazurov, First Secretary of the Belorussian Party, was made a full member of the Presidium and First Deputy Premier of the U.S.S.R.

A number of Khrushchev's organizational measures were reversed in the months immediately after his fall in a way that strongly suggests that political debts were being paid; for example, the Central Asian Council of the National Economy, established in early 1963 at his instigation, was abolished and the Central Asian ministries which it had displaced were reinstated. The split of the Party apparatus into industrial and agricultural sectors was ended. The *sovnarkhozy*, products of the May, 1957, reforms, were ordered dismantled, to be replaced by ministries, in September, 1965.

Khrushchev's final effort to assert his control of Soviet foreign policy was the formal Soviet apology to West Germany for the mustard gas attack of September 12, which was belatedly tendered on October 13.[236] It was a forlorn gesture, however; the preparations for Khrushchev's overthrow had been completed, and a new era in Soviet internal and foreign policy was about to begin.

NOTES

1. Boris I. Nicolaevsky, *Power and the Soviet Elite* (New York: Frederick A. Praeger, 1965), pp. 105–9.
2. *Ibid.*, p. 262.
3. Frol R. Kozlov, "Politicheskaya bditel'nost'—obyazannost' chlena partii," *Kommunist*, XXIX, No. 1 (January, 1953), 46–58.
4. Robert M. Slusser, "Die Sonderstellung Belorusslands," *Osteuropa*, XIV, No. 11 (1964), 851–64.
5. Robert M. Slusser, "Recent Soviet Books on the History of the Secret Police," *Slavic Review*, XXIV, No. 1 (March, 1965), 90–98.
6. The Soviet press reported the shift only after a delay of several years.
7. Hansjakob Stehle, "Polish Communism," in William E. Griffith (ed.), *European Communism* (Cambridge, Mass.: The M.I.T. Press, 1964), I, 105.
8. According to the Chinese People's Republic statement of August 15, 1963; text in *Pravda*, August 21, 1963 (*Current Digest of the Soviet Press* [hereafter cited as *CDSP*], XV, No. 34, 7).
9. David A. Quarles, "The Dismissal of Marshal P'eng Teh-huai," *China Quarterly*, No. 8 (October–December, 1961), pp. 63–76.
10. *Pravda*, September 28, 1959.
11. *Facts on File*, 1959, p. 223.
12. Sidney I. Ploss, *Conflict and Decision-Making in Soviet Russia: A Case Study of Agricultural Policy, 1953–1963* (Princeton, N.J.: Princeton University Press, 1965), pp. 180–81.
13. *Pravda* and *Izvestia*, January 15, 1960 (*CDSP*, XII, No. 2, 3–16, 23). See also Matthew Gallagher, "Military Manpower: A Case Study," *Problems of Communism*, XIII, No. 3 (May–June, 1964), p. 54.
14. *Pravda* and *Izvestia*, January 8, 1960.
15. *Pravda* and *Izvestia*, January 15, 1960.
16. *Ibid.*
17. According to L. F. Ilyichev at the Twenty-second Congress of the CPSU, speech of October 24, 1961, in *XXII syezd Kommunisticheskoi Partii Sovetskogo Soyuza: Stenograficheskii otchet* (Moscow: Gosudarstvennoe Izdatel'stvo Politicheskoi Literatury [hereafter cited as Gospolitizdat], 1962), II, 186.
18. Text in G. F. Hudson, Richard Lowenthal, and Roderick MacFarquhar, *The Sino-Soviet Dispute* (New York: Frederick A. Praeger, 1961), pp. 82–112.
19. Richard Lowenthal, *World Communism: The Disintegration of a Secular Faith* (New York: Oxford University Press, 1964), p. 173.
20. Ploss, *op. cit.*, p. 189.
21. *Ibid.*, p. 184; and Lowenthal, *op. cit.*, p. 222.
22. *Izvestia*, June 3, 1960; and James P. Warburg, *Disarmament: The Challenge of the Nineteen Sixties* (Garden City, N.Y.: Doubleday & Co., 1961), pp. 255–64.
23. On the Peking session of the WFTU, see Lowenthal, *op. cit.*, p. 175; and Donald S. Zagoria, *The Sino-Soviet Dispute* (Princeton, N.J.: Princeton University Press, 1962), pp. 320–25.
24. Zagoria, *op. cit.*, pp. 455–58; and William E. Griffith, *Albania and the Sino-Soviet Dispute* (Cambridge, Mass.: The M.I.T. Press, 1963), p. 42.

25. *Plenum Tsentral'nogo Komiteta Kommunisticheskoi Partii Sovetskogo Soyuza, 13–16 iyulya 1960 goda: Stenograficheskii otchet* (Moscow: Gospolitizdat, 1960), p. 335.

26. *Ibid.*, pp. 335–37.

27. *Facts on File*, 1960, p. 239.

28. *Ibid.*; and *Izvestia*, July 12 and 13, 1960.

29. Boris N. Ponomarev, "Mirnoe sosushchestvovanie—zhiznennaya neobkhodimost'," *Pravda*, August 12, 1960 (*CDSP*, XII, No. 32, 3–5).

30. Publication began in *Borba* (Belgrade) on August 13, 1960; see Viktor Meier, "Yugoslav Communism," in Griffith, *European Communism*, I, 45–47.

31. Review by A. Arzumanyan and V. Koryonov, *Pravda*, September 2, 1960. Meier (*op. cit.*, pp. 47–48) interprets the review as a provisional condemnation of Kardelj's position but not a full-scale agreement with the Chinese on the matter.

32. The Chinese statement was included as an appendix to their statement of September 6, 1963; cited in William E. Griffith, *The Sino-Soviet Rift* (Cambridge, Mass.: The M.I.T. Press, 1964), pp. 419–20.

33. CPC statement of September 6, 1963; cited in Griffith, *Sino-Soviet Rift*, p. 403.

34. *Izvestia*, September 27, 1960 (*CDSP*, XII, No. 39, 22).

35. Analysis of the conference in Alexander Dallin (ed.), *Diversity in International Communism* (New York: Columbia University Press, 1963), pp. 829–30; and Griffith, *Albania*, pp. 52–53.

36. According to the Chinese statement of September 6, 1963; cited in Griffith, *Sino-Soviet Rift*, pp. 406–7.

37. *Pravda*, January 20, 1961 (*CDSP*, XIII, No. 1, 24).

38. Khrushchev's January 6, 1961, speech was published in *Kommunist*, No. 1 (January, 1961), pp. 3–37, and in *World Marxist Review*, No. 1 (1961); for analysis, see Lowenthal, *op. cit.*, pp. 200–202.

39. Ploss, *op. cit.*, pp. 208–9.

40. *Pravda*, December 30, 1960 (*CDSP*, XII, No. 52, 29); and *Yezhegodnik Bol'shoi Sovetskoi Entsiklopedii, 1961* (Moscow: Gosudarstvennoe Nauchnoe Izdatel'stvo "Sovetskaya Entsiklopediya," 1961), p. 94.

41. *Pravda*, April 16, 1961; and *Kommunist Tadzhikistana*, April 14, 1961 (*CDSP*, XIII, No. 15, 9–12).

42. *Pravda*, January 26, 1961 (*CDSP*, XIII, No. 4, 27).

43. *Pravda*, March 20, 1961.

44. *Facts on File*, 1961, pp. 137, 148.

45. Cited by M. A. Suslov in his speech to a CC plenum on February 14, 1964; text in *Pravda*, April 3, 1964 (*CDSP*, XVI, No. 14, 4).

46. The fullest analysis of the development of the Soviet-Albanian dispute is in Griffith, *Albania*.

47. *Ibid.*, pp. 69–76.

48. *Pravda*, May 11, 1961 (*CDSP*, XIII, No. 19, 21). See also Ploss, *op. cit.*, p. 227.

49. *Pravda*, May 30, 1961 (*CDSP*, XIII, No. 22, 22).

50. *Facts on File*, 1961, p. 214.

51. *Ibid.*, p. 221.

52. Penkovsky worked for military intelligence (the GRU), the operations of which were subject to surveillance by the secret police (the KGB). It is

highly unlikely that his leaks to the West escaped detection by the KGB; rather, it is probable that he was permitted to continue them so that the KGB could achieve a double purpose: undermining Khrushchev's efforts to force the West to submit to Soviet pressure in Berlin and/or Cuba, and discrediting the GRU as a step toward absorption of military espionage into the KGB apparatus.

53. *Izvestia*, September 9, 1961 (*CDSP*, XIII, No. 36, 3–5). The quotation from Khrushchev was cited by the Chinese in their statement of August 15, 1963; text in *Pravda*, August 21, 1963 (*CDSP*, XV, No. 34, 3–8).

54. For Shelepin, see *XXII syezd* . . . , II, 402–5; for Mazurov, *ibid.*, I, 290–92.

55. *Ibid.*, III, 6.

56. *Ibid.*, III, 17–18.

57. Jan F. Triska (ed.), *Soviet Communism: Programs and Rules* (San Francisco: Chandler Publishing Co., 1962), p. 181. The significance of this change was first pointed out by Leonard Schapiro, "The Party's New Rules," *Problems of Communism*, XI, No. 1 (January–February, 1962), 351.

58. *Pravda*, November 1, 1961 (*CDSP*, XIII, No. 44, 22); Ploss, *op. cit.*, p. 239; and Boris I. Nicolaevsky, "Padenie Frola Kozlova," *Sotsialisticheskii vestnik*, XLIII, Nos. 9/10 (September–October, 1963), 119.

59. *Pravda*, July 13, 1959 (*CDSP*, XI, No. 28, 31); and *Bakinskii rabochii*, July 11, 1959 (*CDSP*, XI, No. 37, 19–22).

60. See the author's biographical sketch of Semichastny in George W. Simmons (ed.), *World Leaders: The Soviet Union*, forthcoming.

61. *Izvestia*, February 21 and 24, 1962 (*CDSP*, XIV, No. 8, 27).

62. Cited in the CPSU letter of March 30, 1963; text in *Pravda*, April 3, 1963 (*CDSP*, XV, No. 14, 3).

63. *Pravda*, March 4, 1962 (*CDSP*, XIV, No. 9, 20).

64. Dallin, *op. cit.*, p. 651; Griffith, *Albania*, p. 143.

65. Ploss, *op. cit.*, pp. 245–52. For an analysis of the pressure of military expenditures on the budget at the plenum, see Gallagher, *op. cit.*, p. 56.

66. Stewart Alsop, "Kennedy's Grand Strategy," *Saturday Evening Post*, March 31, 1962, pp. 11–17.

67. Ploss, *op. cit.*, p. 255.

68. *Pravda*, April 26, 1962; and Ploss, *op. cit.*, p. 257.

69. *Pravda*, May 4, 1962 (*CDSP*, XIV, No. 18, 19).

70. *Pravda*, April 29, 1962 (*CDSP*, XIV, No. 17, 34).

71. *Khrestomatiya po marksistsko-leninskoi filosofii* (Moscow, 1962), Vol. III. The original title included the words "in two volumes" (*v dvukh tomakh*). Volume I was sent to the printer on March 14, 1960, Volume II on April 12, 1960.

72. Ye. A. Korovin, F. I. Kozhevnikov, and G. P. Zadorozhnyi, "Mirnoe sosushchestvovanie i mezhdunarodnoe pravo," *Izvestia*, April 18, 1962.

73. Mentioned in the CPC letter of March 9, 1963, the CPSU letter of June 15, 1964, and the CPC statement of September 6, 1963; discussed in Dallin, *op. cit.*, p. 651.

74. Griffith, *Albania*, p. 148, citing *Pravda* and *Borba*, April 22, 1962.

75. According to the CPC statement of September 6, 1963; cited in Griffith, *Sino-Soviet Rift*, p. 410.

76. *Pravda*, May 22, 1962 (*CDSP*, XIV, No. 21, 25).

77. For example, Robert Conquest, *Russia After Khrushchev* (New York: Frederick A. Praeger, 1965), p. 180.

78. Heinrich Ziegler in *Osteuropa*, XIII, Nos. 2/3 (1963), p. 186, citing *Borba*, May 13, 1962.

79. *Pravda*, May 20, 1962 (*CDSP*, XIV, No. 20, 7).

80. *Pravda*, June 1, 1962 (*CDSP*, XIV, No. 22, 3–6); and Ploss, *op. cit.*, p. 258. For Khrushchev's explanation of the price rise, see N. S. Khrushchev, *Stroitel'stvo kommunizma v SSSR i razvitie sel'skogo khozyaistva* (Moscow: Gospolitizdat, 1963), VII, 36–37; cited by Jerry Hough in *Problems of Communism*, XIII, No. 4 (July–August, 1964), 31.

81. *Vedomosti Verkhovnogo Soveta SSSR*, No. 23 (June 8, 1962); cited in Gallagher, *op. cit.*, p. 58.

82. *Pravda*, June 4, 1962 (*CDSP*, XIV, No. 22, 22).

83. See, for example, Khrushchev's letter to Premier Ikeda of Japan, June 10, 1962 (text in *Pravda* and *Izvestia*, June 16, 1962 [*CDSP*, XIV, No. 24, 19]); and his speech in Bucharest on June 19, 1962 (text in *Pravda*, June 20, 1962 [*CDSP*, XIV, No. 25, 3–5]). See also Defense Minister Malinovsky's article in *Pravda*, June 22, 1962 (*CDSP*, XIV, No. 25, 14–16).

84. *Pravda* and *Izvestia*, July 11, 1962 (*CDSP*, XIV, No. 28, 3–10).

85. *Pravda* and *Izvestia*, July 14, 1962 (*CDSP*, XIV, No. 28, 18–19).

86. *Pravda* and *Izvestia*, July 22, 1962 (*CDSP*, XIV, No. 29, 9).

87. Griffith, *Albania*, pp. 68–69.

88. Referred to in the CPSU letters of February 21 and March 21, 1963, the CPSU open letter of July 14, 1963, and the CPC statement of September 6, 1963; discussed in Dallin, *op. cit.*, p. 651.

89. Cited in the CPC statement of September 6, 1963; cited in Griffith, *Sino-Soviet Rift*, p. 410.

90. Cited in the Chinese statement of August 15, 1963.

91. Griffith, *Sino-Soviet Rift*, p. 226, citing an article in *People's Daily*, November 2, 1963.

92. *Pravda*, October 21, 1962 (*CDSP*, XIV, No. 40, 5).

93. *Pravda*, May 8, 1963 (*CDSP*, XV, No. 19, 7–8).

94. *The New York Times*, February 4, 1966, p. 12, citing Elie Abel, *The Missile Crisis* (Philadelphia: J. B. Lippincott Co., 1966).

95. *Plenum Tsentral'nogo Komiteta Kommunisticheskoi Partii Sovetskogo Soyuza, 19–22 noyabrya 1962 g.: Stenograficheskii otchet* (Moscow: Gospolitizdat, 1963), pp. 444–52.

96. Khrushchev, *op. cit.*, VII, 163–77, gives Khrushchev's memorandum to the Presidium of September 10, 1962.

97. Provision for the establishment of the Central Asian Bureau was not included in the resolution adopted by the plenum.

98. According to D. Rasulov, First Secretary of the Tadzhik CP, Khrushchev developed the idea of establishing a Central Asian Bureau of the CC during his trip to the Central Asian republics (September 26–October 10, 1962). *Kommunist Tadzhikistana*, November 23, 1962.

99. Decree of ratification by the Supreme Soviet, *Pravda* and *Izvestia*, December 20, 1963 (*CDSP*, XVI, No. 1, 8).

100. On the abolition of the Central Asian Council see *Central Asian Review*, XIII, No. 1 (1965), 87–89, and No. 3, 276–78. "One can naturally only surmise the reasons for the abolition of the joint Central Asian bodies,

but there seems to be little doubt that opposition from the individual republics must have played a large part" (p. 278).

101. *Plenum . . . 19–22 noyabrya 1962 g.*, pp. 451–52.

102. For representative articles in what was a fairly extensive Soviet press campaign, see I. Boyasny, "O sisteme partiinogo i gosudarstvennogo kontrolya," *Kommunist*, XXXVIII, No. 15 (October, 1961), 89–91; and M. Mambetaliev, A. Radvogin, and P. Lavrenkov, "Kontrol'—snizu i sverkhu," *Izvestia*, February 15, 1962.

103. Ralph Blum, "Freeze and Thaw: The Artist in Russia," *The New Yorker*, September 11, 1965, p. 168.

104. *Pravda*, December 2, 1962 (*CDSP*, XIV, No. 48, 20–22).

105. Priscilla Johnson, *Khrushchev and the Arts* (Cambridge, Mass.: The M.I.T. Press, 1965), pp. 11–12.

106. On the Bulgarian Party Congress, see Dallin, *op. cit.*, p. 661; Griffith, *European Communism*, I, 9; *Pravda*, November 6 and 7, 1962 (*CDSP*, XIV, No. 45, 9–12, 32).

107. Dallin, *op. cit.*, p. 662; and Giorgio Galli, "Italian Communism," in Griffith, *European Communism* I, 351–59.

108. *Pravda* and *Izvestia*, December 4, 1962 (*CDSP*, XIV, No. 49, 7).

109. Aldo Garosci, "Palmiro Togliatti," *Survey*, No. 53 (October, 1964), p. 142.

110. Cited in Edward Taborsky, "Czechoslovakia: Out of Stalinism?" *Problems of Communism*, XIII, No. 3 (May–June, 1964), 6.

111. Griffith, *Albania*, pp. 74–76.

112. *Ibid.*, p. 75.

113. Ivo Duchacek, "Czechoslovakia: The Past Reburied," *Problems of Communism*, XI, No. 3 (May–June, 1962), 24; and Taborsky, *op. cit.*, p. 6.

114. *Rude pravo*, April 21, 1962; cited in Duchacek, *op. cit.*, p. 25.

115. Dallin, *op. cit.*, p. 663; and Taborsky, *op. cit.*, pp. 6–7.

116. *Pravda*, December 13, 1962 (*CDSP*, XIV, No. 51, 3–8); and *Izvestia*, December 13, 1962 (*CDSP*, XIV, No. 52, 3–10, 56).

117. Text in Dallin, *op. cit.*, pp. 695–706.

118. In their statement of September 6, 1963 (Griffith, *Sino-Soviet Rift*, p. 411), the Chinese said: "Between December 15, 1962, and March 8, 1963, we published seven such replies [to attacks by other Communist parties]."

119. *Pravda* and *Izvestia*, January 17, 1963 (*CDSP*, XV, No. 3, 3–7); Dallin, *op. cit.*, pp. 746–61.

120. Summarized in Dallin, *op. cit.*, pp. 761–62, citing *Pravda*, January 20 and 23, 1963, and *Peking Review*, No. 4 (January 25, 1963).

121. *Pravda* and *Izvestia*, December 13, 1962.

122. *Pravda*, February 2, 1963; analysis in Gallagher, *op. cit.*, p. 61.

123. *Pravda*, June 12 and 17, 1962 (*CDSP*, XIV, No. 24, 3–8). See also Randolph L. Braham, "Rumania: Onto the Separate Path," *Problems of Communism*, XIII, No. 3 (May–June, 1964); and J. F. Brown, "Rumania Steps Out of Line," *Survey*, No. 49 (October, 1963).

124. *Pravda*, February 23, 1963; and Brown, *op. cit.*, p. 25.

125. *Pravda*, March 14, 1963 (*CDSP*, XV, No. 11, 3–4).

126. *Pravda*, March 14, 1963 (*CDSP*, XV, No. 11, 4–6); and Dallin, *op. cit.*, pp. 820–26.

127. *Pravda*, February 28, 1963.

128. Khrushchev initiated correspondence with Kennedy on December 21, 1962, regarding a ban on nuclear tests. The correspondence was published in *Pravda*, January 21, 1963 (*CDSP*, XV, No. 3, 9–10). The attempt at agreement failed and the Kennedy Administration announced the resumption of nuclear testing on February 8.

129. *Turkmenskaya iskra*, March 27, 1963; and *Pravda*, March 26, 1963 (*CDSP*, XV, No. 12, 26–27).

130. *Pravda* and *Izvestia*, March 14, 1963 (*CDSP*, XV, No. 11, 24–25).

131. *Plenum Tsentral'nogo Komiteta Kommunisticheskoi Partii Sovetskogo Soyuza, 18–21 iyunya 1963 goda: Stenograficheskii otchet* (Moscow: Izdatel'stvo Politicheskoi Literatury, 1964), p. 288.

132. *Pravda*, March 23, 1963 (*CDSP*, XV, No. 12, 22).

133. *Pravda* and *Izvestia*, March 28, 1963 (*CDSP*, XV, No. 13, 21).

134. *Pravda* and *Izvestia*, March 29, 1963 (*CDSP*, XV, No. 13, 23–24).

135. *Pravda* and *Izvestia*, March 30, 1963 (*CDSP*, XV, No. 13, 21–22).

136. *Pravda*, March 17, 1963 (*CDSP*, XV, No. 11, 25).

137. *Pravda*, March 27, 1963 (*CDSP*, XV, No. 13, 20–21).

138. *Izvestia*, March 12–13, 1963 (*CDSP*, XV, No. 11, 21–22).

139. *Pravda*, April 3, 1963 (*CDSP*, XV, No. 14, 3–9); and Griffith, *Sino-Soviet Rift*, pp. 241–58.

140. Griffith, *loc. cit.*

141. *Christian Science Monitor*, April 8, 1963.

142. *Pravda* and *Izvestia*, April 10, 1963 (*CDSP*, XV, No. 15, 26–27).

143. *Pravda*, April 18, 1963 (*CDSP*, XV, No. 15, 26).

144. Blum, *op. cit.*, p. 175.

145. *Izvestia*, April 20 and 21, 1963.

146. *Pravda*, May 14, 1963 (*CDSP*, XV, No. 19, 15).

147. *Pravda*, May 4, 1963 (*CDSP*, XV, No. 18, 30); Conquest, *op. cit.*, p. 115; and Ploss, *op. cit.*, p. 269.

148. Alexander Tvardovsky, "Za ideinost' i sotsialisticheskii realizm," *Novy mir*, XXXIX, No. 4 (April, 1963), 3–10.

149. *Pravda*, May 12, 1963 (*CDSP*, XV, No. 19, 11–13); and Blum, *op. cit.*, pp. 178–81. See also Max Hayward, "The Literary Purge in Retrospect," *Survey*, No. 49 (October, 1963), p. 61.

150. *Pravda*, May 16, 1963 (*CDSP*, XV, No. 20, 19).

151. *Ibid.*

152. *Newsweek*, January 27, 1964, p. 38. Another casualty was Marshal S. S. Varentsov, who lost his posts as chief of the Soviet rocket troops, candidate member of the CC, and deputy to the Supreme Soviet. *Izvestia*, May 30, 1965 (*CDSP*, XV, No. 20, 10).

153. *Pravda*, May 22, 1963 (*CDSP*, XV, No. 21, 22–23).

154. *Izvestia*, May 21, 1963.

155. *New Times* (Russian edition), No. 23 (1963), p. 32; cited in Walter F. Clemens, Jr., *Moscow and Arms Control: Evidence from the Sino-Soviet Dispute* (Cambridge, Mass., 1965), p. 27.

156. Griffith, *Sino-Soviet Rift*, p. 142.

157. Chinese statement of August 15, 1963.

158. *Pravda* and *Izvestia*, June 11, 1963 (*CDSP*, XV, No. 23, 20).

159. *Pravda*, July 14, 1963 (*CDSP*, XV, No. 28, 3–15); Griffith, *Sino-Soviet Rift*, pp. 259–88; for analysis, *ibid.*, pp. 143–48.

160. *Pravda*, June 15, 1963 (*CDSP*, XV, No. 24, 21–23).
161. *Plenum* . . . *18–21 iyunya 1963 g.*, pp. 317–18.
162. *Pravda*, July 14, 1963 (*CDSP*, XV, No. 28, 16–30); Griffith, *Sino-Soviet Rift*, pp. 289–325; for analysis, *ibid.*, pp. 156–59.
163. *Pravda*, July 14, 1963 (*CDSP*, XV, No. 28, 22).
164. *Sovetskaya Moldaviya*, July 6 and 13, 1963.
165. *Ibid.*, October 17, 1963 (*CDSP*, XV, No. 44, 23–24); and *Sovetskaya Moldaviya*, October 20, 1963.
166. *Pravda*, July 12, 1963.
167. *Pravda* and *Izvestia*, July 25, 1963 (*CDSP*, XV, No. 30, 3).
168. Khrushchev, *op. cit.*, VIII, 44–61; cited in Ploss, *op. cit.*, p. 275.
169. *Pravda*, August 14, 1963; and *Izvestia*, August 18, 1963 (*CDSP*, XV, No. 34, 20–30). See also Alexander Tvardovsky, *Kak byl napisan Vasili Terkin: Otvet chitatelyam* (Moscow: Sovetskii Pisatel, 1952).
170. T. W. Wolfe, "Professional Primacy vs. Professional Elan," *Problems of Communism*, XIII, No. 3 (May–June, 1964), 47.
171. Taborsky, *op. cit.*, p. 8.
172. *Pravda*, August 24, 1963 (*CDSP*, XV, No. 34, 37).
173. Griffith, *Sino-Soviet Rift*, pp. 188–89; and Taborsky, *op. cit.*, p. 10, citing *Rude pravo*, September 22, 1963.
174. *Pravda*, July 1, 1963.
175. Soviet approval of Rumanian plans for industrialization was given at a Communist bloc economic conference in Moscow, July 24–26, 1963, which also endorsed the test-ban treaty (July 25). Griffith, *Sino-Soviet Rift*, p. 160, citing *Pravda*, July 27, 1963; and Braham, *op. cit.*, p. 15.
176. See Nancy Nimitz, *Soviet Government Grain Procurements, Dispositions and Stocks, 1940, 1945–63* (Santa Monica, Calif.: The RAND Corporation, November, 1964).
177. Announced by Khrushchev in a speech at Velene, Yugoslavia, August 31, 1963; text in *Izvestia*, September 1, 1963.
178. Griffith, *Sino-Soviet Rift*, p. 211.
179. Ploss, *op. cit.*, p. 277.
180. The reports of the anniversary of the episode of the Baku Commissars as published in *Izvestia*, September 21, 1963, *Komsomolskaya pravda*, September 20, 1963, *Pravda vostoka*, September 21, 1963, *Bakinskii rabochii*, September 20/21, 1963, were notable for their failure to stress the role of Mikoyan.
181. Griffith, *Sino-Soviet Rift*, pp. 211–12, citing *Pravda*, September 24 and 30, 1963.
182. Griffith, *Sino-Soviet Rift*, p. 214, citing *Pravda*, October 3, 1963.
183. *Pravda*, October 19, 1963 (*CDSP*, XV, No. 42, 29).
184. "Marksizm-leninizm—osnova yedinstva kommunisticheskogo dvizheniya," *Kommunist*, No. 15 (October, 1963), pp. 13–47 (*CDSP*, XV, No. 43, 3–14); Griffith, *Sino-Soviet Rift*, pp. 466–74; for analysis, *ibid.*, pp. 217–19.
185. *Ibid.*, pp. 223–24.
186. *Ibid.*, citing *Pravda*, October 3, 1963 (Dutch-Italian CP joint resolution). On October 7, 1963, the Norwegian CP sent both contestants an offer of reconciliation; see Wolfgang Leonhard, "A World in Disarray," *Problems of Communism*, XIII, No. 2 (March–April, 1964), 24, citing

Friheten (Oslo). The Italian CP published a much stronger statement on October 25, 1963; see Galli, _op. cit._, pp. 379–80.

187. _Pravda_, October 2, 1963 (_CDSP_, XV, No. 40, 9–14).
188. _Pravda_, October 27, 1963 (_CDSP_, XV, No. 43, 14–20).
189. Donald G. Bishop, _The Roosevelt-Litvinov Agreements: The American View_ (Syracuse, N.Y.: Syracuse University Press, 1965), p. 103.
190. N. Krylov, "Strategicheskie rakety," _Izvestia_, November 17, 1963 (_CDSP_, XV, No. 46, 29–30).
191. R. V. Allen, "Peace or Peaceful Coexistence?" in E. L. Dulles and R. D. Crane (eds.), _Détente: Cold War Strategies in Transition_ (New York: Frederick A. Praeger, 1965), p. 48.
192. _Pravda_, November 22, 1963 (_CDSP_, XV, No. 47, 23).
193. On Soviet press treatment of the assassination of President Kennedy, see C. M. (Charles Malamuth), "Kennedy Assassination—Communist Version," _Communist Affairs_, I, No. 9 (November–December, 1963), 3–6.
194. Cited in the _Pravda_ editorial of April 3, 1964, and in the CPC letter of May 7, 1964 (text in _Kommunist_, No. 10 [July, 1964], pp. 20–24 [_CDSP_, XVI, No. 30, 3–5]).
195. _Pravda_, December 6, 1963 (_CDSP_, XV, No. 47, 15–19).
196. Cited in R. V. Allen, _op. cit._, in Dulles and Crane, _op. cit._, pp. 56–57.
197. _Encyclopedia Americana Yearbook_, 1964 (New York: Americana Corp., 1964), p. 19.
198. _Pravda_ and _Izvestia_, December 10, 1963 (_CDSP_, XV, No. 49, 12).
199. _Ibid._
200. Ploss, _op. cit._, p. 277.
201. _Pravda_ and _Izvestia_, December 15, 1963 (_CDSP_, XV, No. 49, 12).
202. T. W. Wolfe, _op. cit._, in Dulles and Crane, _op. cit._, p. 72, cites an article by Marshal Grechko, "On a Leninist Course" (_Krasnaya zvezda_, December 22, 1963), as "rather restrained." See also an interview with A. Petrosyants, Chairman of the Soviet Atomic Energy Commission, in _Izvestia_, December 12, 1963 (_CDSP_, XV, No. 50, 23); and an article by N. Inozemtsev, "Nadezhdy i trevogi amerikantsev," _Pravda_, December 25, 1963 (_CDSP_, XV, No. 52, 3–5).
203. _Pravda_, December 27, 1963 (_CDSP_, XV, No. 52, 25).
204. _Pravda_ and _Izvestia_, December 31, 1963 (_CDSP_, XV, No. 52, 24–25).
205. "The CPSU leaders are the greatest splitters of our time": _Red Flag_ and _People's Daily_, February 4, 1964; extract in _Problems of Communism_, XIII, No. 2 (March–April, 1964), 15; referred to in Suslov's plenum speech of February 14, 1964, and the _Pravda_ editorial of April 3, 1964; analysis in Harry Gelman, "The Conflict: A Survey," _Problems of Communism_, XIII, No. 2 (March–April, 1964), 3–15.
206. Coverage of the plenum was given in _Pravda_, February 11–16, 1964 (_CDSP_, XVI, No. 6, 3–15, 28; XVI, No. 7, 3–22; XVI, No. 8, 10–15; XVI, No. 9, 13–24).
207. _Pravda_, April 3, 1964 (_CDSP_, XVI, No. 13, 13).
208. Mentioned in the CPC letter of May 7, 1964.
209. _Ibid._
210. _Ibid._
211. Mentioned in the _Pravda_ editorial of April 3, 1964, the CPC letter of May 7, 1964, and the CPSU letter of June 15, 1964.

212. Mentioned in the *Pravda* editorial of April 3, 1964, and the CPC letter of May 7, 1964.
213. Mentioned in the *Pravda* editorials of April 3, 1964, and of April 28–29, 1964 (*CDSP*, XVI, No. 17, 20).
214. *Pravda*, March 28, 1964 (*CDSP*, XVI, No. 13, 25).
215. *Pravda* and *Izvestia*, April 17, 1964 (*CDSP*, XVI, No. 16, 6).
216. *Problems of Communism*, XIII, No. 3 (May–June, 1964), 2.
217. *Pravda*, June 2, 1964 (*CDSP*, XVI, No. 22, 21–22).
218. *Pravda*, April 4, 1964 (*CDSP*, XVI, No. 15, 6–8).
219. *Pravda*, June 27, 1964 (*CDSP*, XVI, No. 26, 17).
220. The CPC letter of May 7, 1964.
221. *Kommunist*, No. 10 (July, 1964), pp. 9–20; and *Pravda*, July 17, 1964 (*CDSP*, XVI, No. 30, 5–10).
222. *Partiinaya zhizn*, No. 14 (July 14, 1964), pp. 8–30 (*CDSP*, XVI, No. 32, 11–16).
223. *The New York Times*, July 16, 1964, p. 4; and *Pravda*, July 24, 1964 (*CDSP*, XVI, No. 30, 22).
224. *Pravda*, July 9, 1964 (*CDSP*, XVI, No. 28, 3–8).
225. *Pravda*, July 22, 1964, p. 3 (*CDSP*, XVI, No. 30, 11–13).
226. *Pravda*, July 16, 1964.
227. Boris N. Ponomarev, "Proletarian Internationalism—A Powerful Force in the Revolutionary Transformation of the World," *World Marxist Review*, VII, No. 8 (August, 1964), 59–70; cited in Uri Raanan, "Moscow and the 'Third World,'" *Problems of Communism*, XIV, No. 1 (January–February, 1965), 28.
228. *Pravda* and *Izvestia*, August 8, 1964 (*CDSP*, XVI, No. 32, 29).
229. Eric Sevareid, "Final Troubled Hours of Adlai Stevenson," *Look*, November 30, 1965, pp. 81–84.
230. *Pravda*, August 9, 1964 (*CDSP*, XVI, No. 33, 10–12).
231. *Pravda*, August 28, 1964 (*CDSP*, XVI, No. 36, 3–5).
232. *Ibid.*, p. 4.
233. "Bortsy za velikoe delo: Predsedatel' OGPU," *Izvestia*, September 1, 1964; and "Besstrashnyi borets za kommunizm: K 90-letiyu so dnya rozhdeniya V. R. Menzhinskogo," *Pravda*, September 1, 1964.
234. Viktor Maevsky, "Tovarishch Rikhard Zorge," *Pravda*, September 4, 1964 (*CDSP*, XVI, No. 36, 10–11); and N. Pekelnik, "Podvig Rikharda Zorge," *Izvestia*, September 5, 1964 (*CDSP*, XVI, No. 36, 11–13).
235. Boris Meissner, "Chruschtschowismus ohne Chruschtschow," *Osteuropa*, XV, Nos. 1/2 (1965), 13.
236. P. B. Reddaway, "The Fall of Khrushchev: A Tentative Analysis," *Survey*, No. 56 (July, 1965), p. 15.

Index